IMAGES
of America

THE WEIRS

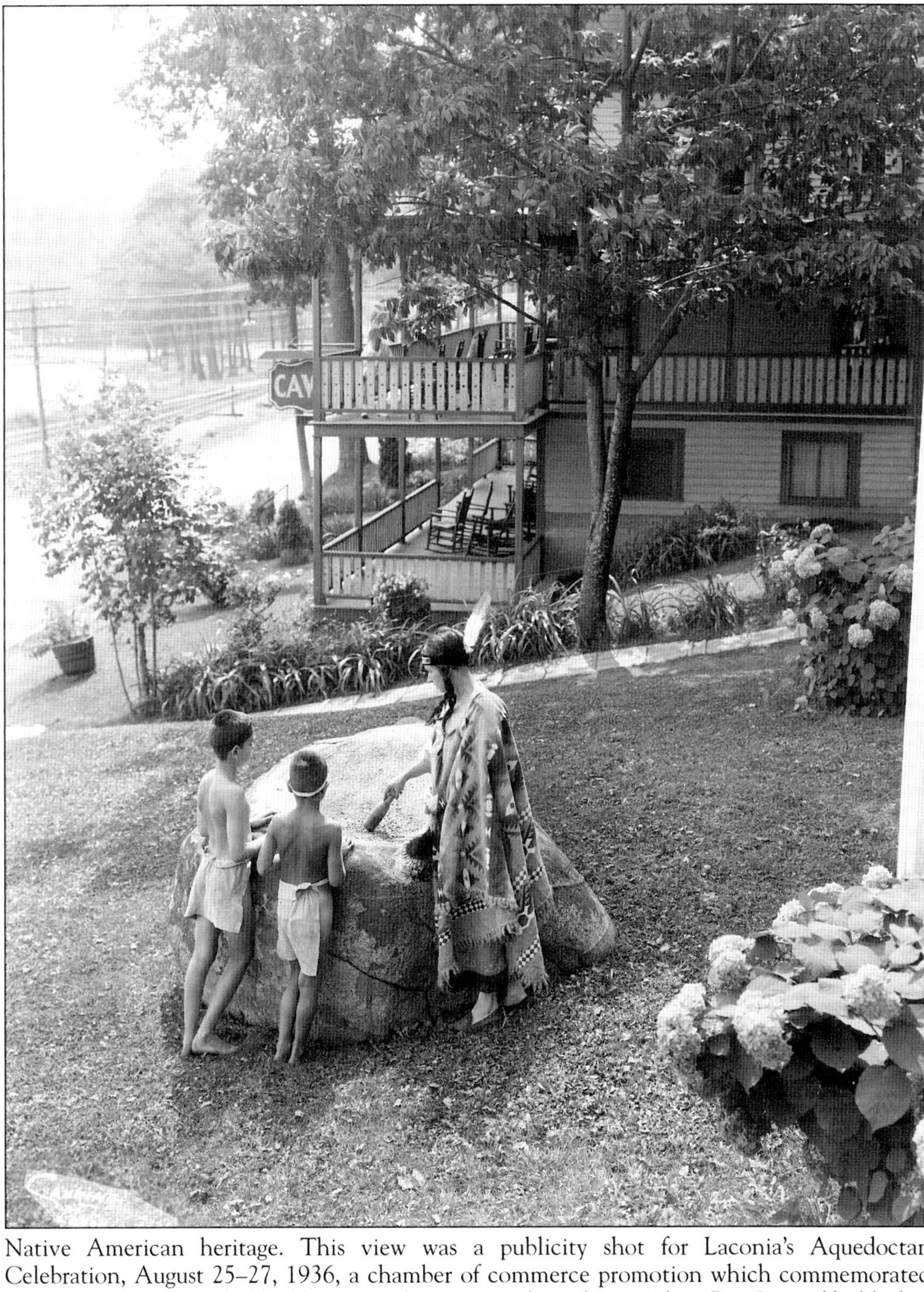

Native American heritage. This view was a publicity shot for Laconia's Aquedoctan Celebration, August 25–27, 1936, a chamber of commerce promotion which commemorated the 1736 garrisoning of a blockhouse at The Weirs and another at Alton Bay. Legend holds that American Indians of Aquedoctan Village, at The Weirs, used this stone mortar to grind corn. The "Indians" in the photograph are Laconia residents Nina (Mrs. Allen G.) Veazey and her sons Bill and John. Unfortunately, the stone mortar was destroyed in the early 1990s, during land development operations following a 1991 fire which destroyed Story's Hotel (known as Cawley's in 1936), here visible in the background (see pp. 36–37).

IMAGES
of America

THE WEIRS

Warren D. Huse

ARCADIA
PUBLISHING

ISBN 978-0-7385-8954-1

Published by Arcadia Publishing
Charleston, South Carolina

Printed in the United States of America

Library of Congress Control Number: Applied for

For all general information contact Arcadia Publishing at:
Telephone 843-853-2070
Fax 843-853-0044
E-mail sales@arcadiapublishing.com
For customer service and orders:
Toll-Free 1-888-313-2665

Visit us on the Internet at www.arcadiapublishing.com

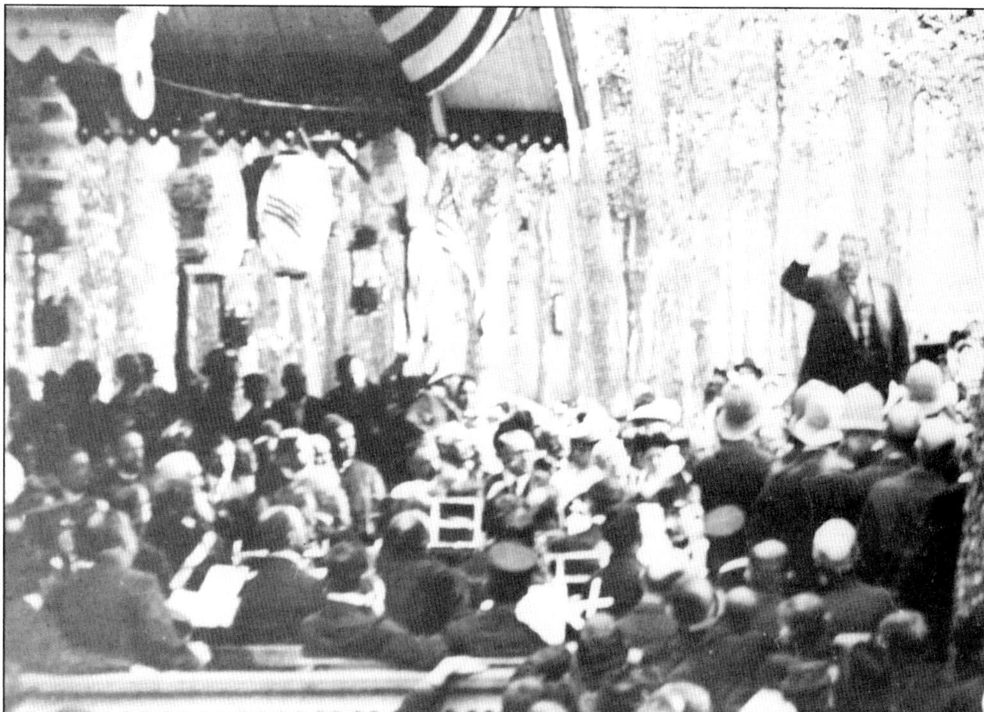

Presidential address. In this detail from the photograph on pp. 52–53, Theodore Roosevelt emphasizes a point in his address to the New Hampshire Veterans Association at The Weirs, August 28, 1902.

Cover Photograph: New Hotel Weirs. With 230 rooms, dining, banquet, and music rooms, and other amenities, this establishment was Laconia's "grand hotel" until 1924, when the ornate structure burned to the ground (see pp. 55–64).

Contents

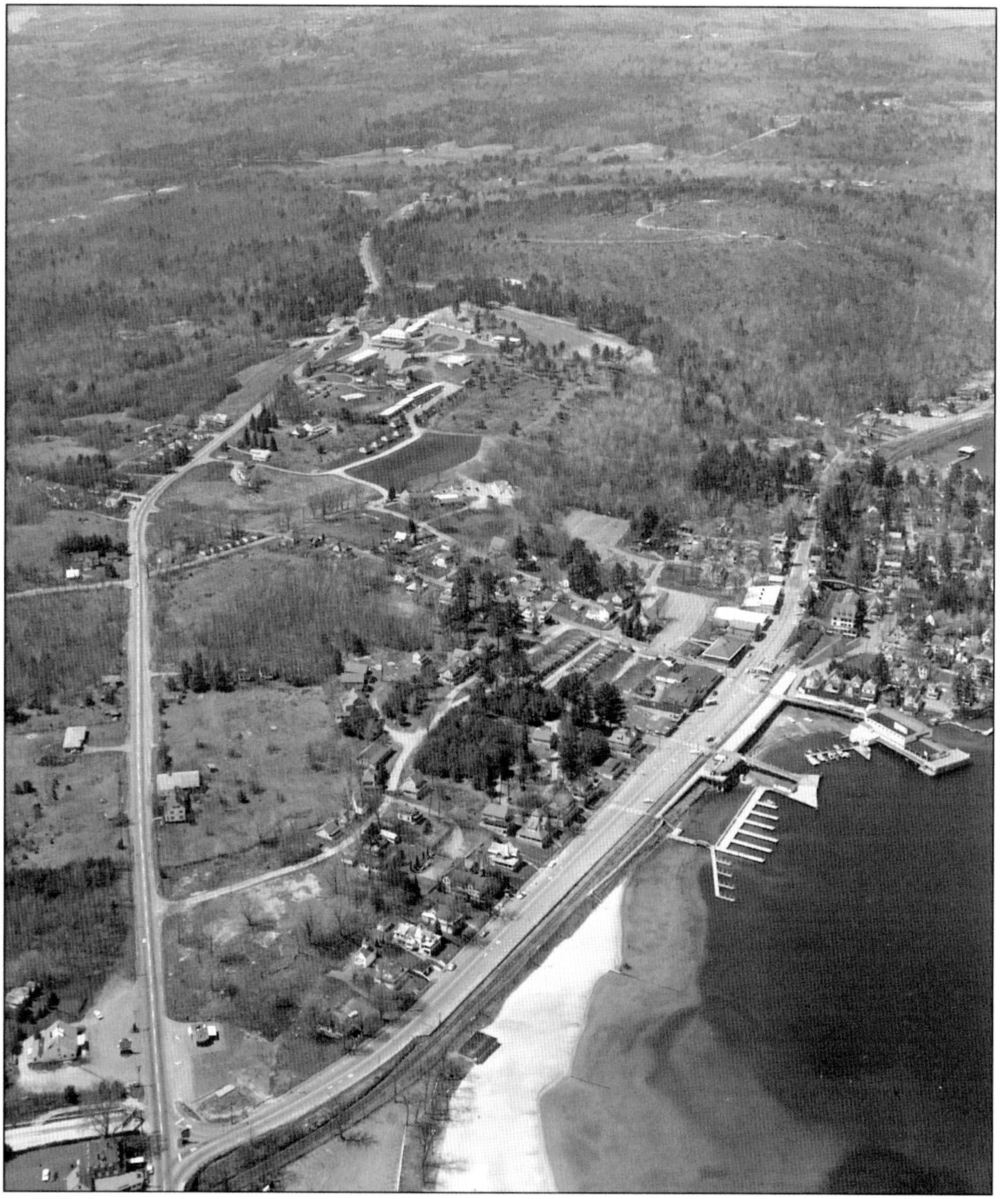

Aerial photograph of The Weirs, looking north, 1960s. U.S. Route 3 is on the left and Lakeside Avenue branches off to the right. The former Aquedoktan Hotel (today's Sand Bar Beach Resort) and, above it, Howard Johnson's Restaurant (burned October 7, 1984), are visible in the lower left corner. The major complex to the upper left of center was the Shangri-La (originally the Hotel Winnicoette), later the Brickyard Mountain Resort. The New Hampshire Veterans Association grounds appear at lower center, fronting on Lakeside Avenue. The Methodist Campground and other residential settlements are right of center, beyond the boatslips and pier containing Irwin's Winnipesaukee Gardens, more recently once again called Winnipesaukee Pier (see p. 83). The brickyard (see pp. 118–121) was located to the west (left) of Lakeside Avenue, beyond the curve to the right, where Scenic Drive begins, just north of the residential area. The train wreck of September 15, 1900 (see pp. 124–126), occurred on the tracks just off the photograph's upper right edge.

Introduction

The Weirs is the second volume in a planned series on the city of Laconia, New Hampshire. As with *Laconia* (published in 1995), it was necessary to concentrate on the period of the late-1870s through the first decades of the twentieth century, because of the wealth of imagery available from that period. Continuing the story will be the subject of a future endeavor.

Home for 10,000 years to Native Americans, who established the seasonal village of Aquedoctan, The Weirs takes its name from the fish weirs built in the channel at the outlet of Lake Winnipesaukee, to catch the shad in their yearly migrations to and from the ocean.

In July 1652, a daring expedition ventured up the Merrimack River in search of the headwaters of the Merrimack. Their goal was to ascertain the northerly line of the jurisdiction of the Massachusetts Bay Colony. Captain Simon Willard, a captain of militia, headed the party, which included Captain Edward Johnson, a politician and author; Jonathan Ince, a scholar and 1650 graduate of Harvard College, who had "a singular faculty to learn and pronounce the Indian tongue;" John Sherman, a prominent resident and land surveyor of Watertown; James Prentiss and another colonist, who went along as laborers; and two Indians, Pontauhum and Ponbakin, characterized as "very intelligent and well-acquainted with the river and lake." Upon their arrival, the party observed a well-shaped boulder exactly at the head of the river, on which they cut the name of "Worshipful" Governor Endicott and their own initials in deep letters. In the 1760s, settlers from the Seacoast took up residence in the area, but it was not until 1833, during excavation of the channel to permit passage of the first lake steamer, the *Belknap*, that the boulder was rediscovered. It was then another fifty-nine years before the granite canopy was dedicated, in 1892—240 years after those early surveyors set the northern limit of the Massachusetts Bay Colony as a line 3 miles north of Endicott Rock. (Later, however, an English court ruled that the charter of the colony had envisioned the boundary as 3 miles north of the mouth of the river—which is where it is today, between Seabrook and Salisbury, Massachusetts.)

The Weirs was one of the earliest sections of today's city to be settled by colonists from the Seacoast. A sawmill and a gristmill were established here in the early 1760s. Agriculture and lumbering were the occupations of the first settlers, when the land on the north of the Weirs Channel was part of Meredith and that on the south, part of Gilmanton (after 1812, part of Gilford). Because of its accessibility by water from other communities around the lake, The Weirs also became a trading center at an early date.

In 1848–49, the rails of the Boston, Concord & Montreal Railroad reached The Weirs. The tracks were extended to Woodsville by 1852, and soon The Weirs was included on the main line between Boston and Montreal. A quarter-century later, the ease of access provided by the railroad greatly facilitated the development of the area as a tourist destination.

In the 1870s, the Winnipisiogee Campmeeting Association (Methodist) and the New Hampshire Veterans Association established campgrounds here. In the 1880s, the New Hampshire Music Teachers Association began several decades of annual music festivals. Beginning in the late 1870s, and enjoying tremendous growth in the 1880s and 1890s, resort hotels sprang up, catering to the tourists who came to enjoy the scenery, steamboat trips, fishing, and other attractions.

The Laconia Street Railway extended its tracks from Lakeport to The Weirs in 1899, allowing local residents easy access to the resort area and visitors a similar ease in visiting Lakeport and Downtown Laconia.

Within the space available, it has not been possible to do more than hint at the rich fabric of life at The Weirs during those years. Nonetheless, the photographs provide a tantalizing overview.

Several hundred hours have been spent verifying the dates of construction and other particulars of principal landmarks. Two areas of inquiry, however, have eluded resolution. The first concerns the various wharves or piers prior to construction of the Winnipesaukee Pier shown on p. 83. A definitive and pictorial chronology of these structures must await future research. The second problem area concerns the photographs of early aviation at The Weirs. Initially, it was thought that all of the photographs included on pp. 85–89 chronicled Harry Atwood's 1912 visit. Closer inspection discloses, however, at least two different seaplanes and the particulars of the second plane likewise await further clarification.

Readers of *Laconia* have expressed a desire to see maps included in these books. Although an 1892 map of The Weirs is available, its inclusion would be in too minuscule a form to be of much assistance. It is hoped that the aerial photographs and panoramic views provided will help in identifying locations. No attempt has been made to present definitive coverage of steamboats and other lake craft, as these are admirably detailed in other publications.

Specific attribution of photographs is contained in the acknowledgments (see p. 128). However, it should be noted that the images have been drawn principally from collections at the Laconia Public Library and Laconia Historical Society, with significant additions from the private collections of Robert F. Dearborn and Douglas B. McGowan, along with choice material from others. The pioneering work of Andrew L. Childs and Theo S. Jewett in identifying and indicating the significance of many of these images is again noted, along with the early cataloging of Barbara B. Cotton, former librarian at Laconia Public Library.

The work, more than a century ago, of T.C. Moon, F. and M. Moulton, George H. Tebbetts, Frederick W. Fowler, and a host of unknown photographers must be credited with making this book possible.

Once again, the support and enthusiasm of Carol Sykes, director, and the trustees of the Laconia Public Library, as well as of the officers and directors of the Laconia Historical Society, have been of material assistance.

As with the preparation of *Laconia*, I owe much to Gilbert S. Center for his incisive comments, at several stages, upon the captions. Likewise, Julie Upham and a number of others, especially Beth Lavertue and Rolland R. Gove, have made constructive suggestions. At Arcadia, Sarah Maineri and Michael Joseph Guillory were responsible for editing the text; while Aaron Faulkner, technical supervisor; and Paul Webb, scanning operator, reproduced the photographs. To all, I express deep appreciation.

Finally, tribute must be paid, once again, to Winnifred N.A. Hackettt (1926–1994), whose dogged determination played a major part, in 1980, in re-establishing the Laconia Historical Society as a force for preserving the heritage of the city, and to longtime Laconia Deputy Chief of Police Burlon F. McGowan (1918–1993) who was, for six years, a director of the society. To Burlon's memory, this volume is dedicated.

Warren D. Huse

One

Overview and Approaches

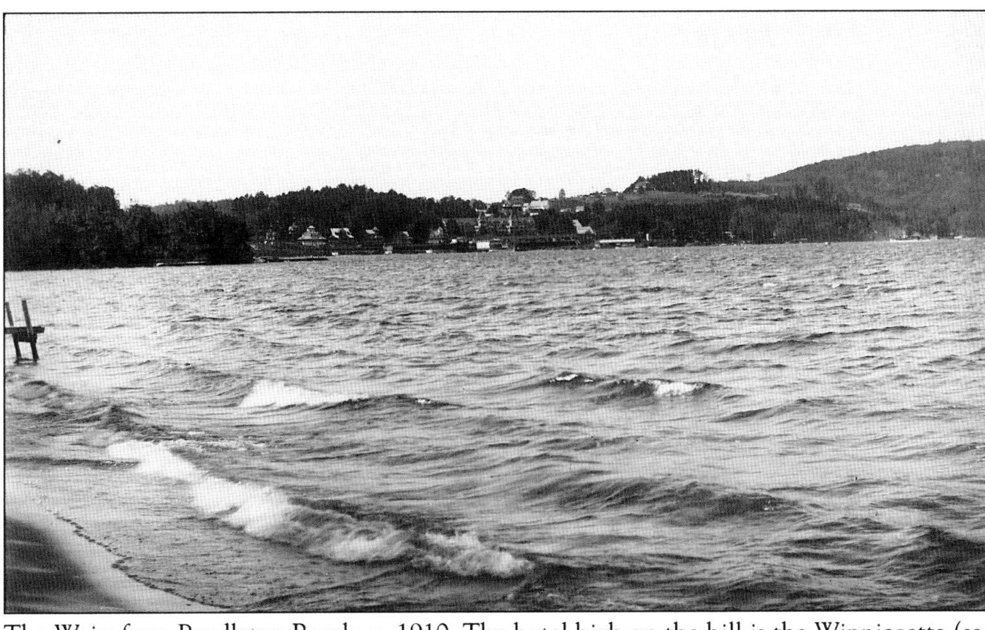

The Weirs from Pendleton Beach, *c.* 1910. The hotel high on the hill is the Winnicoette (see p. 16), later the Shangri-La and the Brickyard Mountain Resort. Although The Weirs had experienced an intense boom beginning in the late 1870s, the resort area still enjoyed a bucolic atmosphere at the time of this photograph.

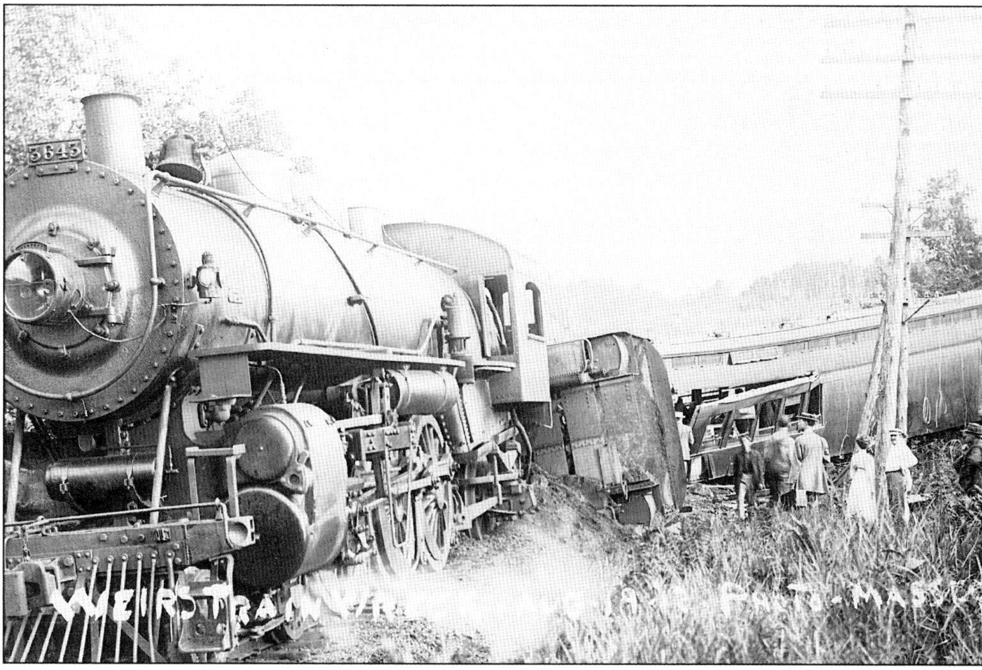

Railroad wreck on the west side of Lake Paugus, August 19, 1912. The northbound White Mountain Express, en route to The Weirs, left the rails at a curve "on the shore of the lake about halfway between Lakeport and The Weirs and made a nasty wreck, plowing up the right of way and tumbling the forward cars into the ditch," according to *The Laconia Democrat* for August 23, 1912.

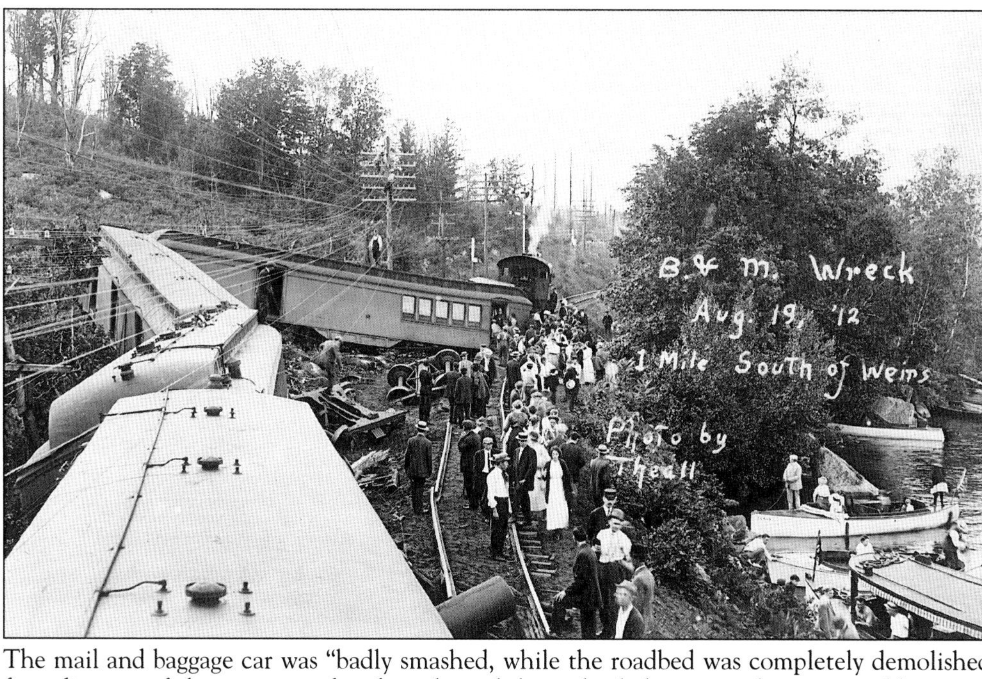

The mail and baggage car was "badly smashed, while the roadbed was completely demolished for a distance of about seventy-five feet, the rails being hurled in every direction and bent and twisted out of shape."

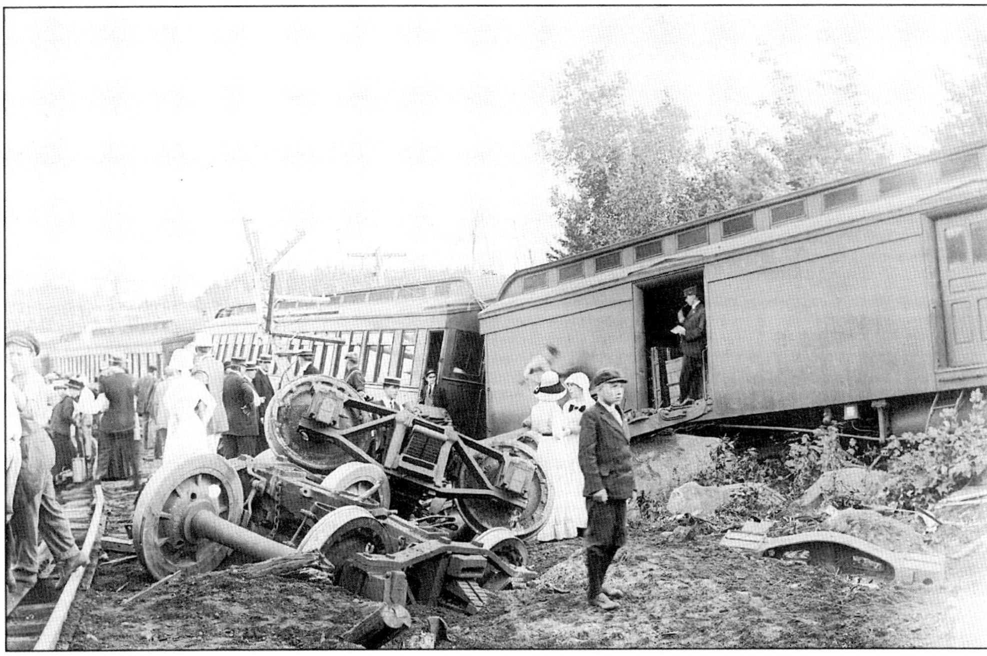

Miraculously, the only persons injured were the mail clerk, baggage man, and the express messenger, "and none of their injuries were very serious." Wrecking crews cleared up the site in a few hours and traffic resumed.

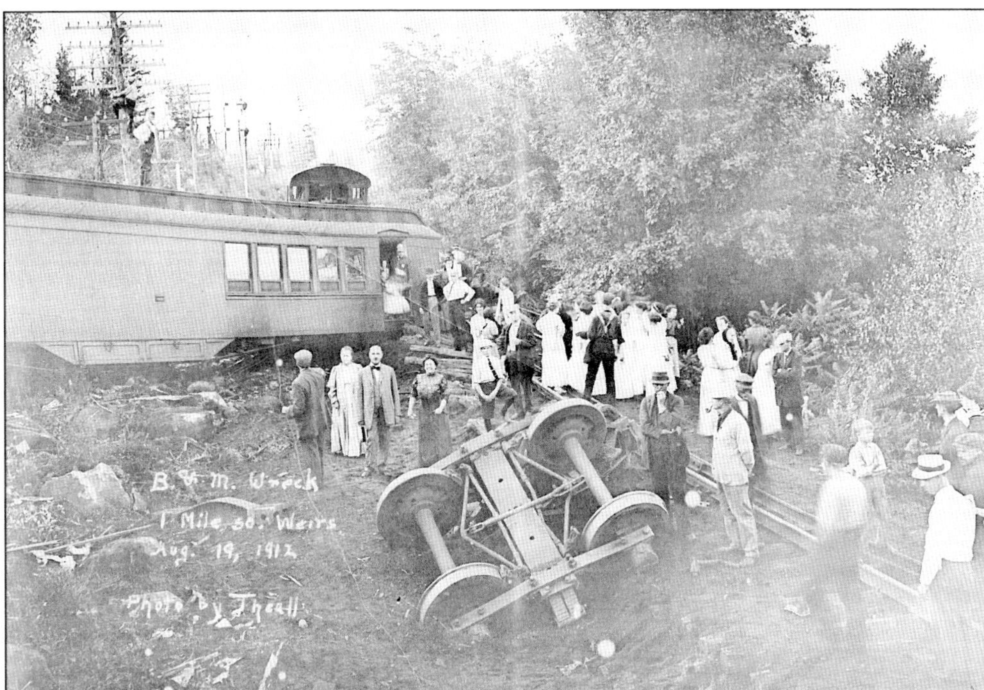

"It was fortunate that the train jumped towards the land side of the track, for if the cars had started down the bank into the lake, the accident would have been a serious disaster for the water is deep at that point and the train would probably have gone under water."

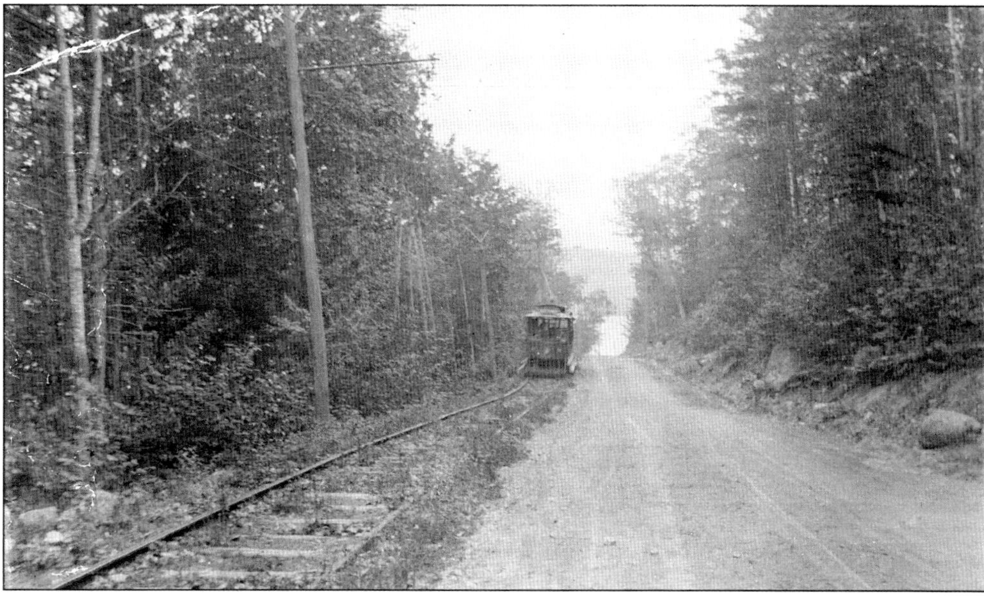

Open Car No. 16 of the Laconia Street Railway, 1904. The car was traveling along the Weirs Boulevard, with the upper (northeast) end of Lake Paugus visible in the distance. The trolley tracks and boulevard were built in 1899. The trolleys, which transported large numbers of Laconia residents and visitors to and from The Weirs every summer, ceased operation in 1925.

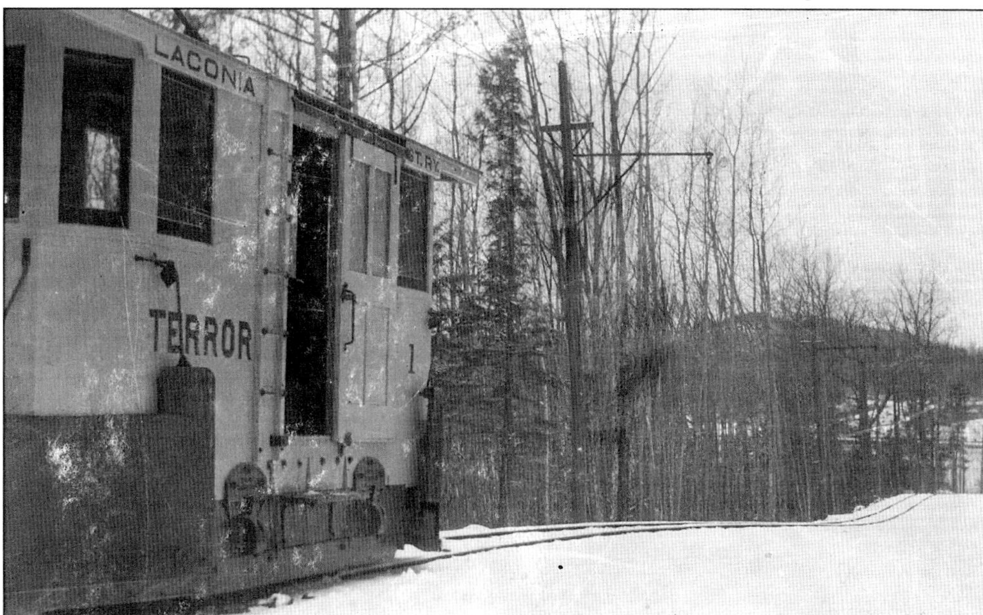

The snowplow Terror of the Laconia Street Railway. Here, the snowplow traverses the same stretch of the line on a run early in the season. Service to The Weirs was normally suspended during the winter months. Today's Lazy E Motor Inn and the Quarterdeck Motel would be located to the left of the tracks in this photograph.

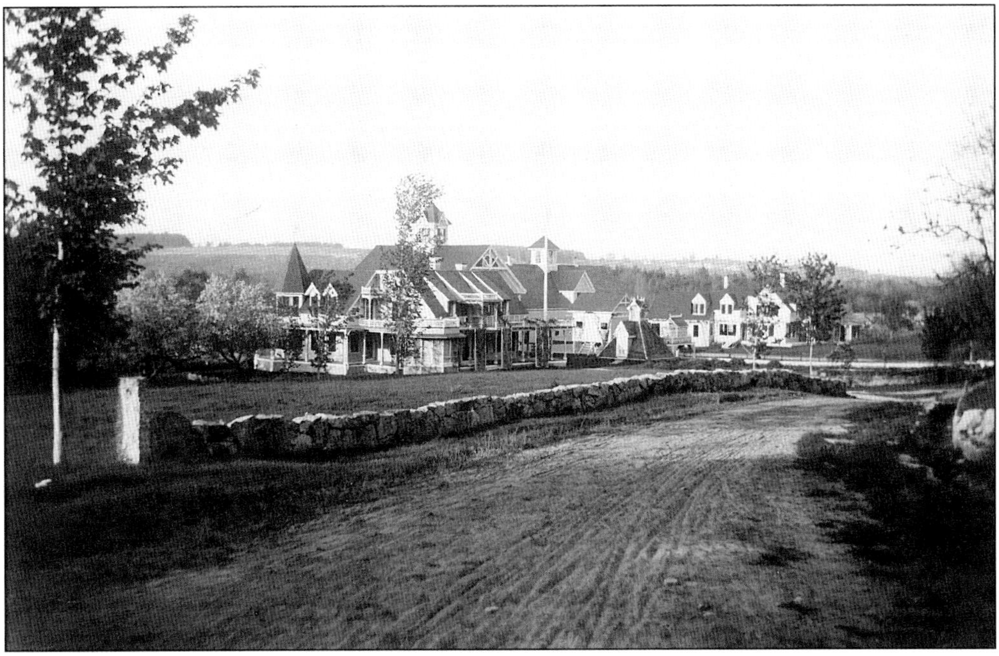

Nestledown, c. 1899. The summer residence of Mrs. John F. Zebley was located on Route 11B, about a mile south of The Weirs, near today's St. Helena Church. Mrs. Zebley's father, Loammi Bean, purchased the property in 1861, moving his family there to reside during his absence with the 8th New Hampshire Volunteer Regiment (see pp. 42–44).

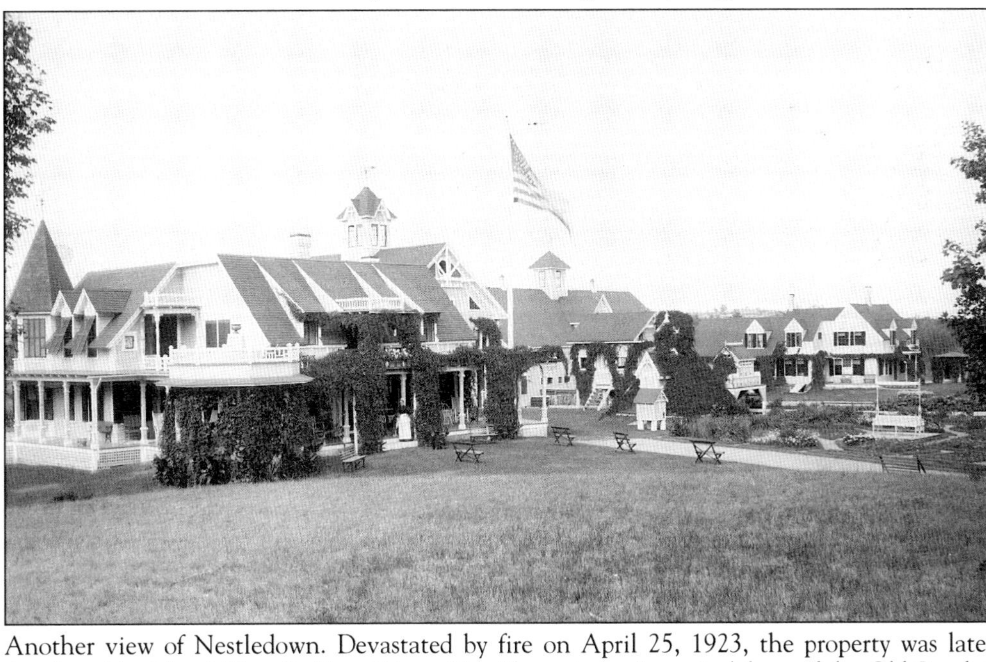

Another view of Nestledown. Devastated by fire on April 25, 1923, the property was later developed by Mrs. Lillian B. Carroll into The Plantation—"a typical farm of the Old South." Accommodating sixty-eight guests, the grounds covered 150 acres and included a private beach. Southern cooking was a specialty. The last of the buildings burned on October 7, 1954. Today the site is occupied by the Sundown Condominiums.

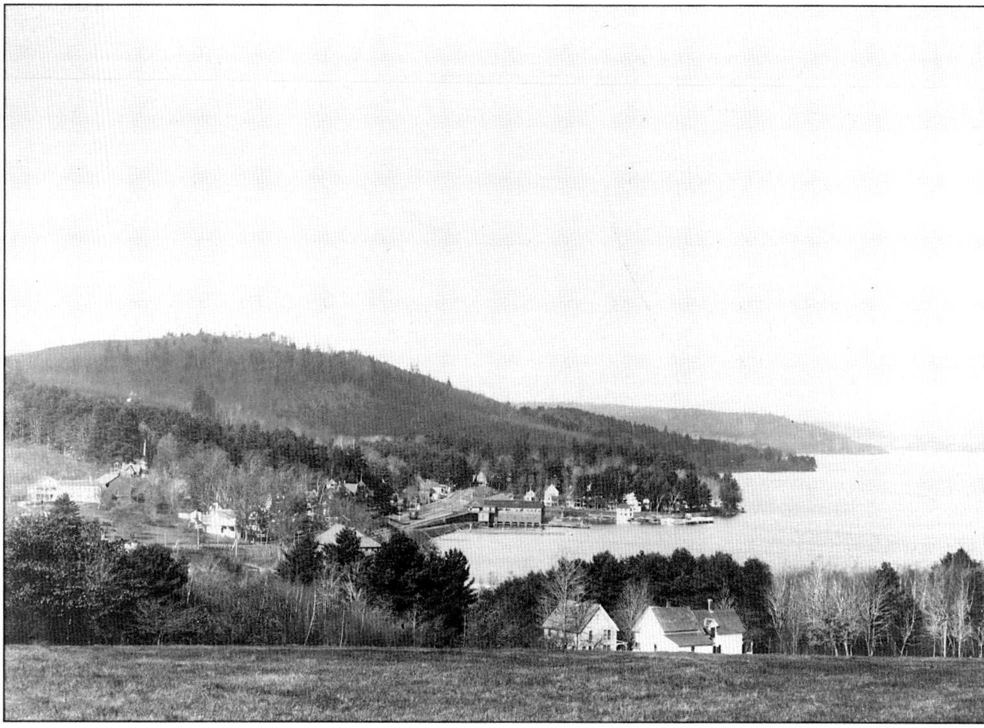

A view of The Weirs, *c.* 1890. Weirs Cafe dominates the waterfront.

Another view from Interlaken Park, around the turn of the century. A much-enlarged New Hotel Weirs looms over the cafe and waterfront.

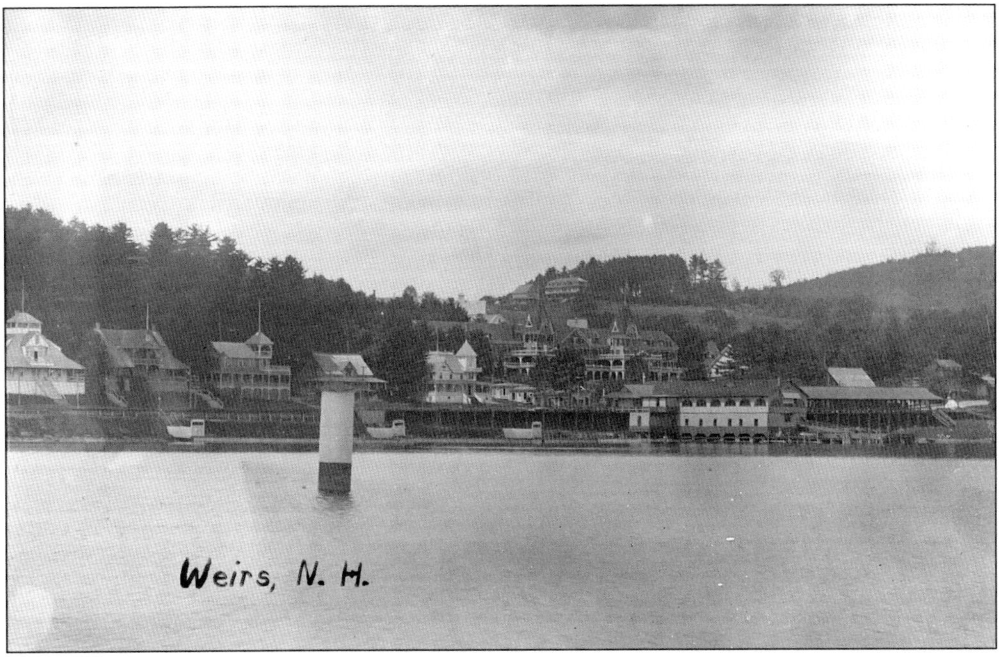

A third view from Interlaken Park. This photograph affords a clear view of the Hotel Winnicoette (center, above New Hotel Weirs) atop Doe (later known as Brickyard) Mountain.

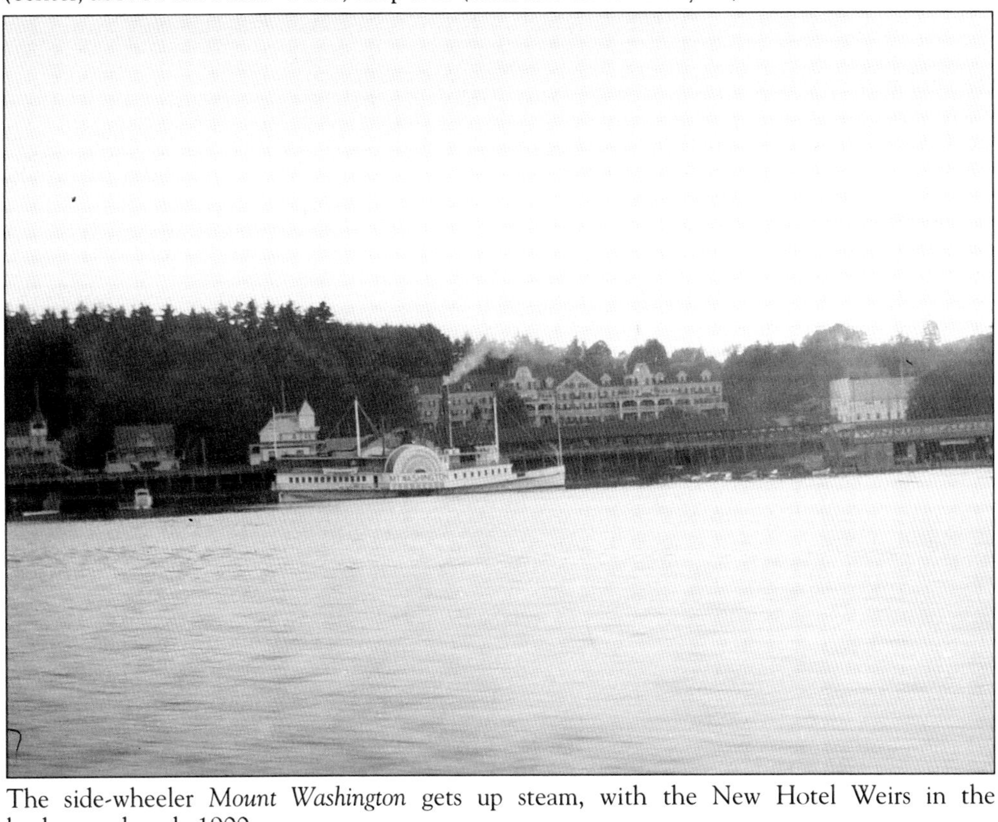

The side-wheeler *Mount Washington* gets up steam, with the New Hotel Weirs in the background, early 1900s.

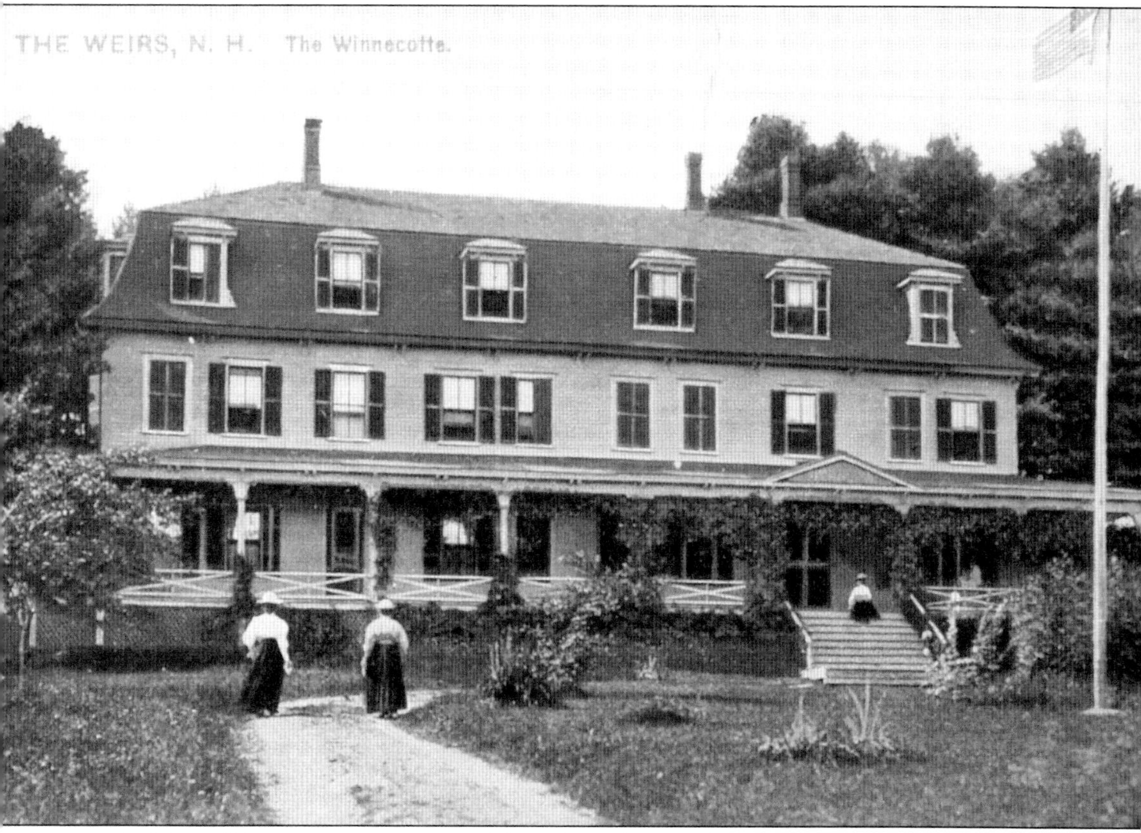

The Hotel Winnicoette, opened in 1879. As with other hotels of the period, ample porches were provided for viewing the panorama of lake and mountains from high on the hill and for promenading—that Victorian essential of resort life. In the mid-twentieth century, the structure underwent alterations and enlargement as the Shangri-La and, later, the Brickyard Mountain Resort. Ultimately, fire destroyed the hotel on March 16, 1989.

Two

The Channel

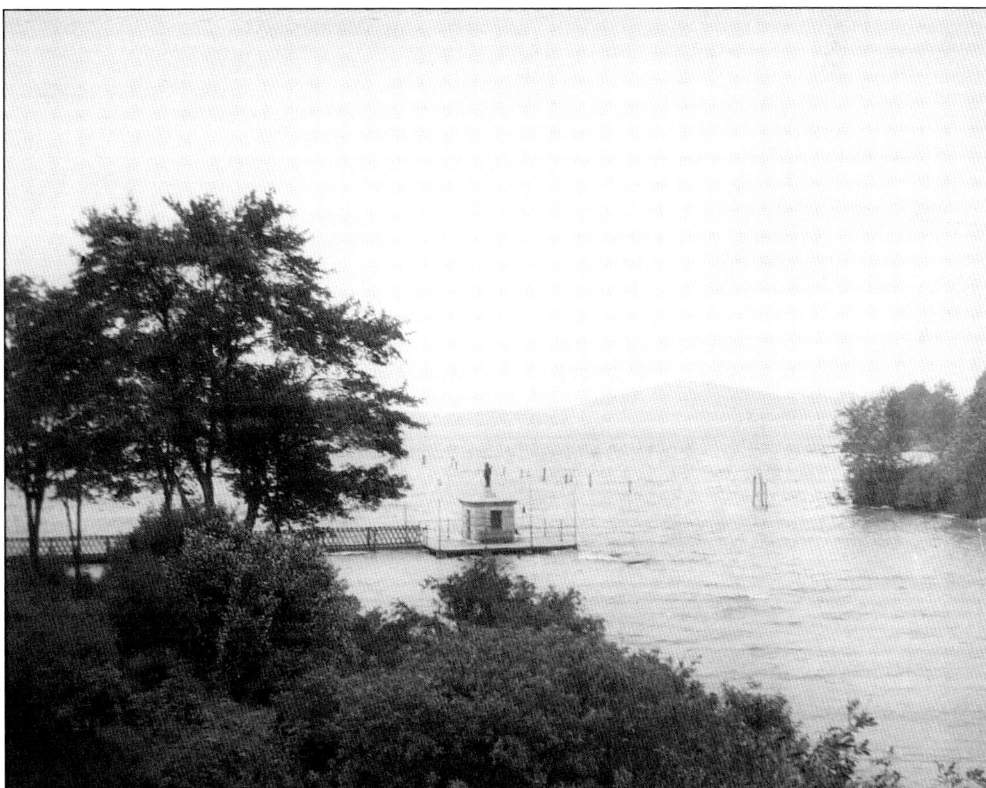

Weirs Channel, looking east toward Lake Winnipesaukee, with Endicott Rock monument at the center, *c.* 1901. The iron footbridge and Indian statue atop the 1892 granite canopy were dedicated in July 1901. Marking the visit of a Colonial surveying party here on August 1, 1652—only thirty-two years after the landing of the Pilgrims at Plymouth—the stone (see pp. 27–34) is "the oldest public monument in New England," declared Laconia lawyer and historian, Erastus Perry Jewell, in his address at the 1901 dedication.

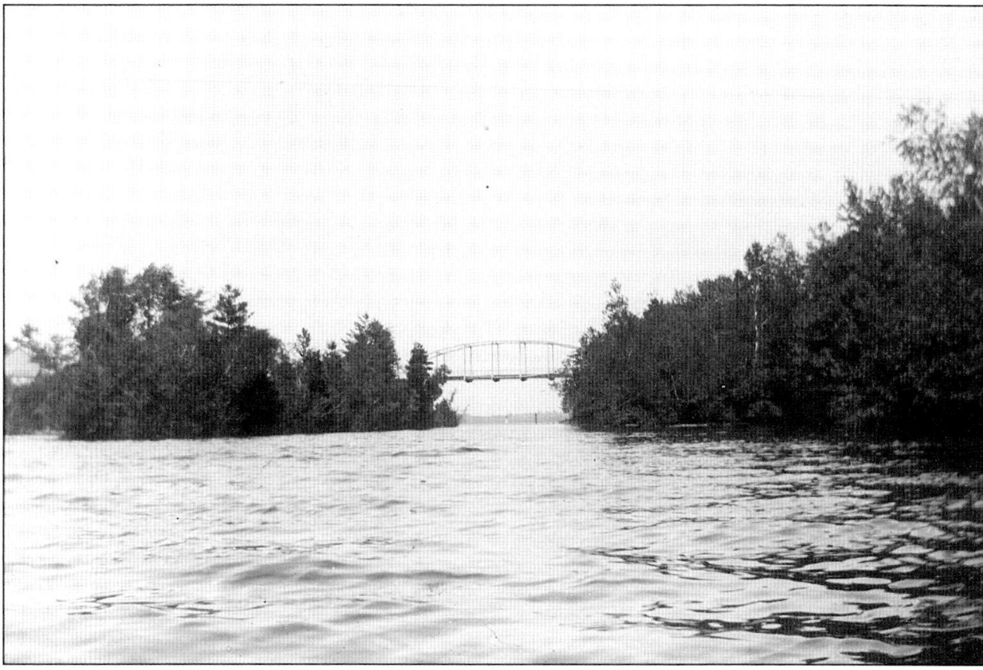

Weirs Bridge, from Lake Paugus and the channel, *c.* 1890. In 1883, this steel-truss suspension bridge replaced a succession of earlier wooden bridges, including at least one covered bridge. With a span of nearly 100 feet, the roadbed of the new bridge was 4 feet higher than the old.

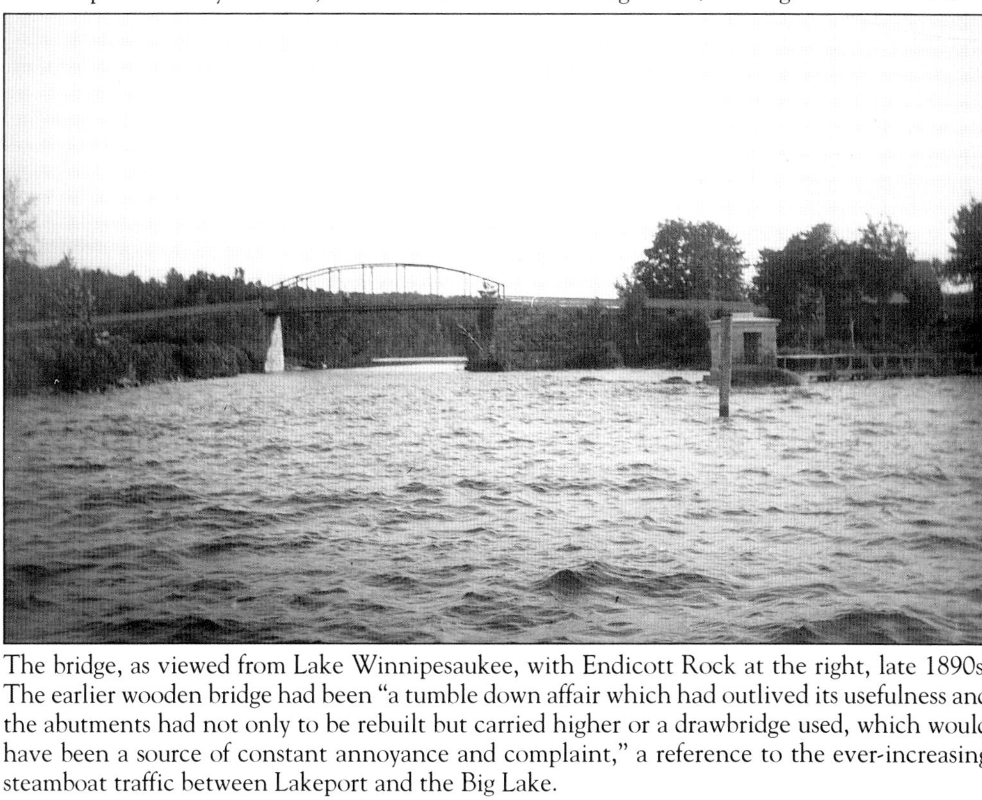

The bridge, as viewed from Lake Winnipesaukee, with Endicott Rock at the right, late 1890s. The earlier wooden bridge had been "a tumble down affair which had outlived its usefulness and the abutments had not only to be rebuilt but carried higher or a drawbridge used, which would have been a source of constant annoyance and complaint," a reference to the ever-increasing steamboat traffic between Lakeport and the Big Lake.

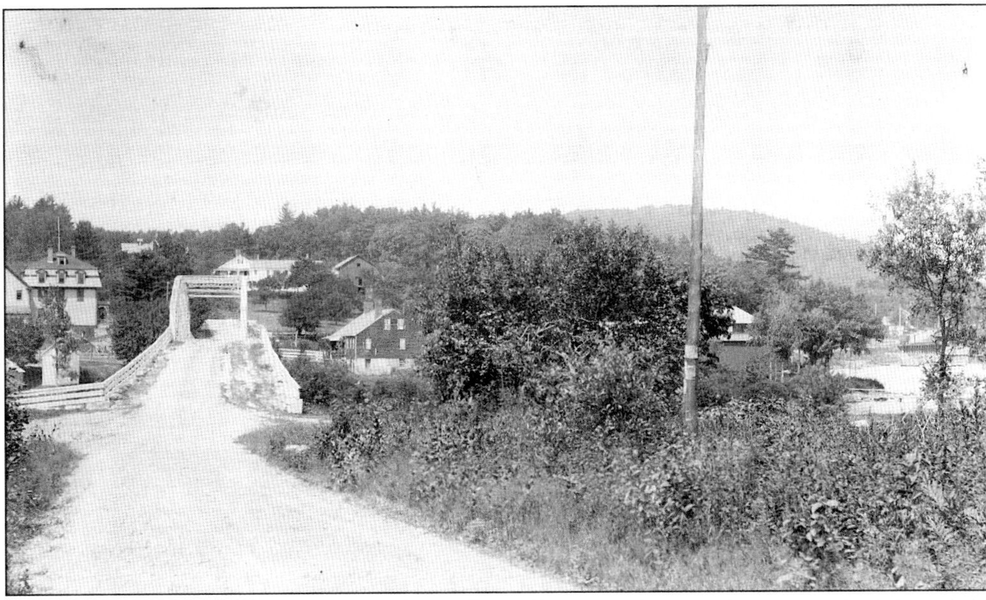

Weirs Bridge, as viewed from the south, *c.* 1890. The Aquedoktan Hotel is at the left and the "Old Red House" (see p. 26) is to the immediate right of the bridge.

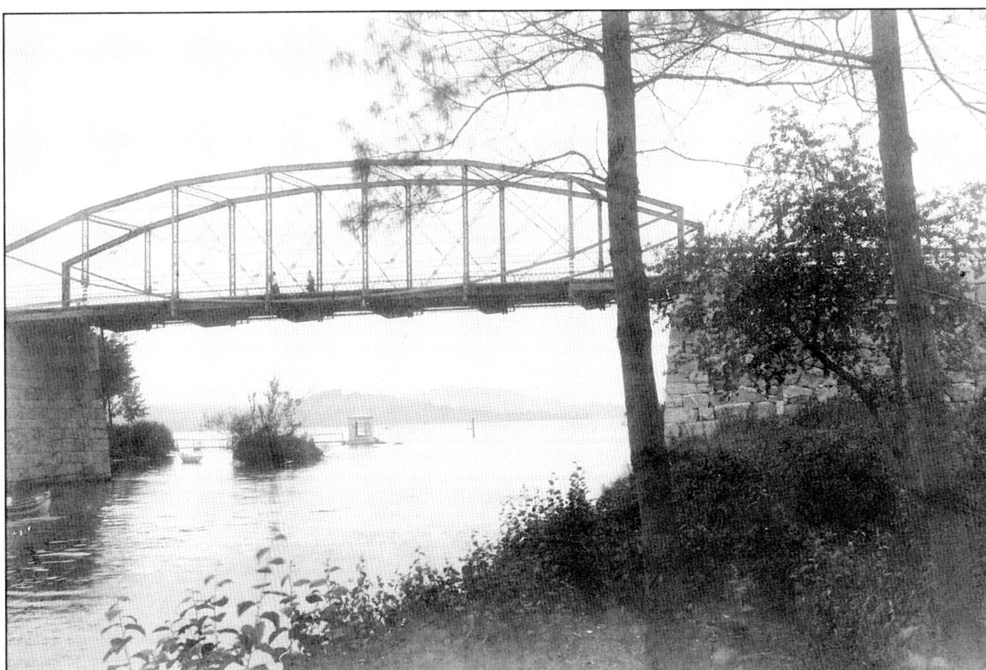

Another view of the 1883 bridge, with Endicott Rock in the distance, mid-1890s. The abutments at both ends were "of the most solid and substantial kind and taken in connection with the long wing walls, extending back on the Laconia side [left] 200 feet and on the Gilford side [right], nearly as far, contain an immense amount of stone work."

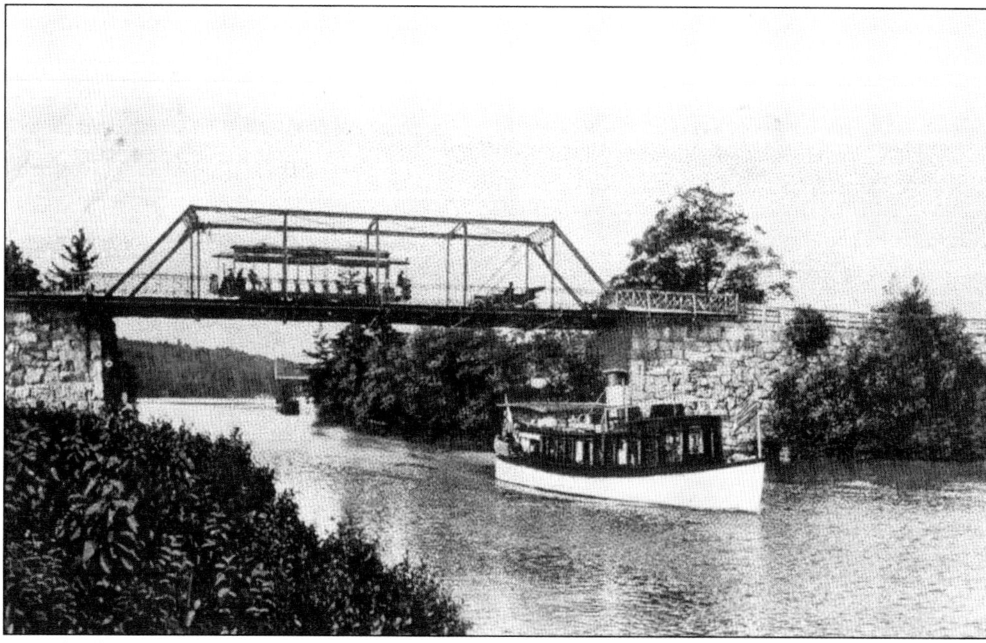

New bridge, about 1906. Although the 1883 bridge was expected to last for many years, the extension of the Laconia Street Railway to The Weirs in 1899 necessitated a heavier span to accommodate the electric cars. The new bridge and trolley line, which ran all the way to the Lakeside House, opened in June of that year. Here, an open trolley crosses the bridge and the U.S. mailboat *Uncle Sam* heads toward Lake Winnipesaukee.

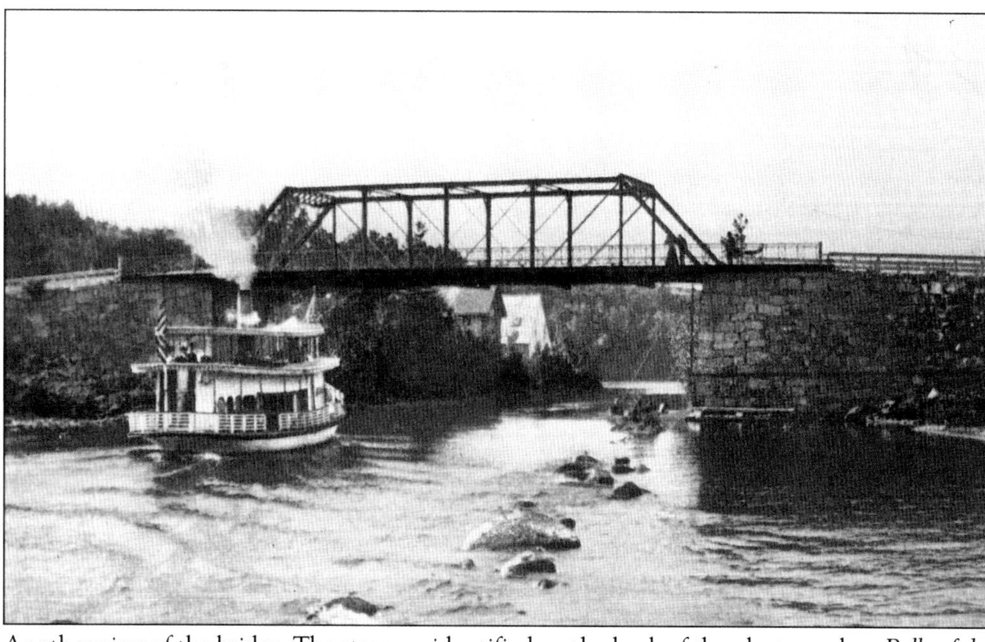

Another view of the bridge. The steamer, identified on the back of the photograph as *Belle of the Isles*, heads through the channel toward Lake Paugus, *c.* 1910.

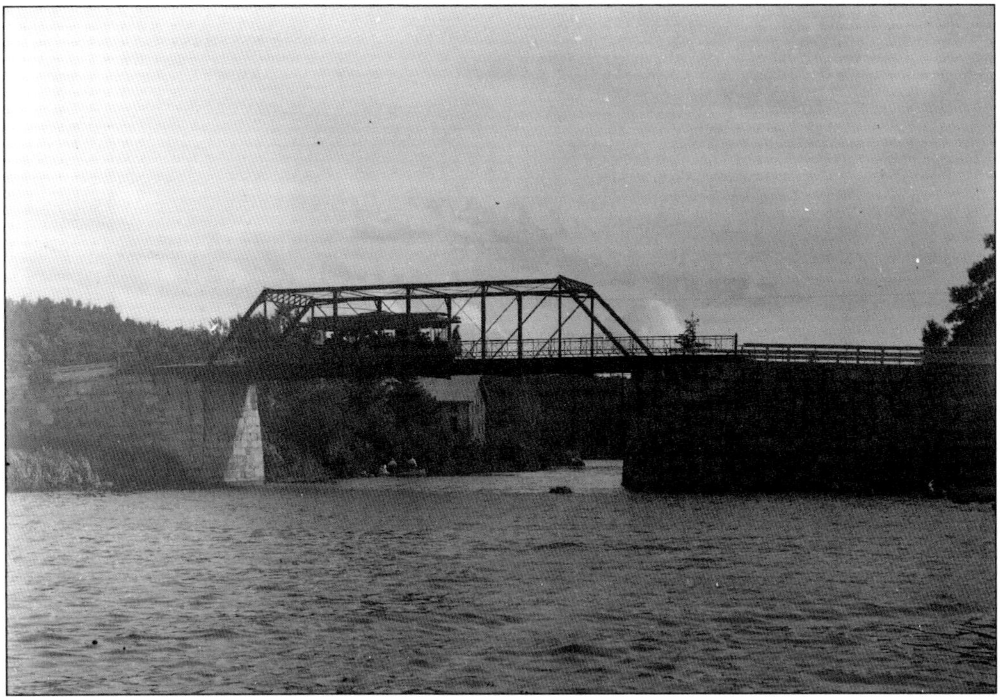

A trolley crossing the bridge. For twenty-six years, the electric cars of the Laconia Street Railway provided daily summer service between Laconia, Lakeport, and The Weirs, carrying thousands of local residents and summer visitors.

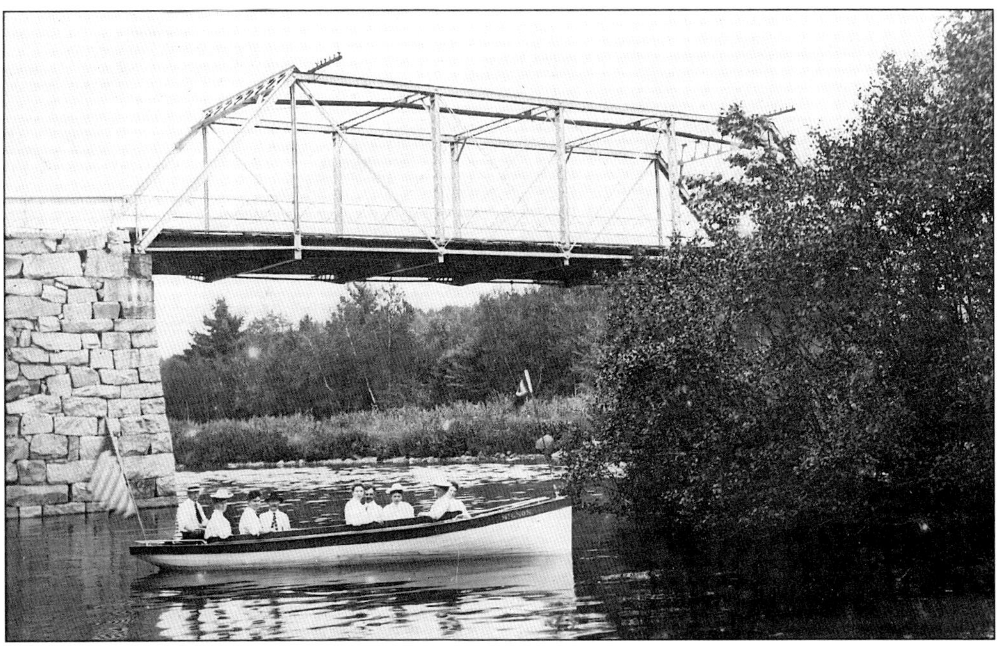

One more view of the bridge, with a party of boaters in the foreground.

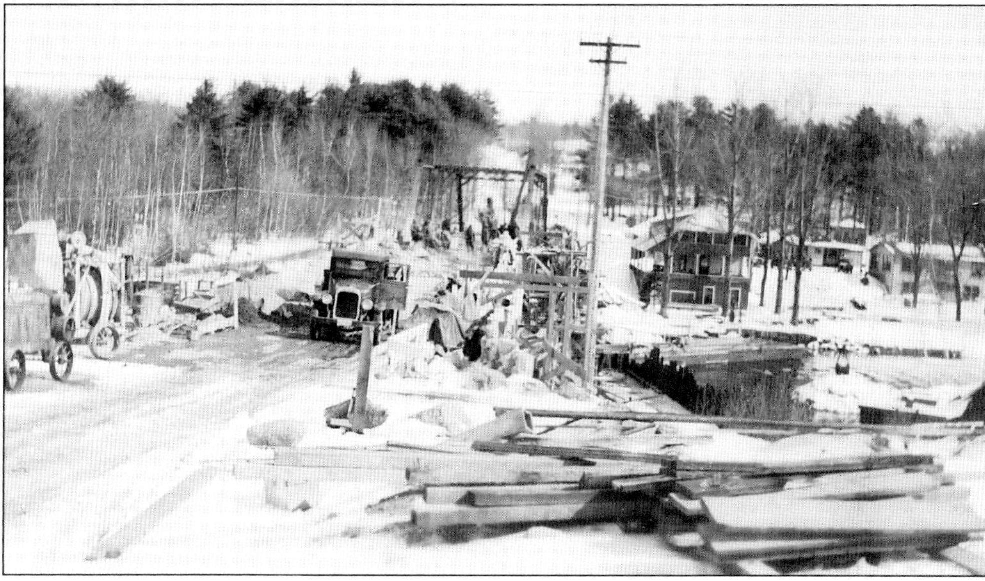

Preparations for the construction of today's bridge, 1932–33.

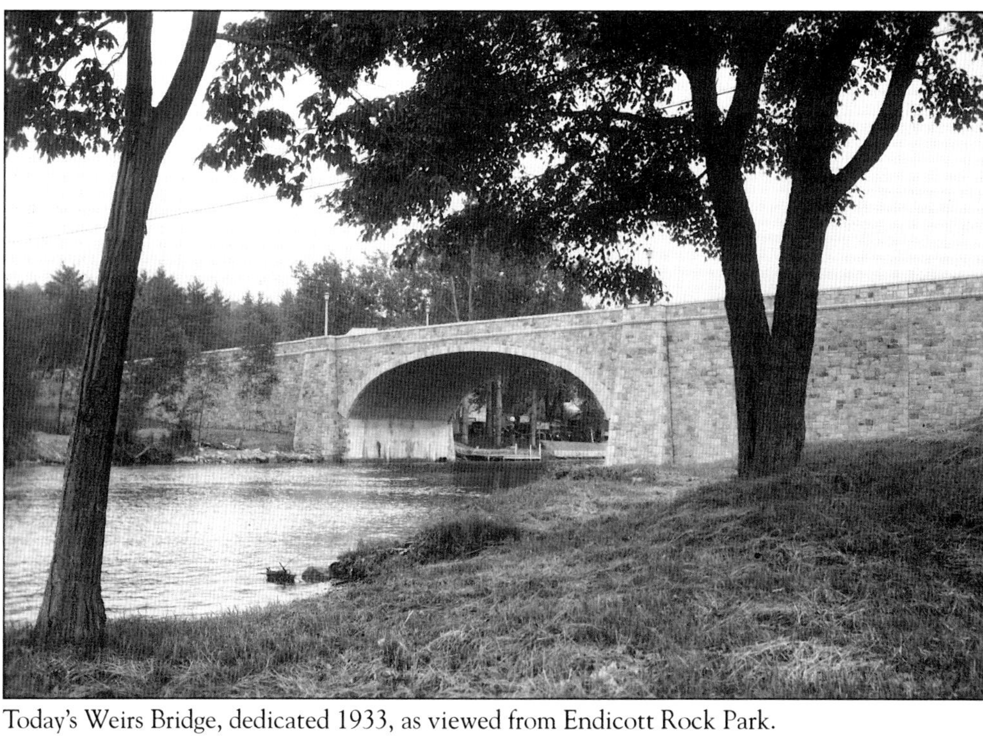

Today's Weirs Bridge, dedicated 1933, as viewed from Endicott Rock Park.

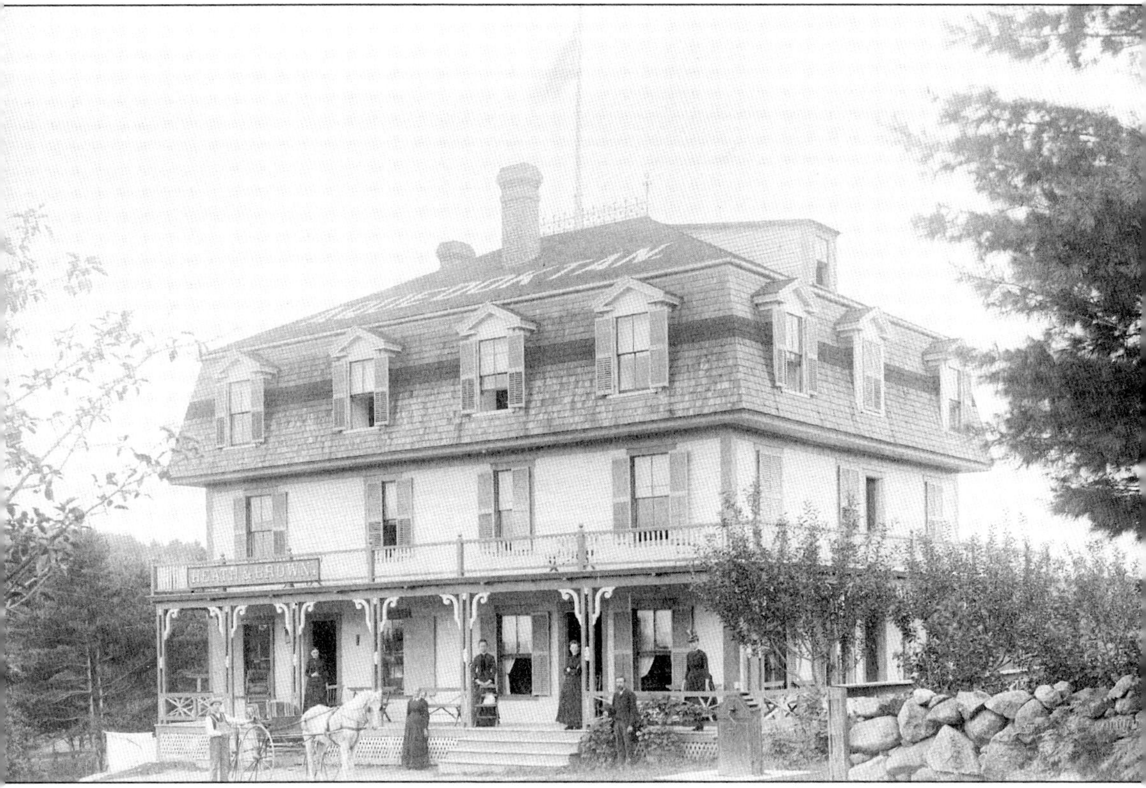

The Aquedoktan Hotel, *c.* 1890. Opened in 1886, it was later known for more than a quarter-century as the Pleasant View Hotel and, after that, as the Park View. The structure still stands as today's Sand Bar Beach Resort. Today's Channel Lane would be to the left, with the entrance to the Weirs Drive-In Theater to the right.

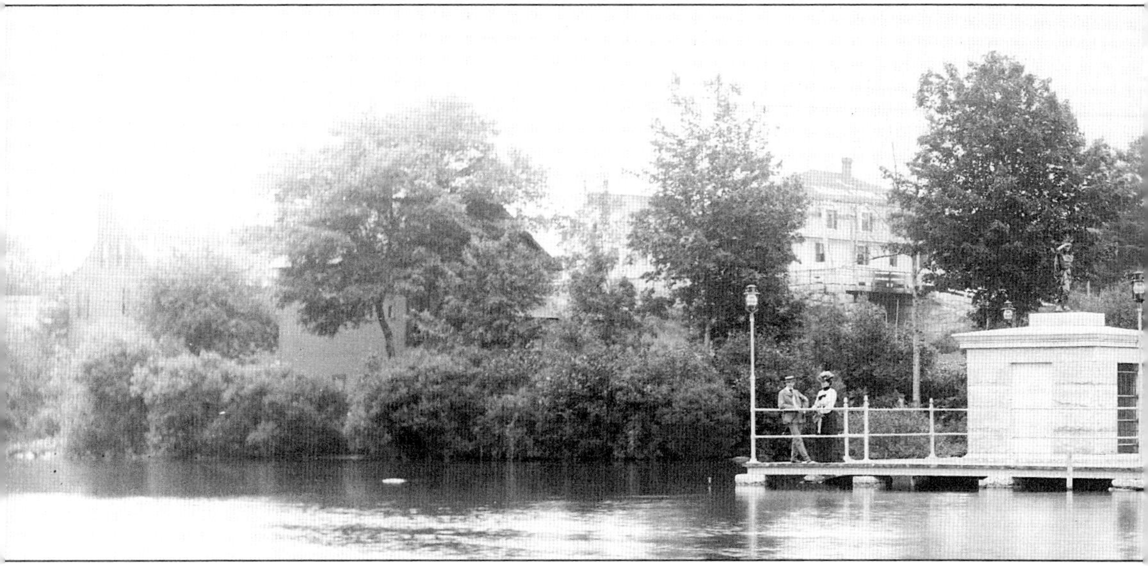

Panoramic view of the area comprising today's Endicott Rock Park. The Aquedoktan Hotel is visible at the top and the Music Hall is to the right. Formerly a roller-skating rink in Concord, the latter structure was taken down and reassembled at The Weirs in July 1886, where it was used for several years for the annual one-week festivals of the New Hampshire Music Teachers

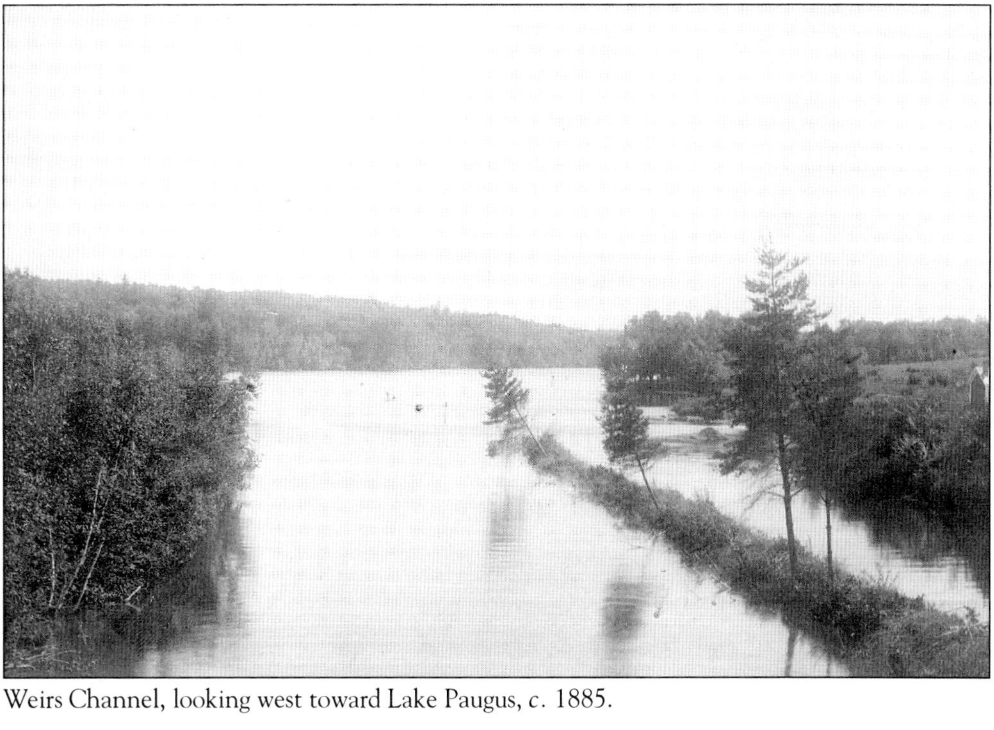

Weirs Channel, looking west toward Lake Paugus, *c.* 1885.

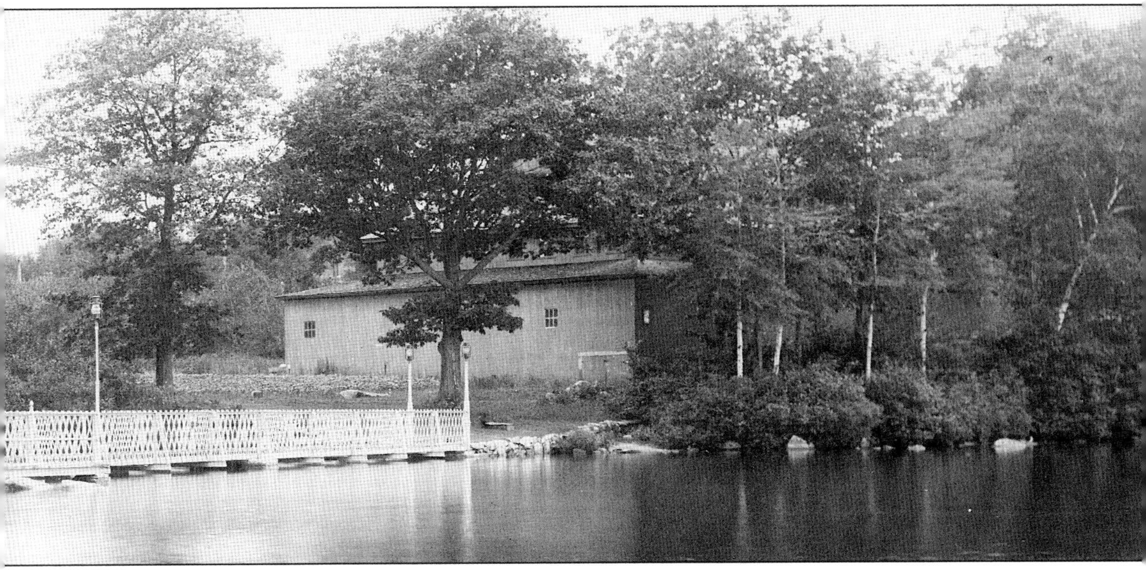

Association. During the rest of the season, the rink reverted to its original purpose, at least in the early years. When the building collapsed "during a winter gale" in 1902–1903, a new Music Hall (see p. 101) was built on Tower Street, next to the Trinity Methodist Episcopal Church.

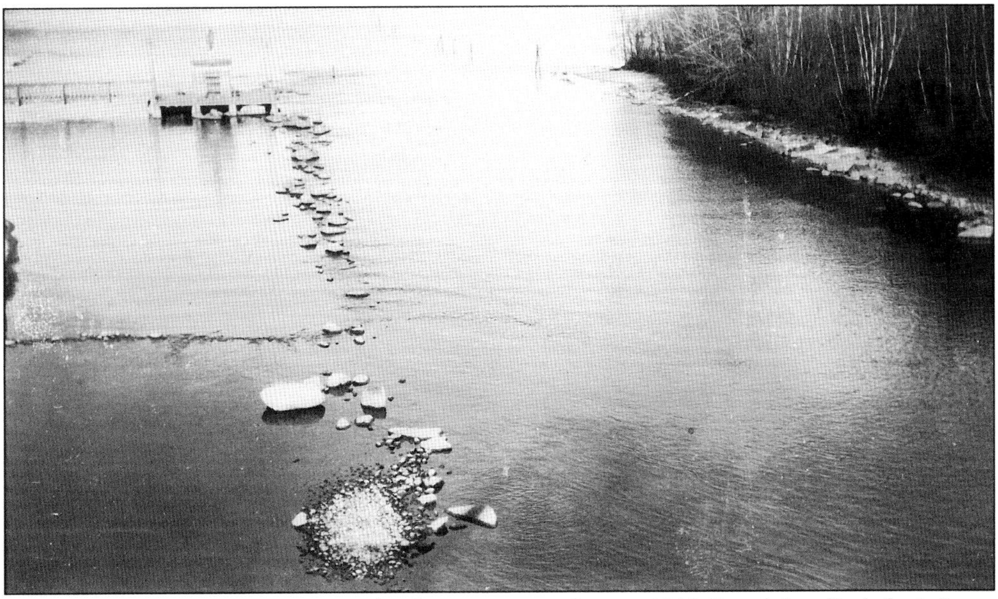

Weirs Channel, looking east toward Lake Winnipesaukee, *c.* 1905. Interlaken Park (right) was an early 1890s subdivision, with its 40 acres laid out into streets and lots for summer cottages.

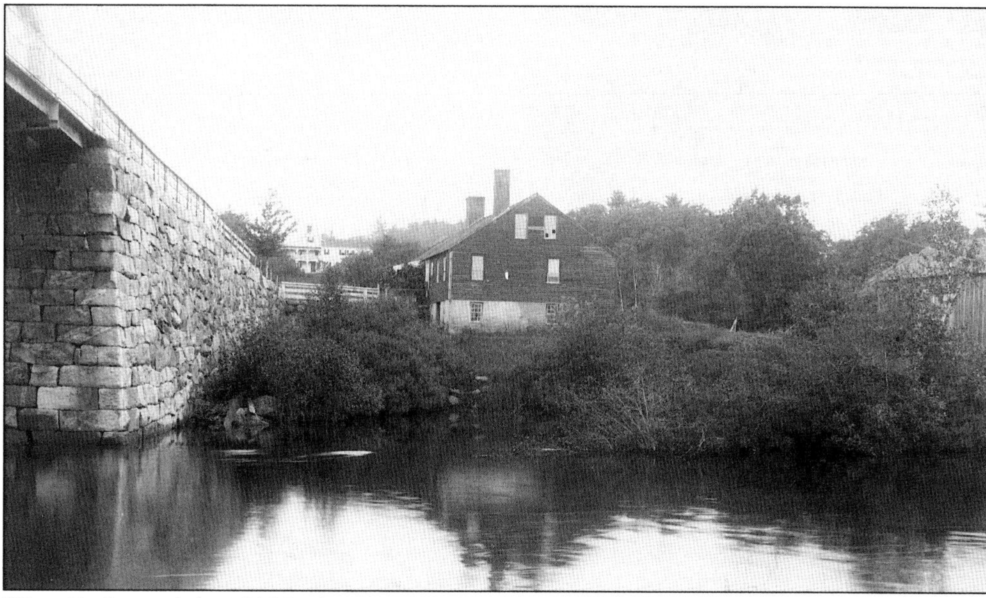

Weirs Bridge and the "Old Red House," at the entrance to today's Endicott Rock Park, c. 1900. Torn down in 1902, the house was old long before The Weirs came into prominence as a summer resort in the late 1870s, "when the place was little more than a cow pasture with a plank walk extending a few feet on the side of the lake and known to the traveling public as Weirs Steamboat Landing." The Old Red House was an important trading post. "Over its counter has been sold in years gone by many dollars' worth of West India goods, etc., to say nothing of many gallons of old New England rum."

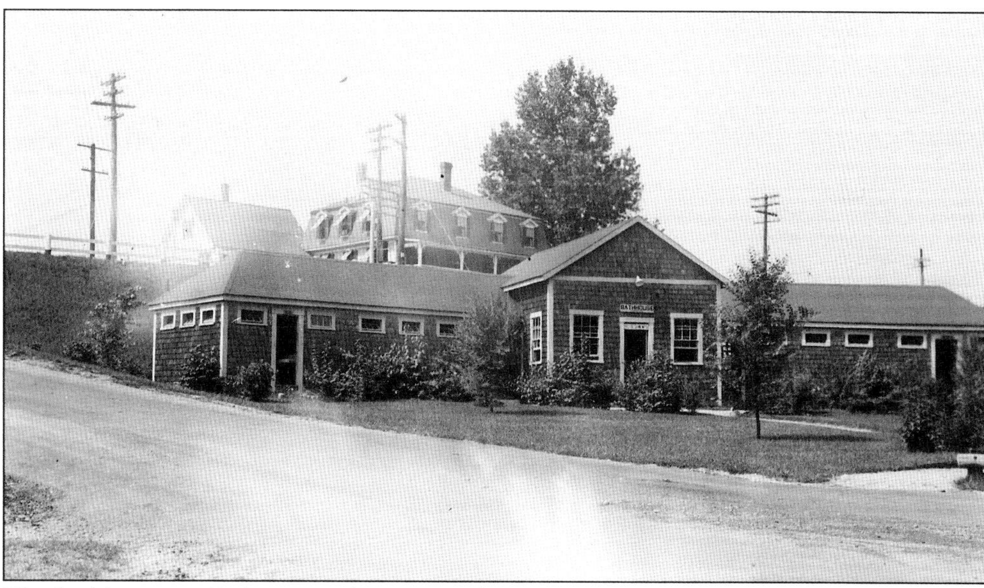

The bathhouse at Endicott Rock State Park, c. late 1930s. Pleasant View (originally the Aquedoktan) Hotel is in the distance. The bathhouse was replaced in May 1962 by a new facility nearer the beach.

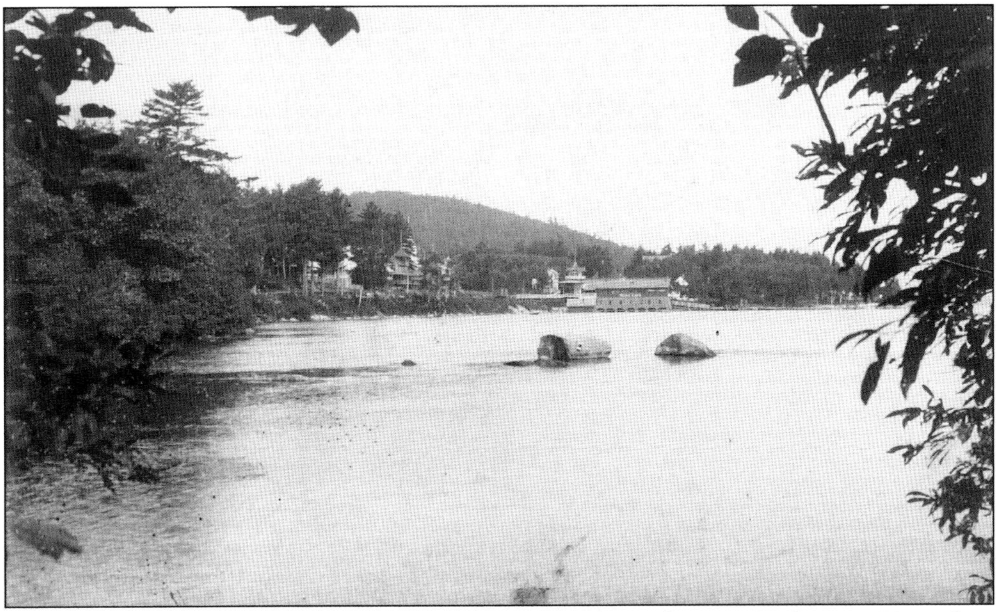

Endicott Rock, to the left of another boulder in Weirs Channel, *c.* 1885. The New Hampshire Veterans Association buildings can be seen in the distance to the left, and the 1885 Weirs Cafe to the right. The New Hampshire Legislature was spurred to take action to protect Endicott Rock by enclosing it in the granite canopy because passing boats had been bumping into the historic relic.

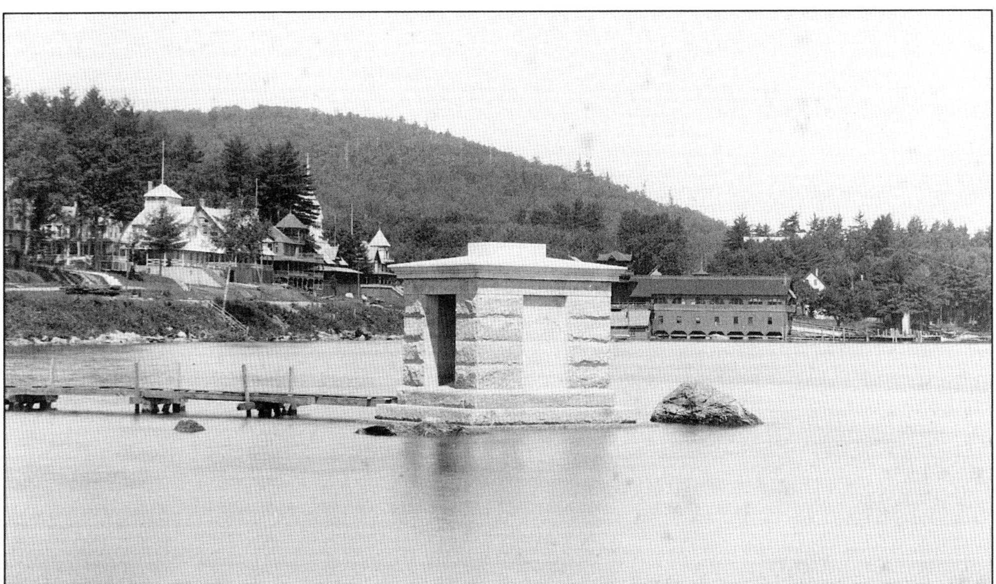

The granite canopy over Endicott Rock, erected by the state and dedicated with elaborate ceremonies in 1892. The wooden footbridge served as access to the monument until replaced by one made of steel in 1901. In the distance, the buildings of the New Hampshire Veterans Association on Lakeside Avenue, Weirs Cafe, and the steamboat landing can be seen.

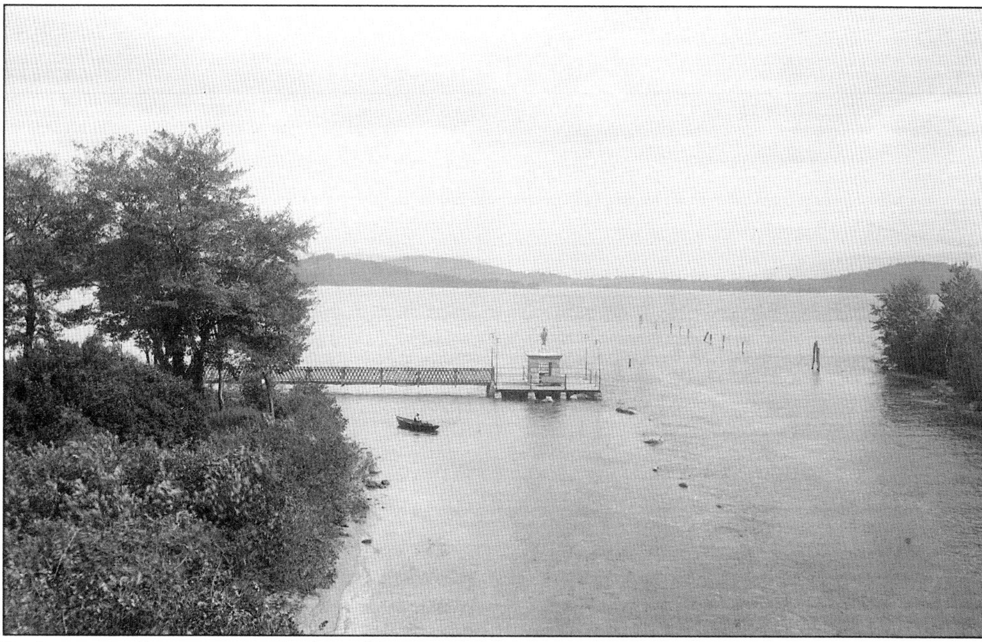

Endicott Rock canopy, with the addition of the Indian statue now known as "Captain Jack." The statue, a gift of Dr. J. Alonzo Greene (see p. 62), was added in 1901, along with a steel footbridge that replaced the earlier wooden walkway.

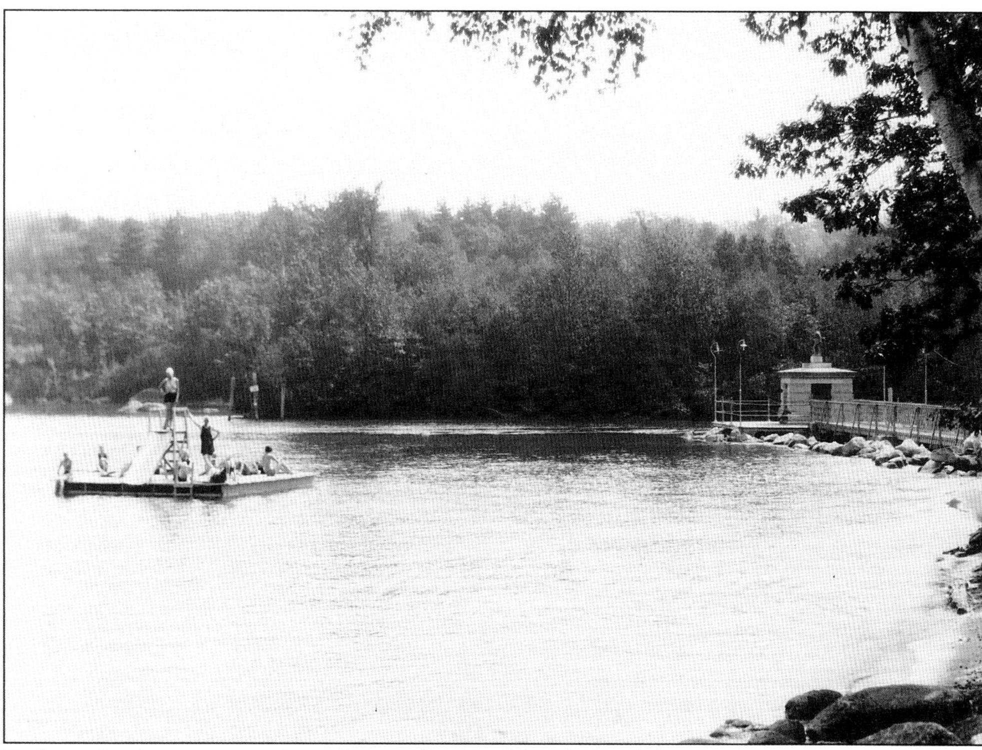

Endicott Rock monument from the north side of the channel, late 1920s or early 1930s.

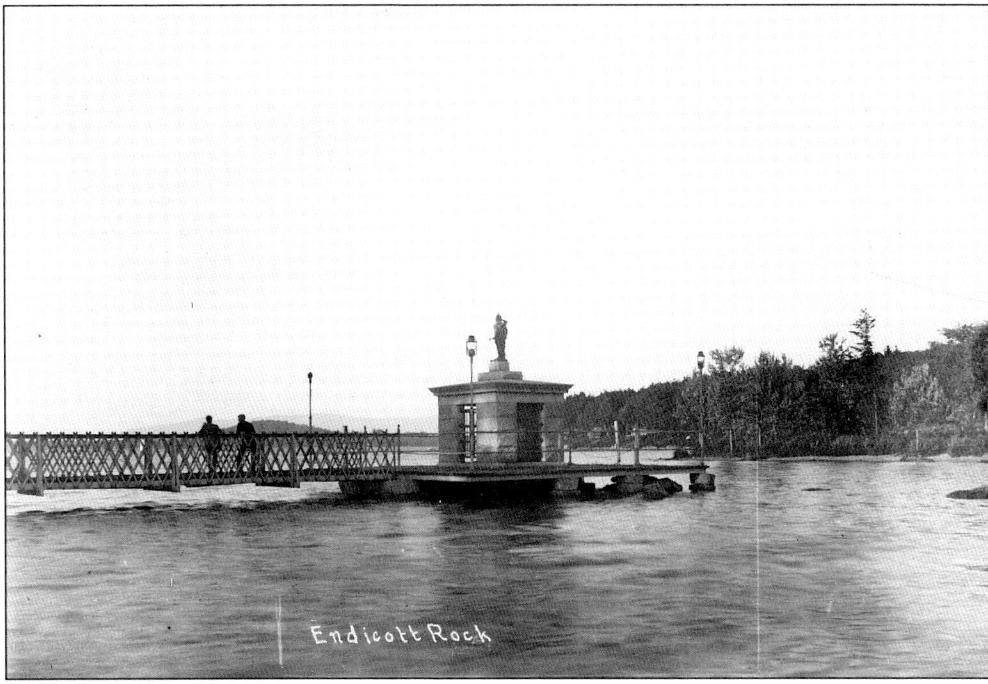

Another view of Endicott Rock monument, at the end of the 1930s, before the land for part of today's Endicott Rock Park was filled in.

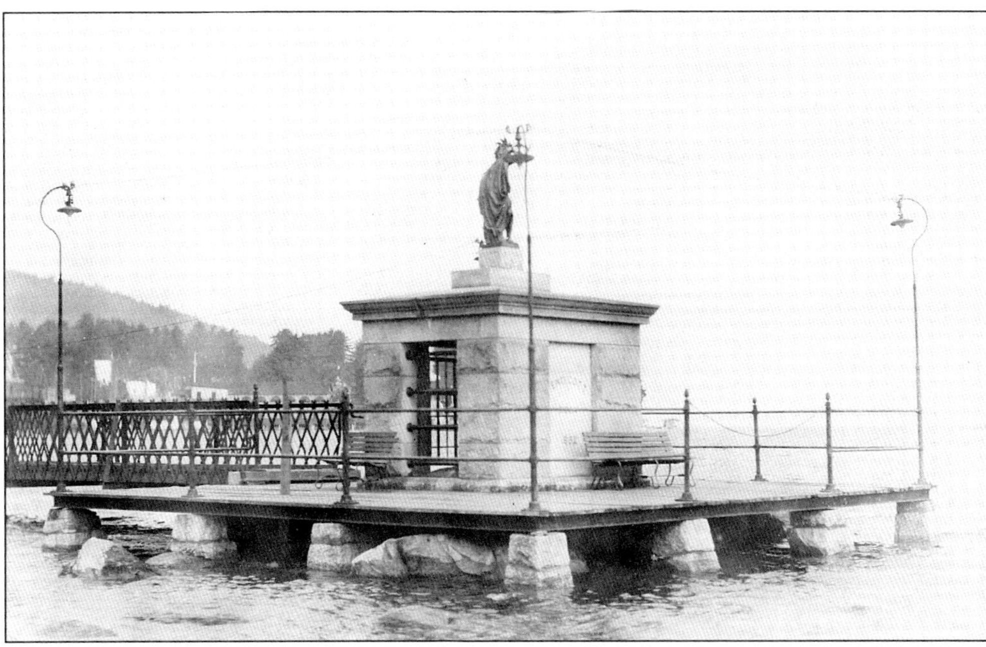

A closer view of the monument.

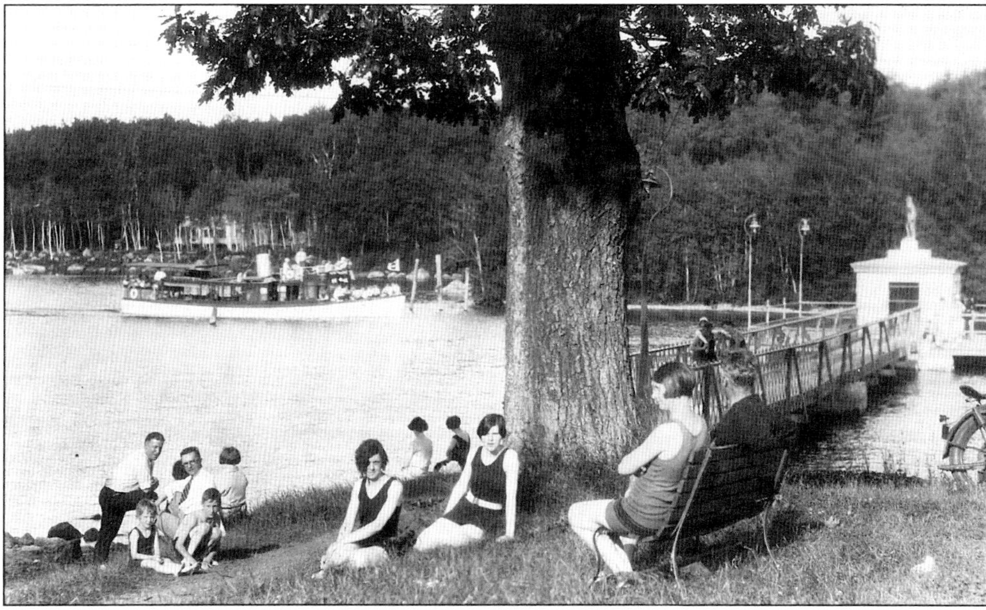

Bathers relax on the shore near Endicott Rock, 1926.

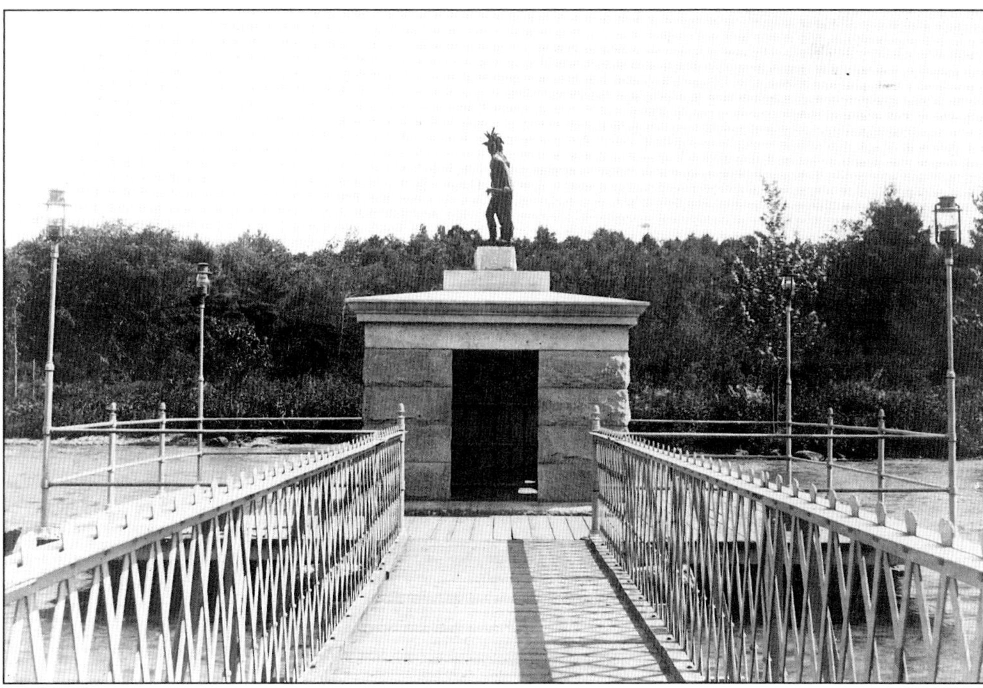

The approach to the monument, *c.* 1912.

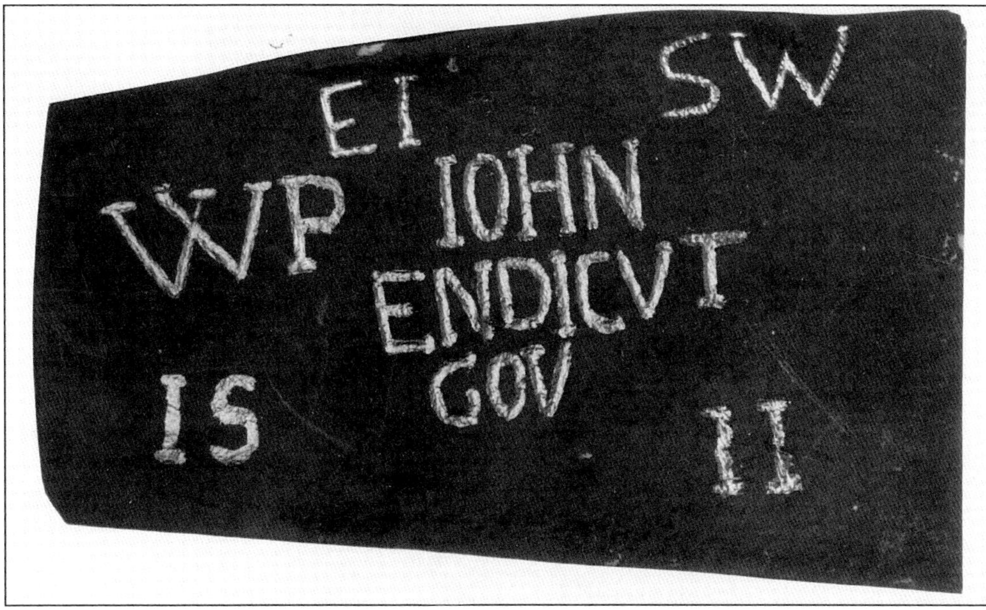

The inscription on Endicott Rock, documenting the 1652 visit by a surveying party sent out by Massachusetts Bay Colony Governor John Endicott. Surrounding the governor's name are the initials of members of the surveying party. A description of the inscription was entered into the colony's records, which helped identify the boulder when it was rediscovered in 1833, while the channel was being deepened to allow the steamboat *Belknap* to pass between Lake Paugus and Lake Winnipesaukee.

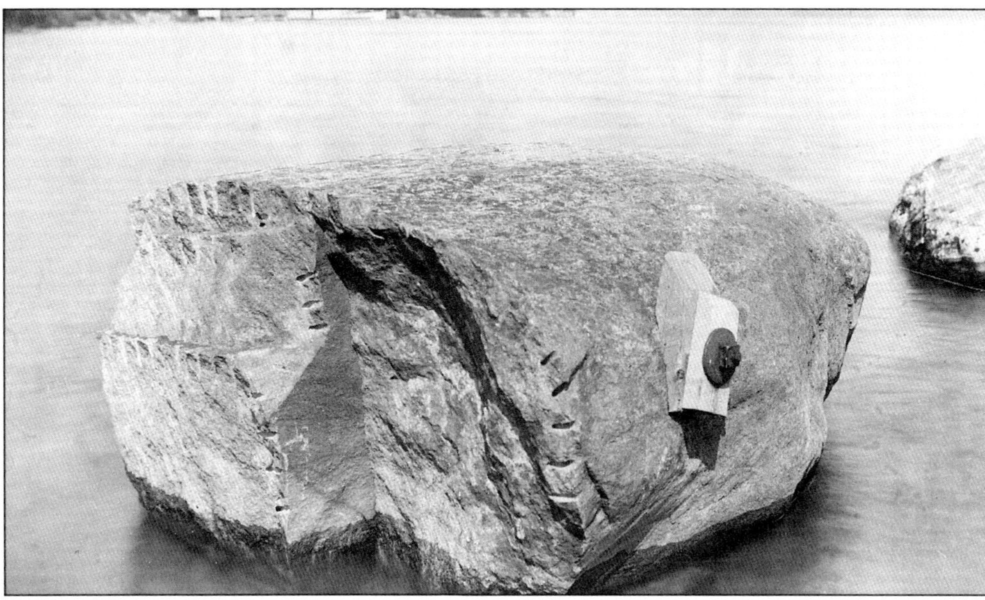

Endicott Rock, prior to construction of the granite canopy. Elevated several feet above its former position, a firm support of stone was built beneath it "and all danger of fracture, on account of a seam formed therein, to be averted by an iron band passed around and an iron bolt passed through it from one side to the other." This photograph was taken on August 28, 1885, by F.W. Fowler of Salisbury, Massachusetts, later a longtime distinguished resident of Laconia.

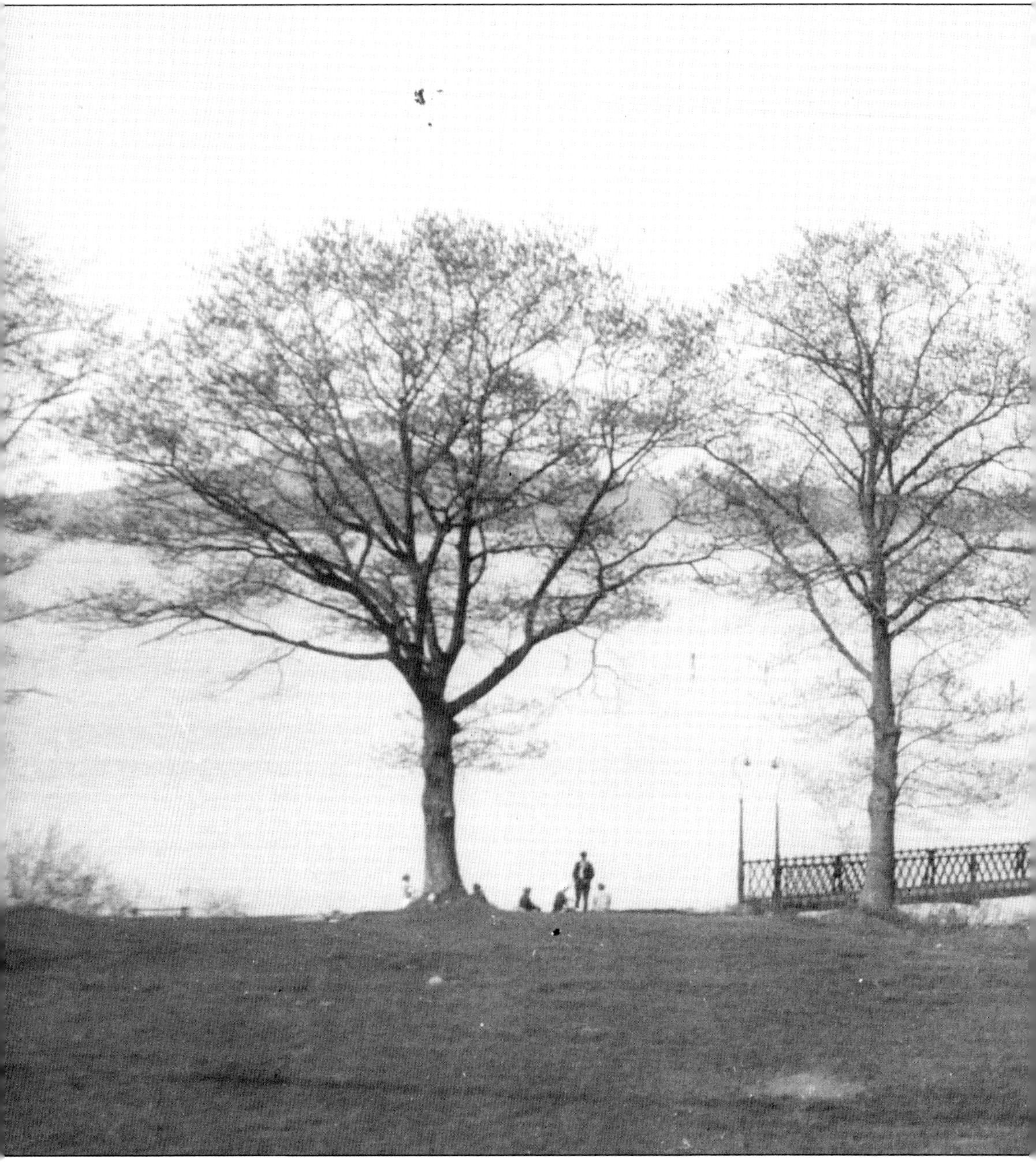

Endicott Rock Park, before part of the channel (right) was filled in. In 1903, the remains of the 1886 Music Hall (see p. 25) were torn down and the land began to be used as a park. In May 1908, the Boston & Maine Railroad formally donated the use of its land adjoining Endicott Rock monument for a park and furnished one hundred shrubs for landscaping. This photograph was probably taken between 1901 and 1908. The space portrayed in this tranquil scene was the site, 350 years ago, of part of the Native American village of Aquedoctan. (The village extended west, along the Channel, past the area of today's Weirs Drive-In Theater and probably north along Lakeside Avenue as well.) Archeological investigations here in 1976–77 determined that the site had been occupied as early as 9,800 years ago. Shad, caught in the fish

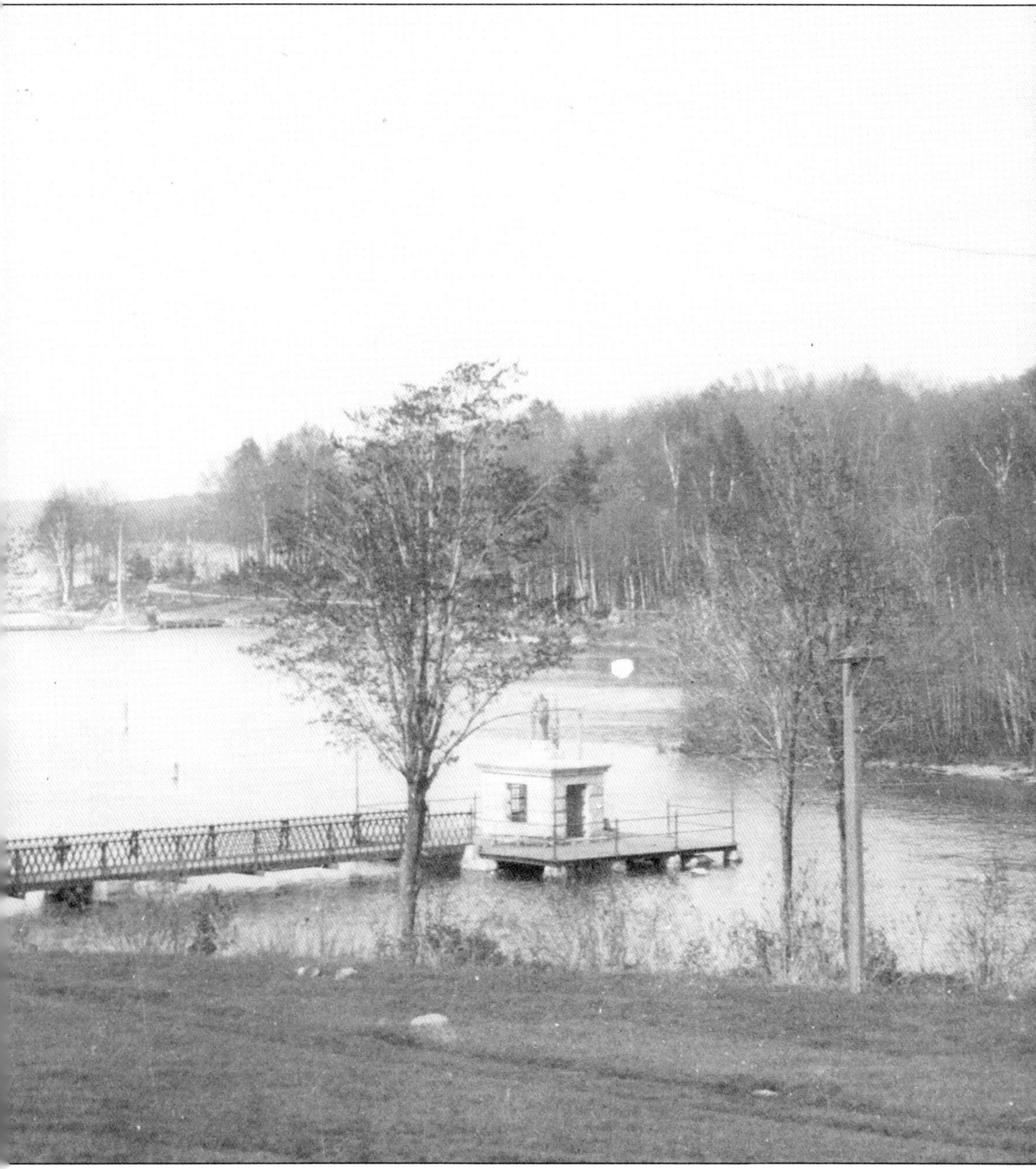

weirs in the channel, comprised a major part of the Indians' diet. Evidence was also found of pottery made from the same clay deposits later used by the Weirs Brickyard at the northern end of Lakeside Avenue. Old accounts indicate that by 1696—only forty-four years after the visit of Governor Endicott's surveying party—Aquedoctan had been abandoned, most of its residents victims of European diseases or Colonial scalp hunters, the few survivors having relocated to Maine or Canada. Somewhere in the vicinity, a Colonial fort was briefly garrisoned in 1736. Most of the area depicted is now covered with the asphalt parking lot of Endicott Rock Park.

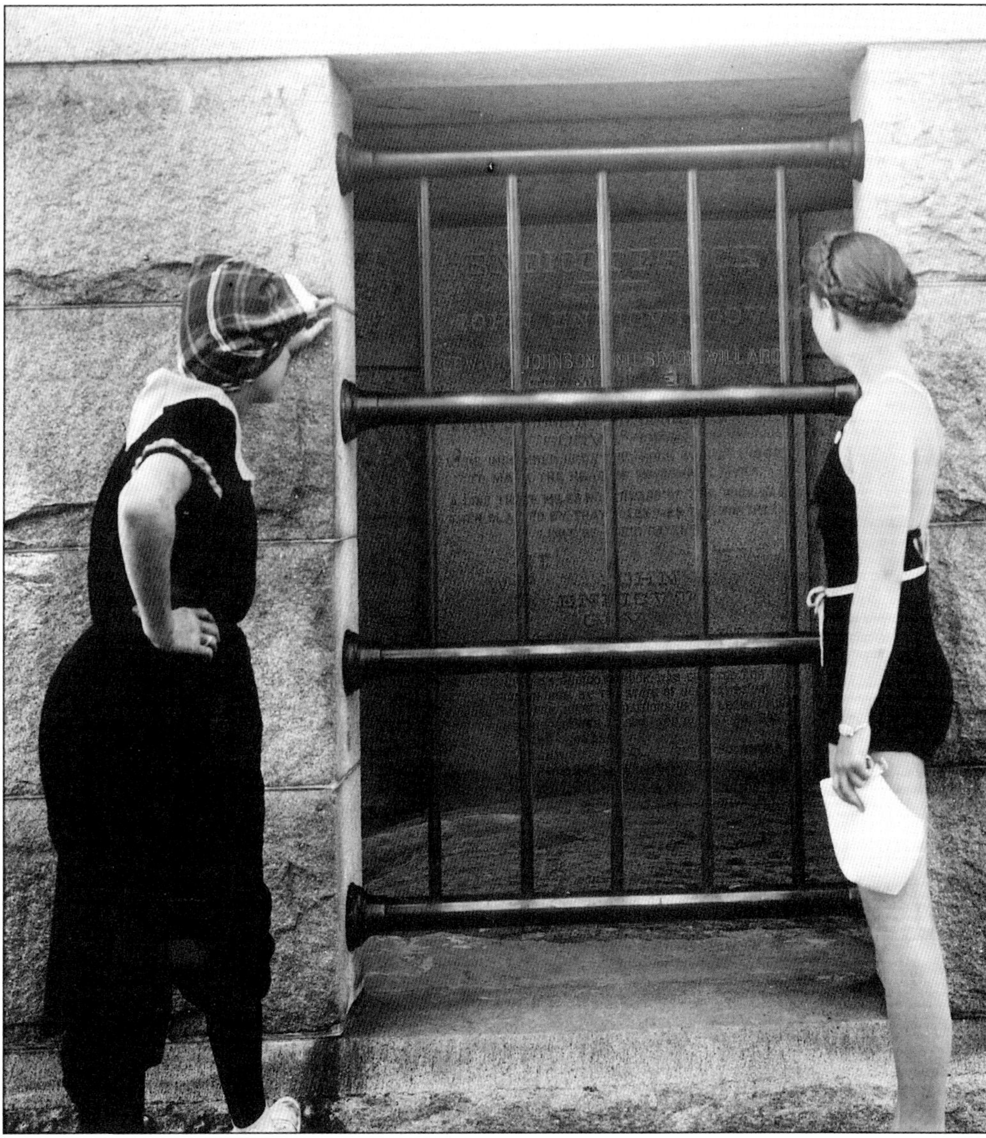

Another publicity shot from the 1936 Aquedoctan Celebration. Here, Mary Louise Plummer of Pleasant Street, Laconia, dressed as an old-fashioned bathing girl, tells Anne Little of The Weirs and Melrose, Massachusetts, in more modern garb, the interesting story of this old boulder.

Three

Lakeside Avenue to Tower Street

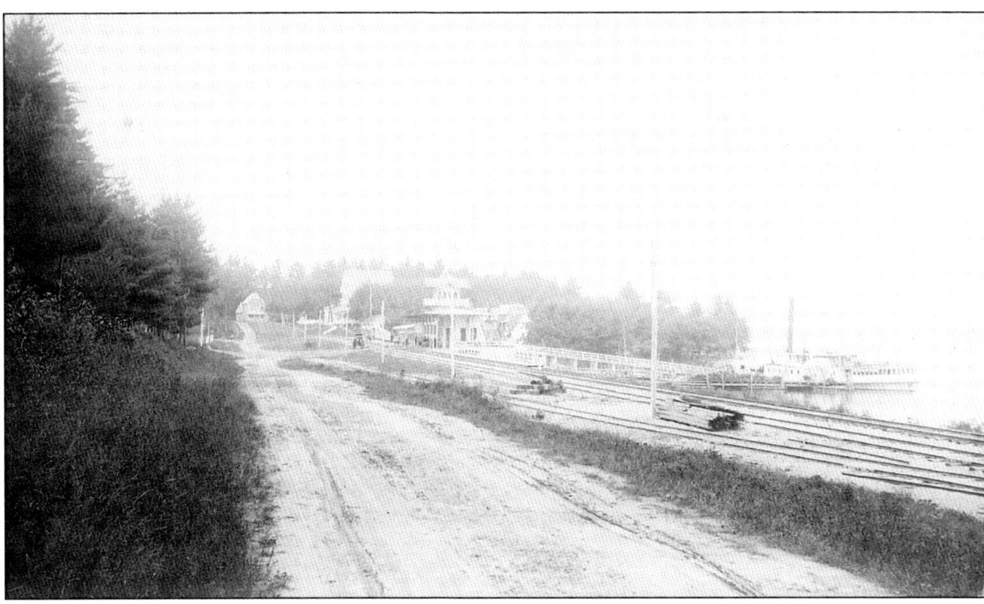

Lakeside Avenue, *c.* 1880. This was The Weirs just before the rapid expansion of the 1880s and early 1890s, which included construction of the Weirs Cafe in 1885 and culminated in the renovation and expansion of the 1880 depot (center). Renovations included the addition of a 500-by-30-foot canopy over the boardwalk in 1893 and raising the grade of the avenue some 3 feet, a year or so thereafter.

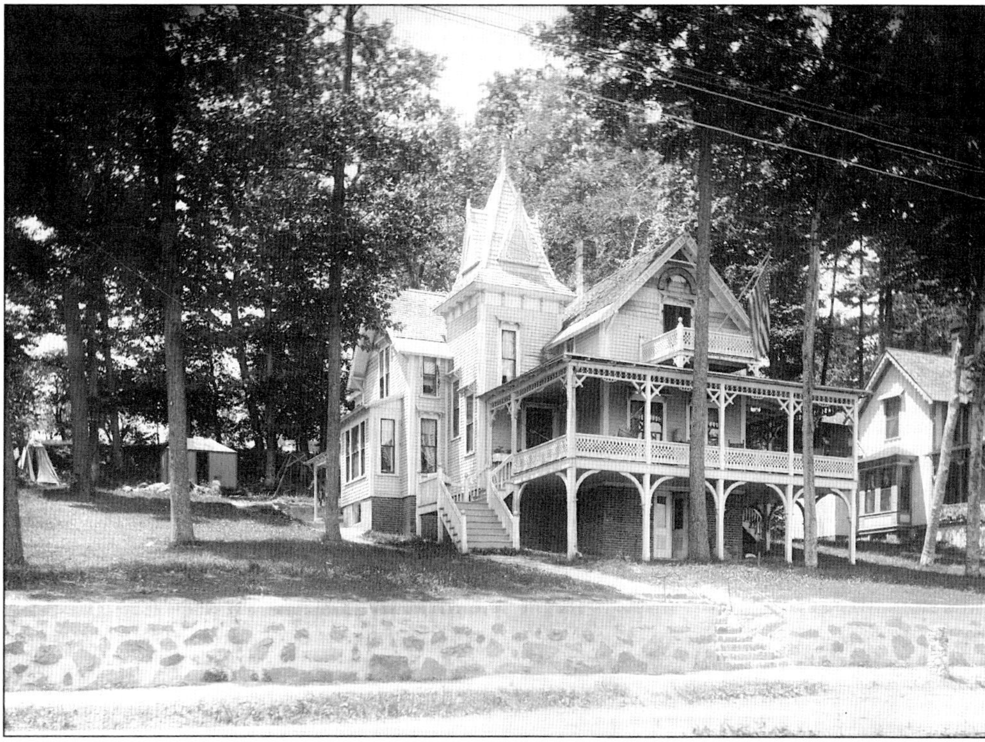

"Castle Rest," Lakeside Avenue. This was the home of George W. Tarlson, and later of George W. Tarlson Jr., both merchants, politicians, and civic leaders. George Jr. was also a prominent musician in the Lakes Region for decades, with his Tarlson's Tune Toppers. His sister Hazel, a member of the Tune Toppers, was a noted pianist and organist in the area.

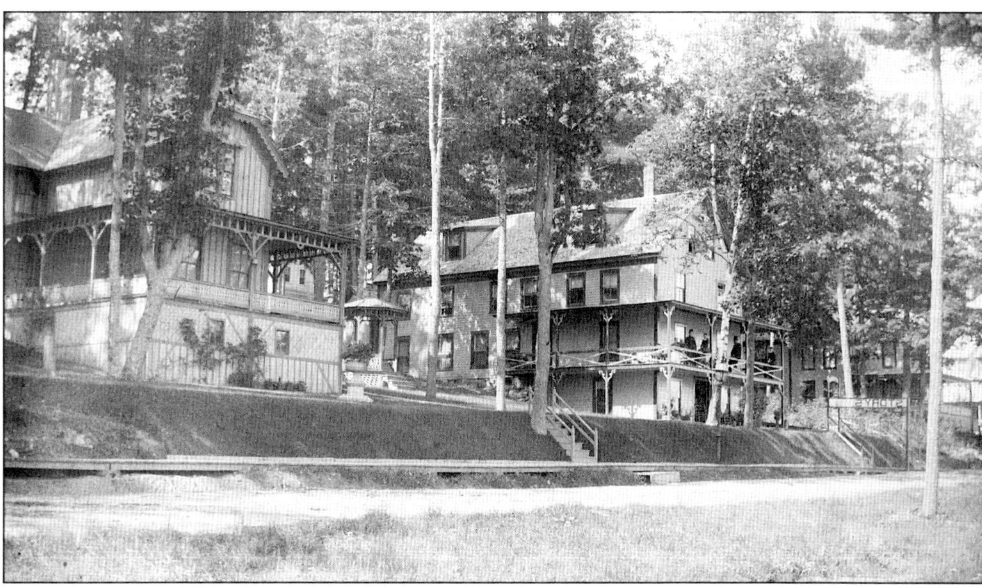

Clyde Cottage (left), one of several private cottages on the south end of Lakeside Avenue, and Story's Hotel (right) as they appeared in 1889.

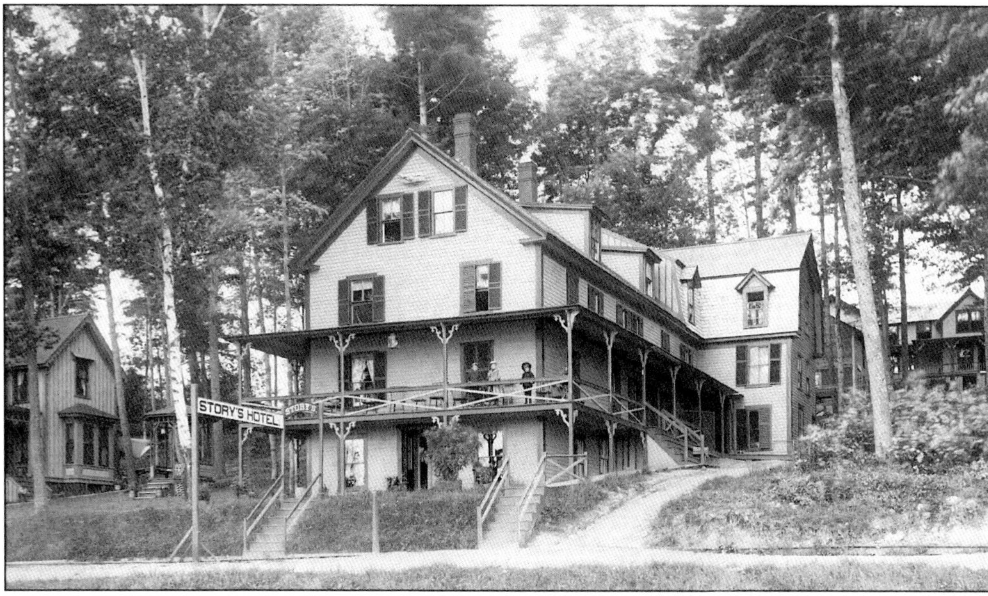

Story's Hotel, 1890. Proprietor David B. Story, already an experienced hotelkeeper in Laconia and Lakeport, was also landlord of the Hotel Weirs for some years. His son, J. Henry Story, was proprietor of the downtown Laconia drugstore that for many years bore the Story name.

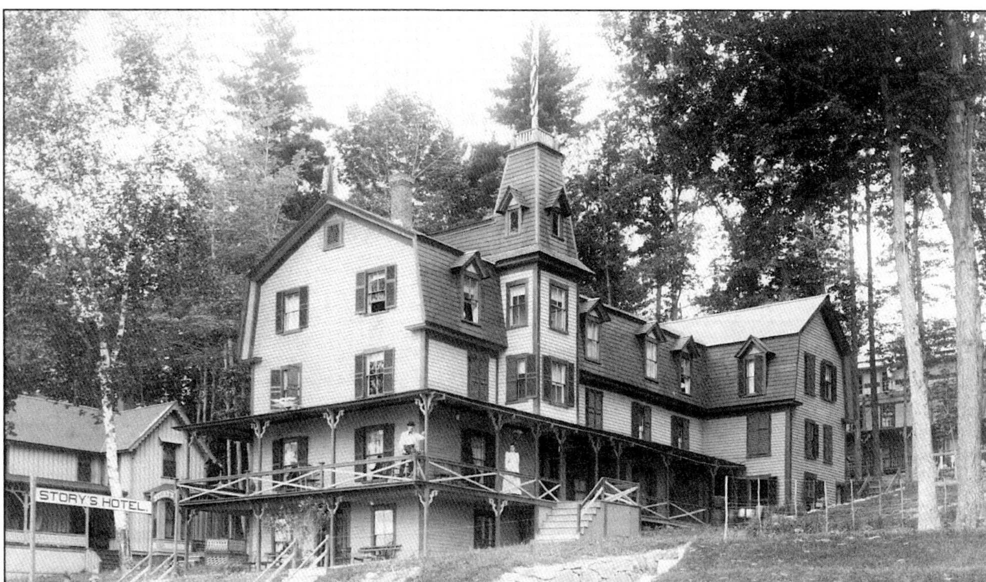

Story's Hotel, 1892, after considerable enlargement. In later years, it was known as Cawley's, as the Carroll Arms, and, at the end, even as the Hotel Weirs. The building was destroyed by fire, September 27, 1991.

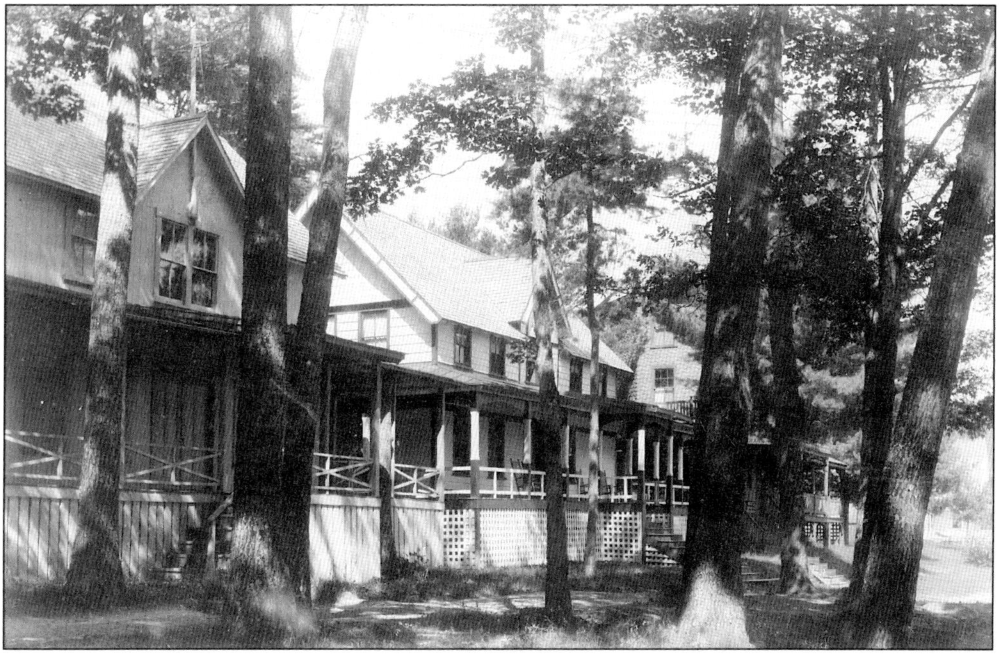

From the left: The 5th Regiment, Lowell, and Manchester Buildings on the New Hampshire Veterans Association grounds. The Lowell Building, the first of some thirty-five structures ultimately built on the grounds, is located directly opposite the upper end of New Hampshire Avenue. It appears prominently in a number of photographs, in the distance beyond the arch over the entrance to the grounds (see p. 46). The Manchester Building no longer exists.

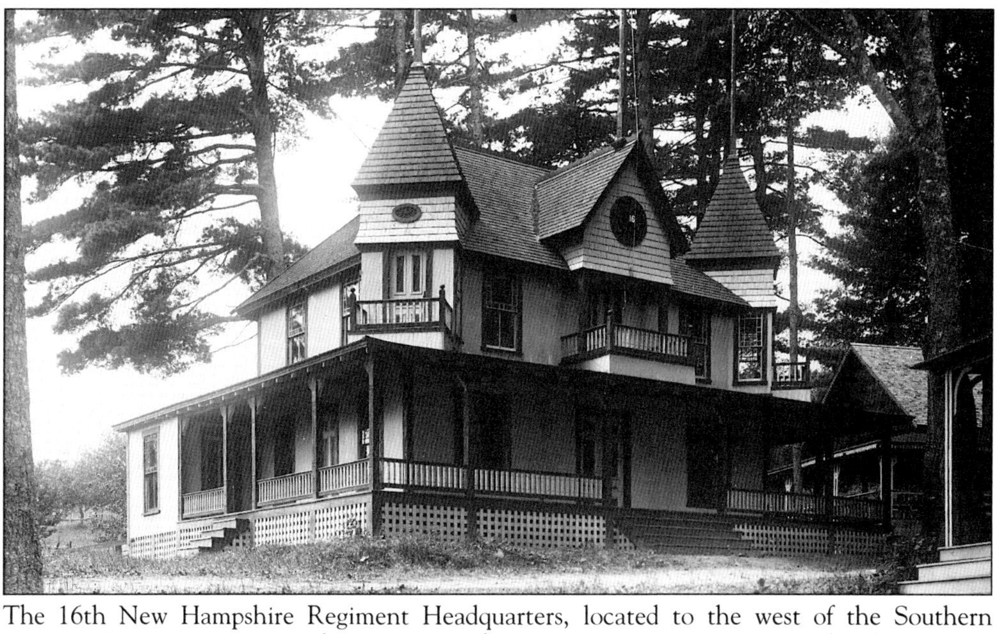

The 16th New Hampshire Regiment Headquarters, located to the west of the Southern Veterans Avenue entrance to the New Hampshire Veterans Association grounds. The building burned in January 1995. Although the annual veterans' reunions were usually held during the last week of August, regimental association buildings like this were available to members for accommodations during the rest of the summer season.

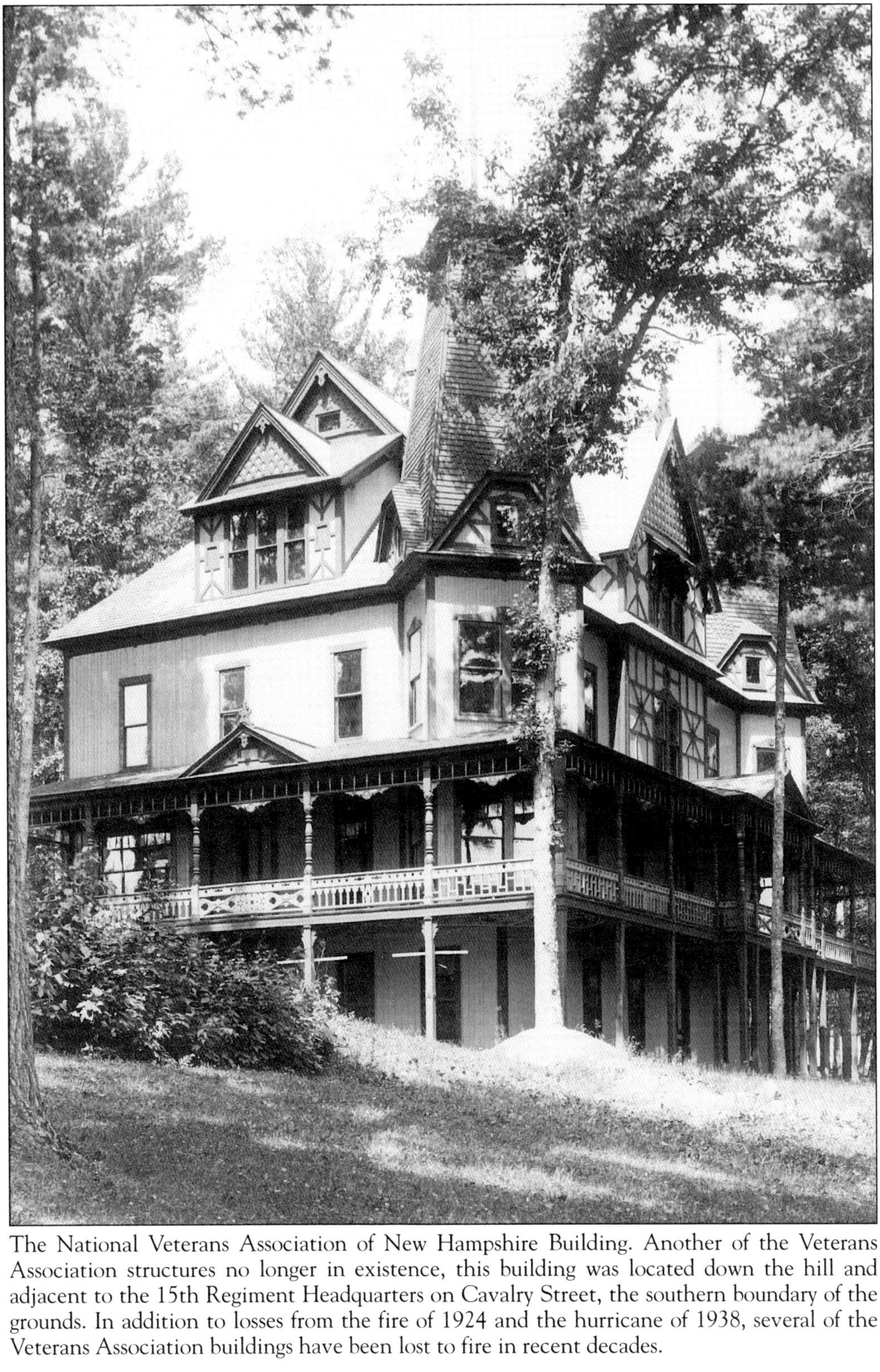

The National Veterans Association of New Hampshire Building. Another of the Veterans Association structures no longer in existence, this building was located down the hill and adjacent to the 15th Regiment Headquarters on Cavalry Street, the southern boundary of the grounds. In addition to losses from the fire of 1924 and the hurricane of 1938, several of the Veterans Association buildings have been lost to fire in recent decades.

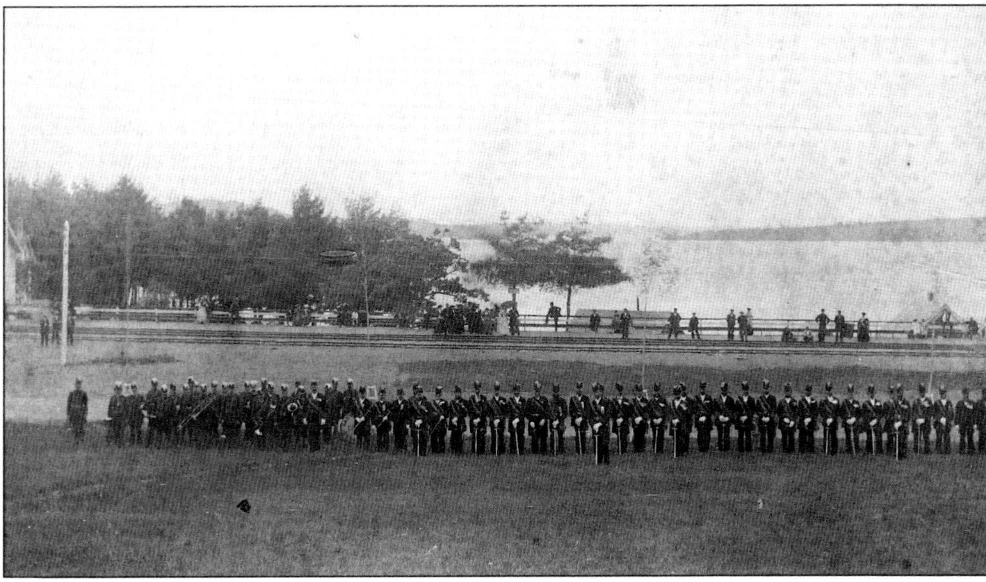

Early veterans' reunion exercises on Lakeside Avenue, *c.* 1880.

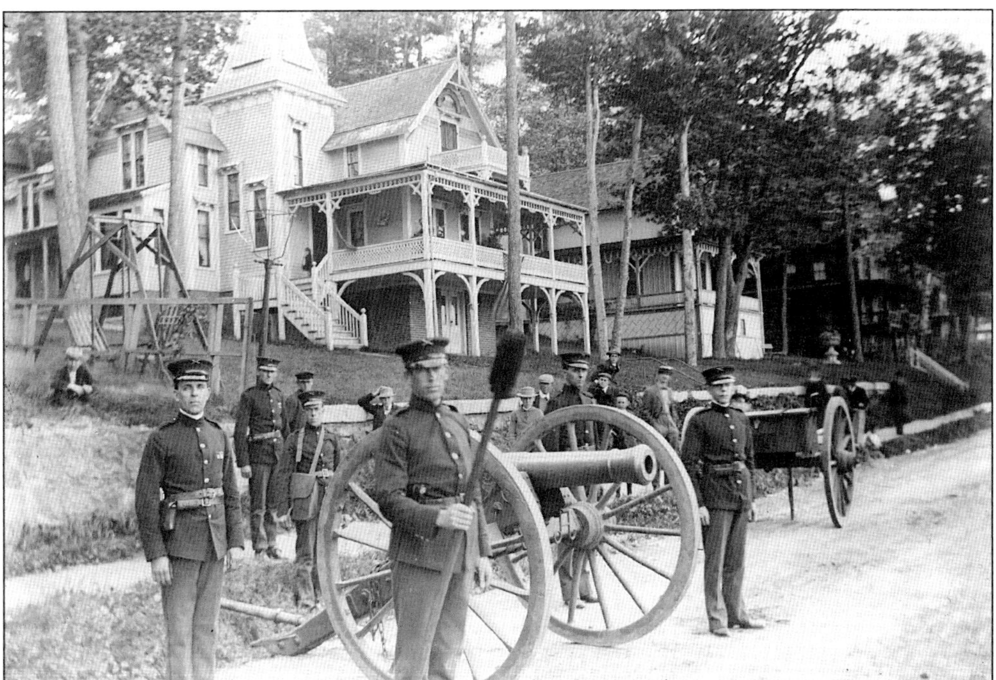

Ceremonial field piece and crew on Lakeside Avenue, early 1900s, with "Castle Rest" in the background.

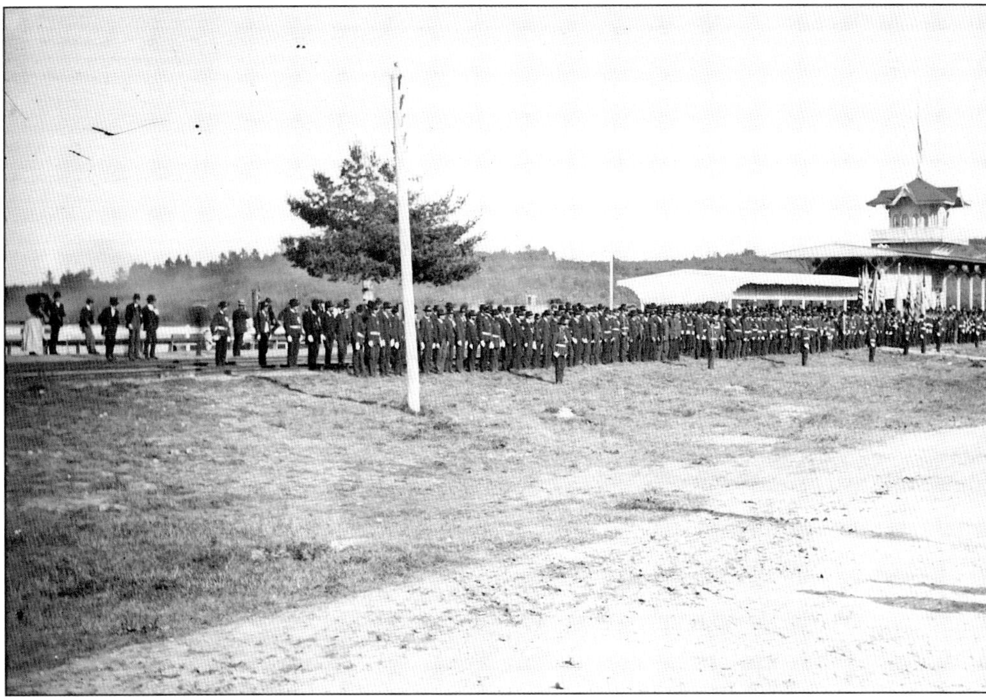

Veterans review, early 1880s. To the right is the Concord & Montreal Railroad station.

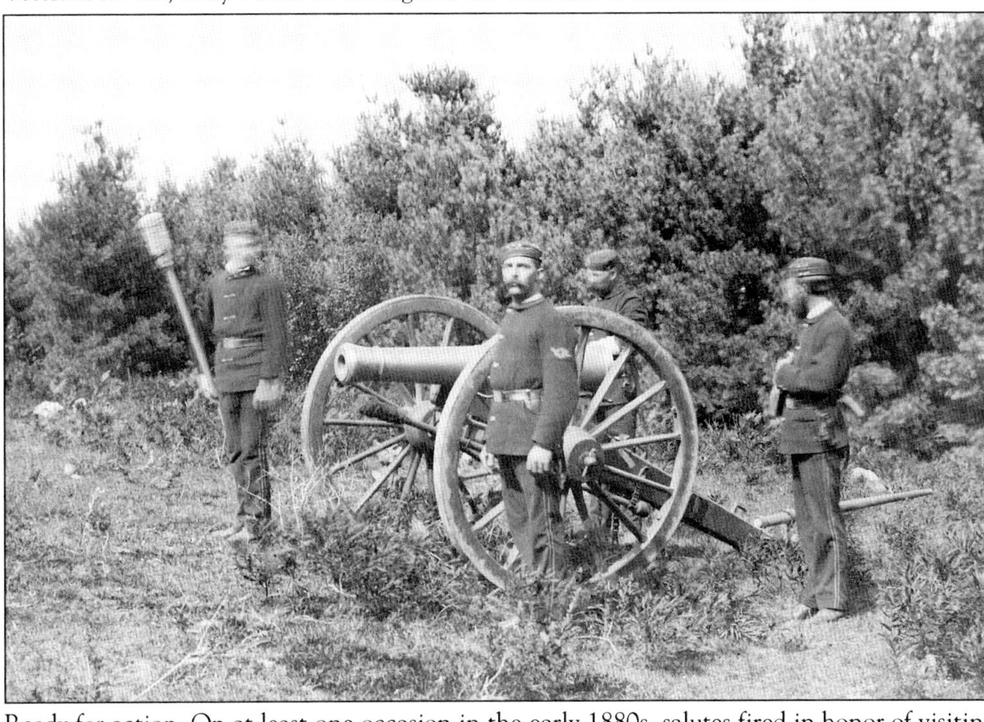

Ready for action. On at least one occasion in the early 1880s, salutes fired in honor of visiting dignitaries shattered windows in passenger cars at the railroad station. In addition to ceremonial firings, early reunions featured sham battles conducted in and around Lakeside Avenue and the Veterans Association grove.

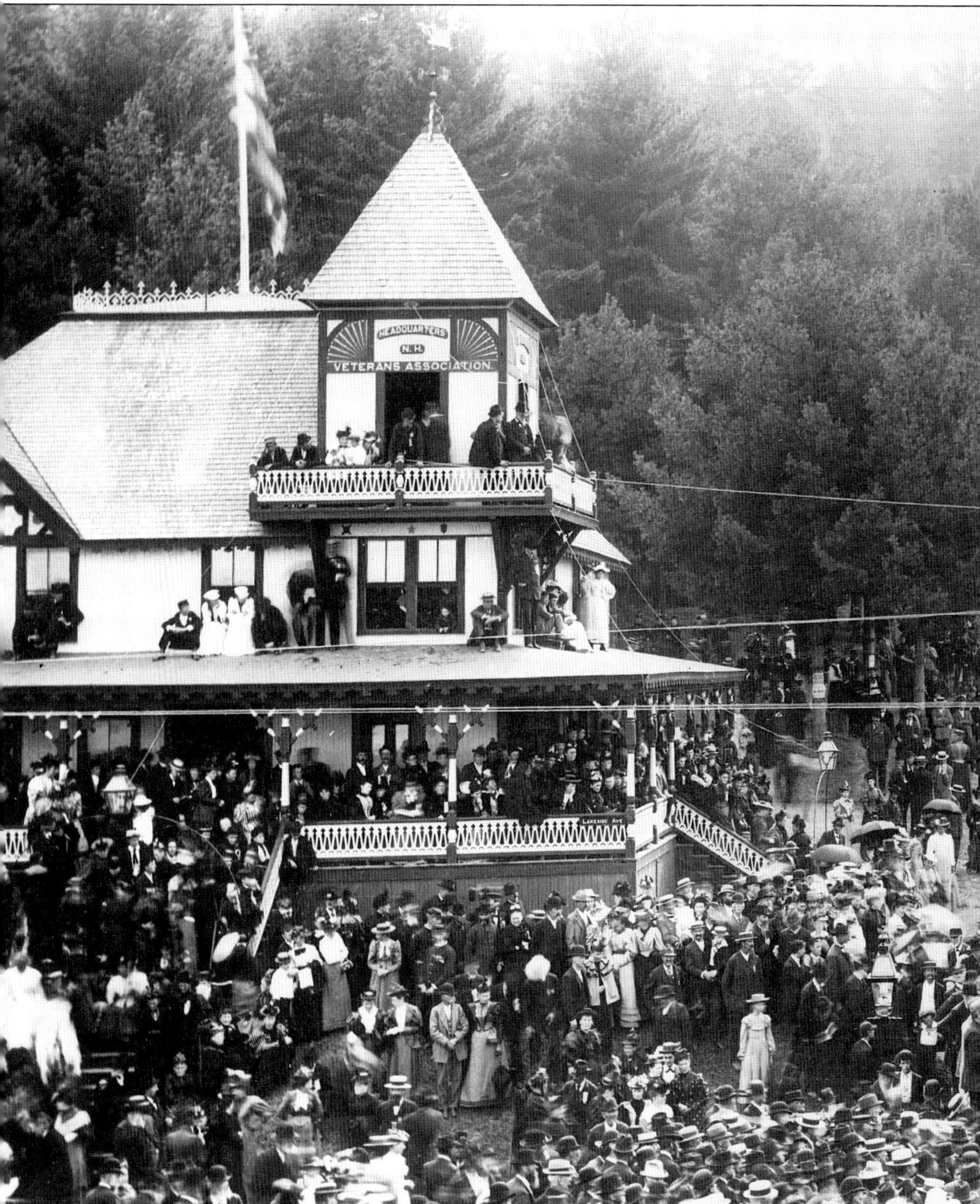

Eighteenth encampment, New Hampshire Veterans Association, Camp Mason W. Tappan, August 1894. Hon. Charles A. Busiel (holding script), mayor of Laconia, delivers his address just to the left of the soldier's monument. Unveiled August 29, 1894, the Loammi Bean soldiers' monument, combination fountain and watering trough, stood at the entrance to the New

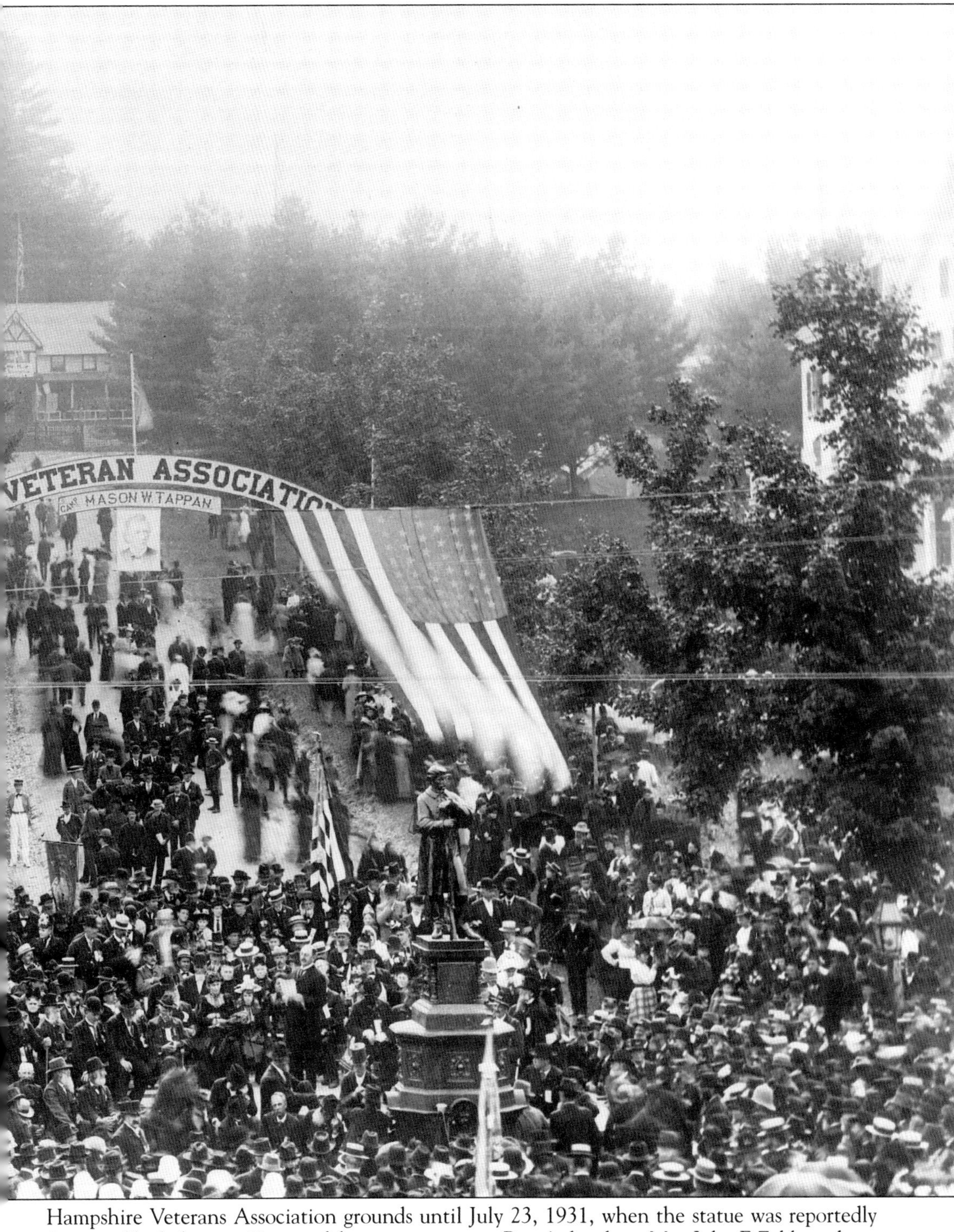

Hampshire Veterans Association grounds until July 23, 1931, when the statue was reportedly destroyed by lightning. Donor of the monument was Bean's daughter, Mrs. John F. Zebley, whose Zebley Farm (or Nestledown) on Route 11B (see p. 13) was a longtime Weirs area landmark.

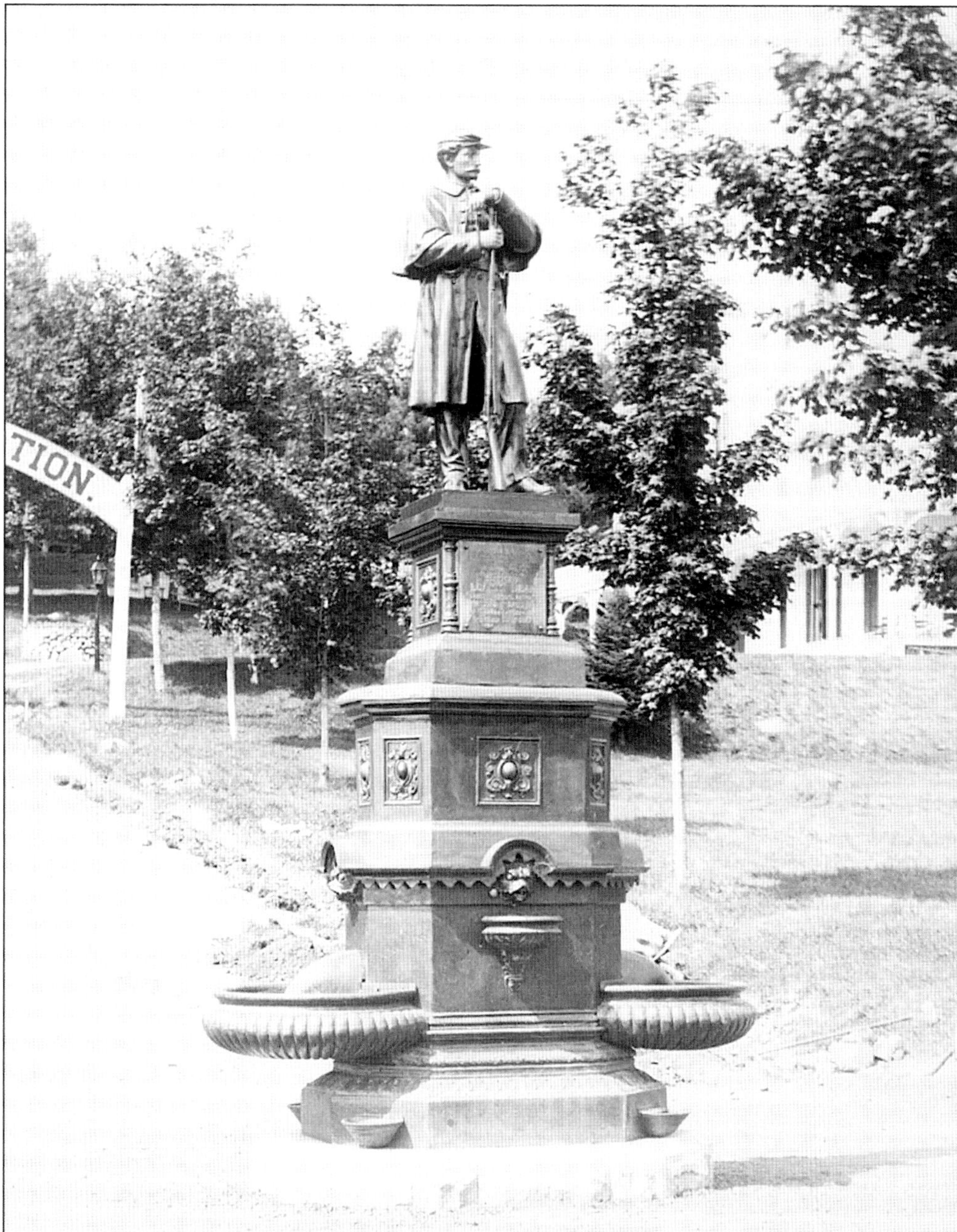

Soldiers' monument. Loammi Bean was thirty-seven when the call came for volunteers, and he promptly enlisted in the 8th New Hampshire Volunteer Regiment for three months. In October 1861, he re-enlisted for three years' service in the regiment. Just a year later, on October 27, 1862, he was killed in the Battle of Georgia Landing, Louisiana. It was the first battle in which the 8th participated, and Private Bean was one of the first men to fall. In his honor, "and to the memory of thousands of other gallant soldiers who laid down their lives that the Union might be preserved," his daughter erected the handsome monument, dedicated at exercises conducted by the 8th New Hampshire Volunteer Regiment Association on August 29, 1894.

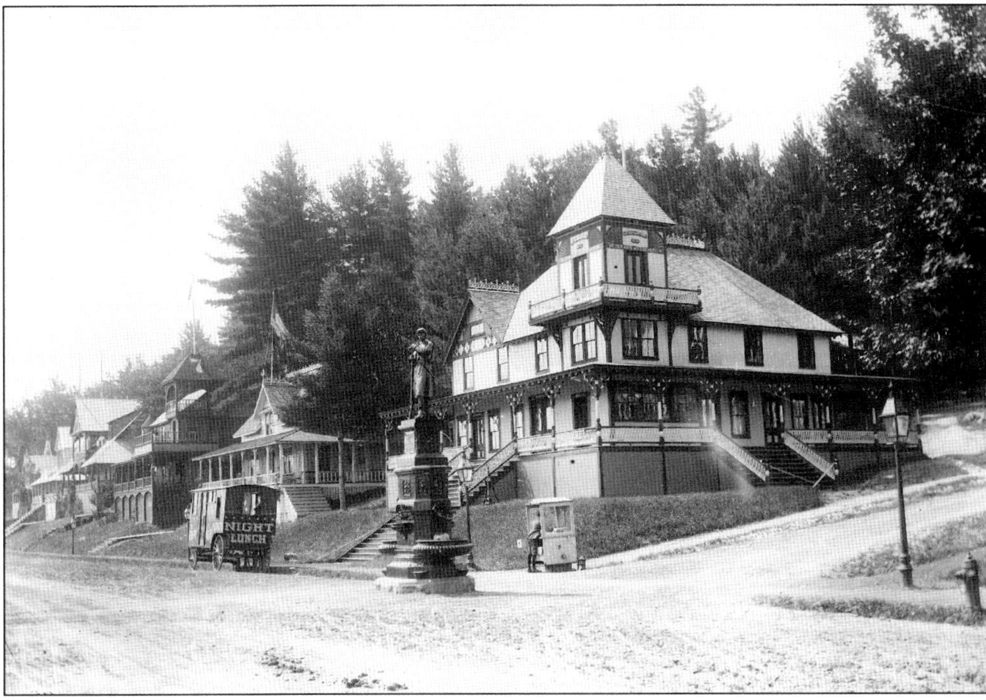

Headquarters Building, New Hampshire Veterans Association, at the corner of New Hampshire Avenue, *c.* 1895. From right to left, the other headquarters buildings are those of the 3rd, 7th, and 11th regiments and of the Cavalry (at the corner of Cavalry Street, to the extreme left). Two lunch carts of the era flank the soldiers' monument.

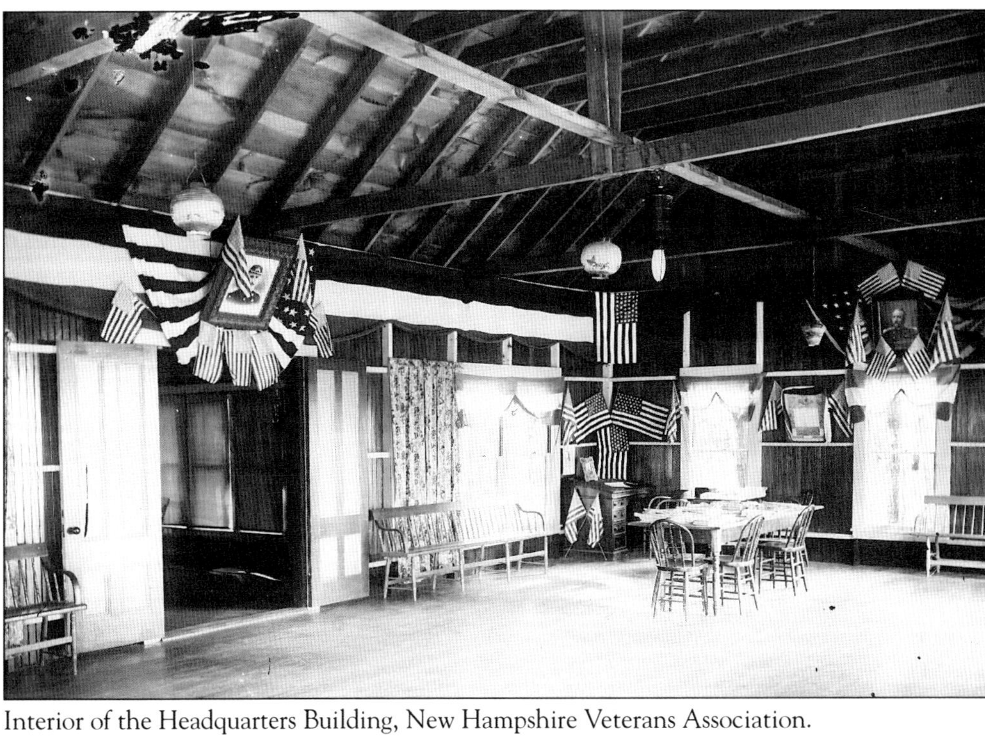

Interior of the Headquarters Building, New Hampshire Veterans Association.

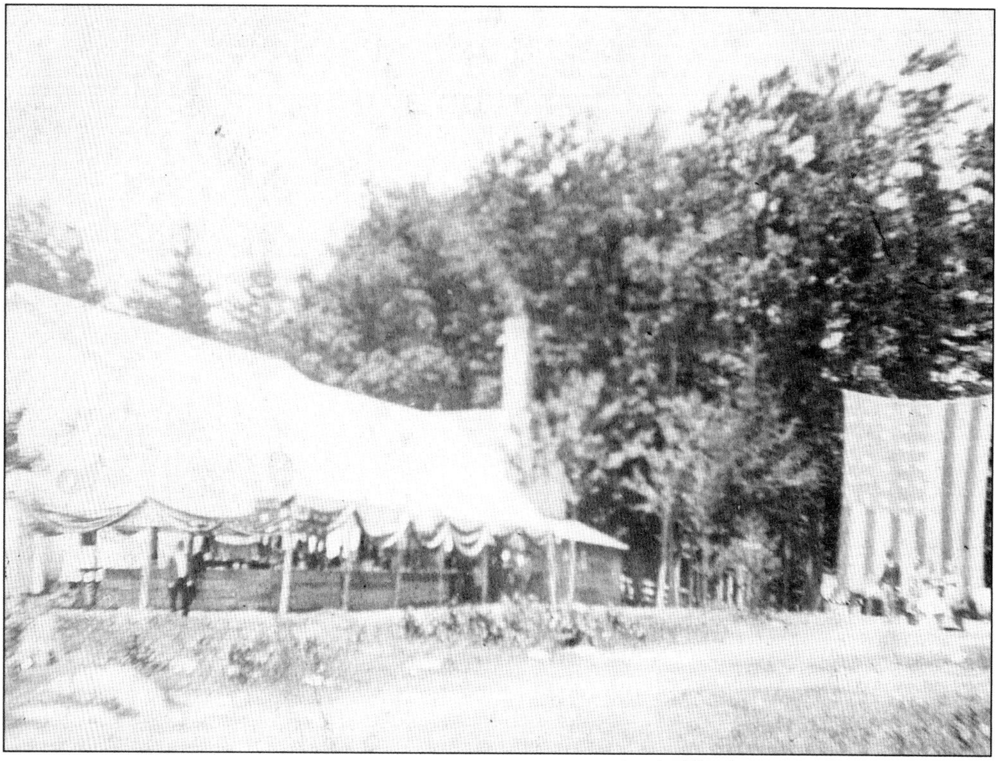

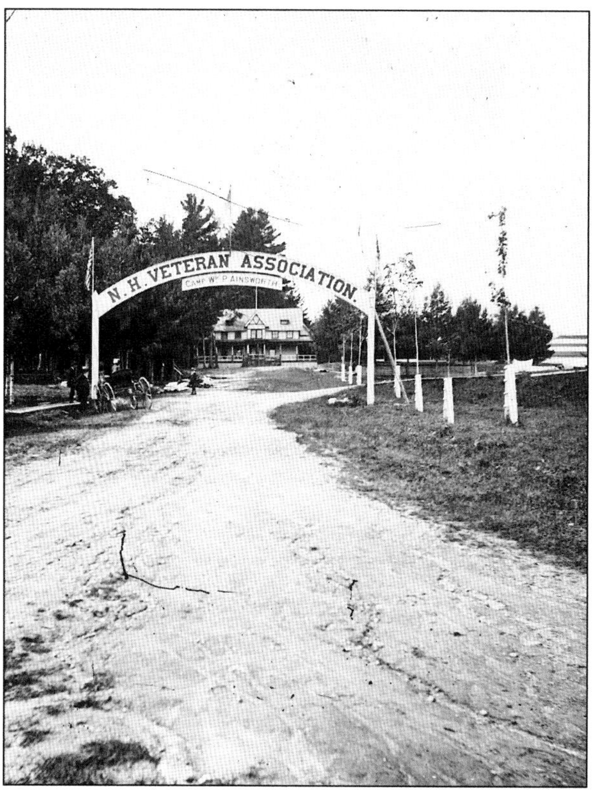

Probably the second veterans encampment, 1879. This was a year before the Concord & Montreal Railroad made available the land which today comprises the New Hampshire Veterans Association grounds. Tents provided shelter for the first two reunions, with company "streets" laid out in regulation Civil War army manner.

Entrance to the New Hampshire Veterans Association grounds, early 1880s. The property is now listed as a historic district in the National Register of Historic Places. Lowell Building can be seen in distance. The Hotel Weirs is off the photograph to the right.

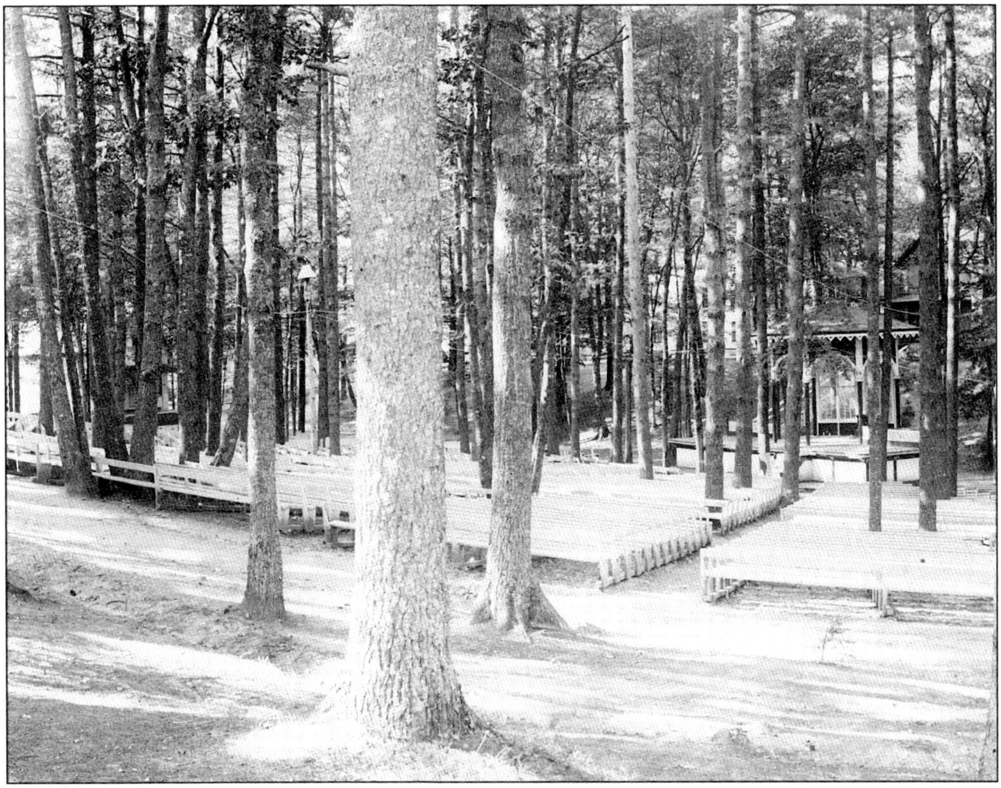

The veterans grove, with the speaker's stand (see p. 48) in the distance. The benches could accommodate 3,000 persons.

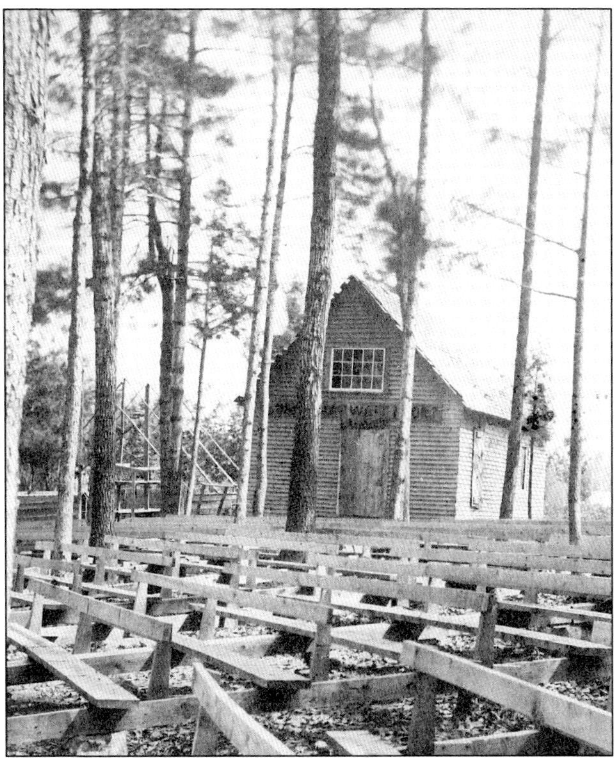

Another view of the grove.

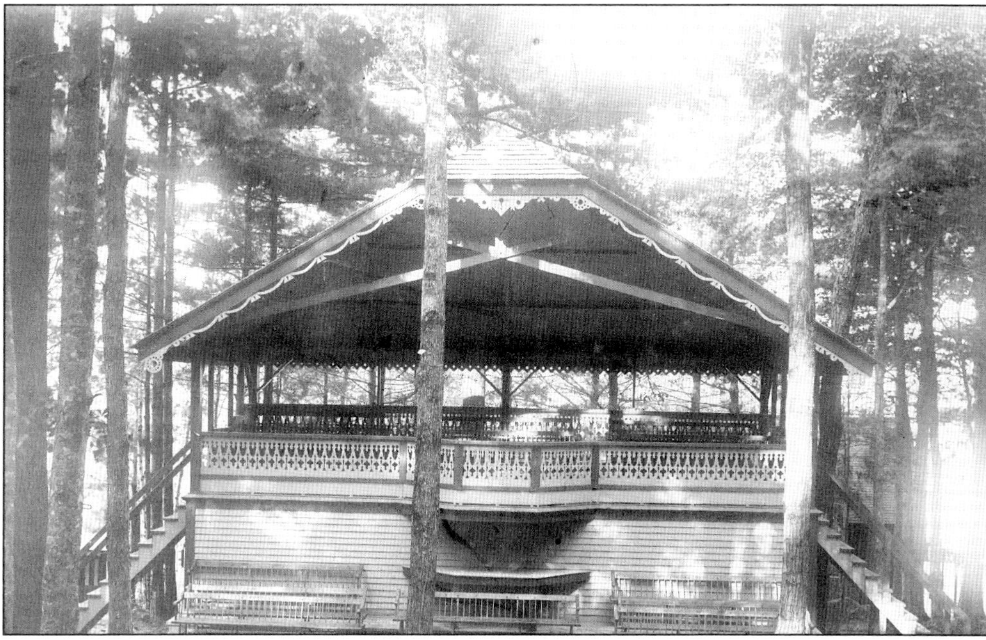

The bandstand and speaker's platform, New Hampshire Veterans Association. The ornate structure and most of the benches were ultimately casualties of the 1938 hurricane.

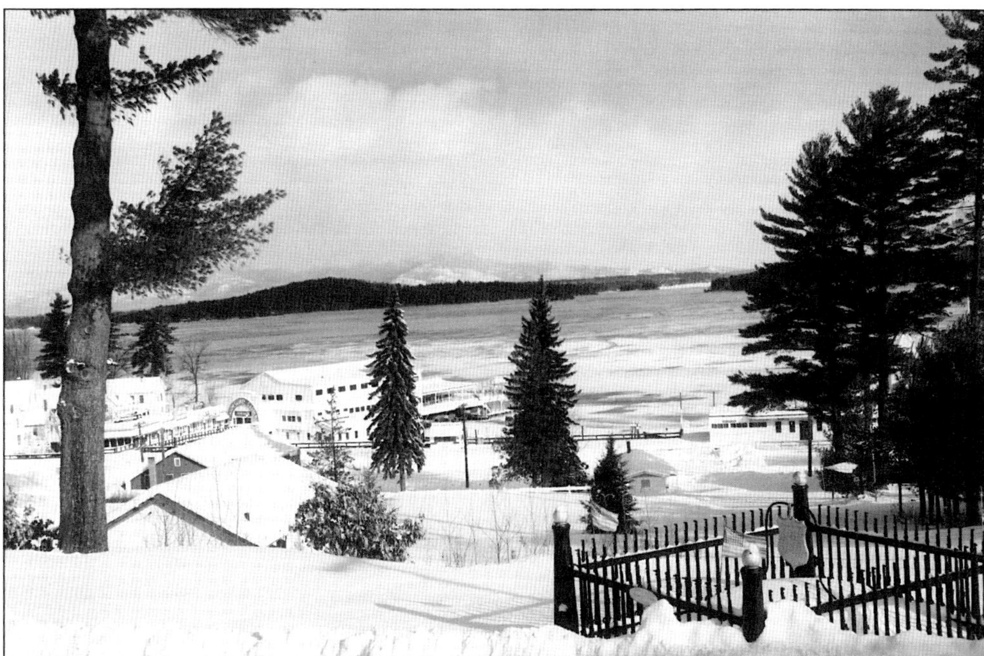

Woodbury Sanborn Memorial. The boulder, inscribed in 1882 with the designations of the New Hampshire volunteer regiments, was the gift of Sanborn, sutler (civilian purveyor of food, liquor, and other comfort items) to the 12th New Hampshire Regiment. The stone was surrounded in 1883 by a cast- and wrought-iron fence featuring pickets of cast-iron muskets, complete even to lock, ramrod, and bayonet, and cornerposts of vertical iron cannons, topped by cannonballs

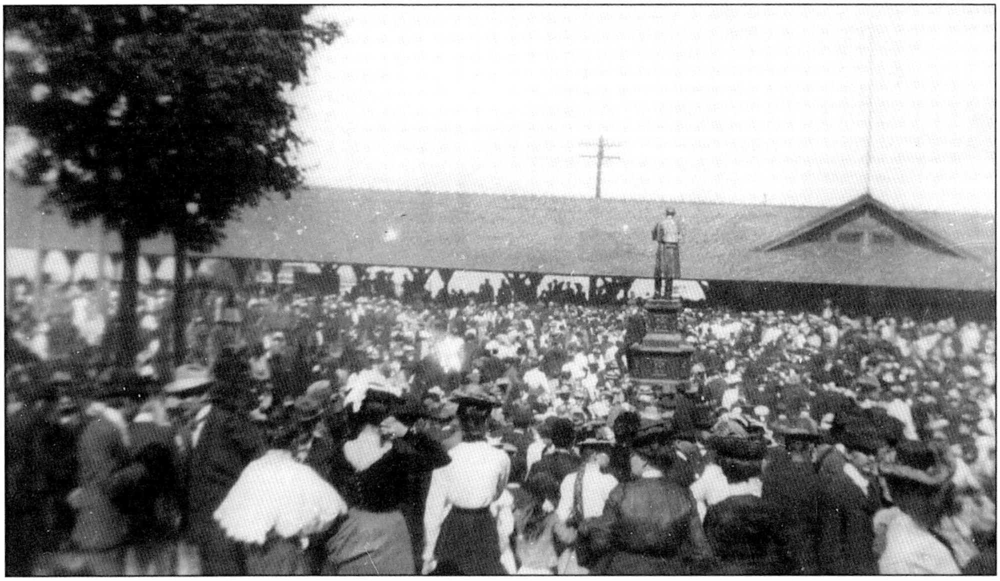

Visit of Theodore Roosevelt. Crowds, variously estimated at between 20,000 and 40,000 people, thronged The Weirs for a two-hour visit by the president on August 28, 1902. The railroad station appears in the background. "The president's special train pulled into The Weirs right on schedule time, twelve o'clock to the very minute," reported *The Laconia Democrat* of August 29, 1902.

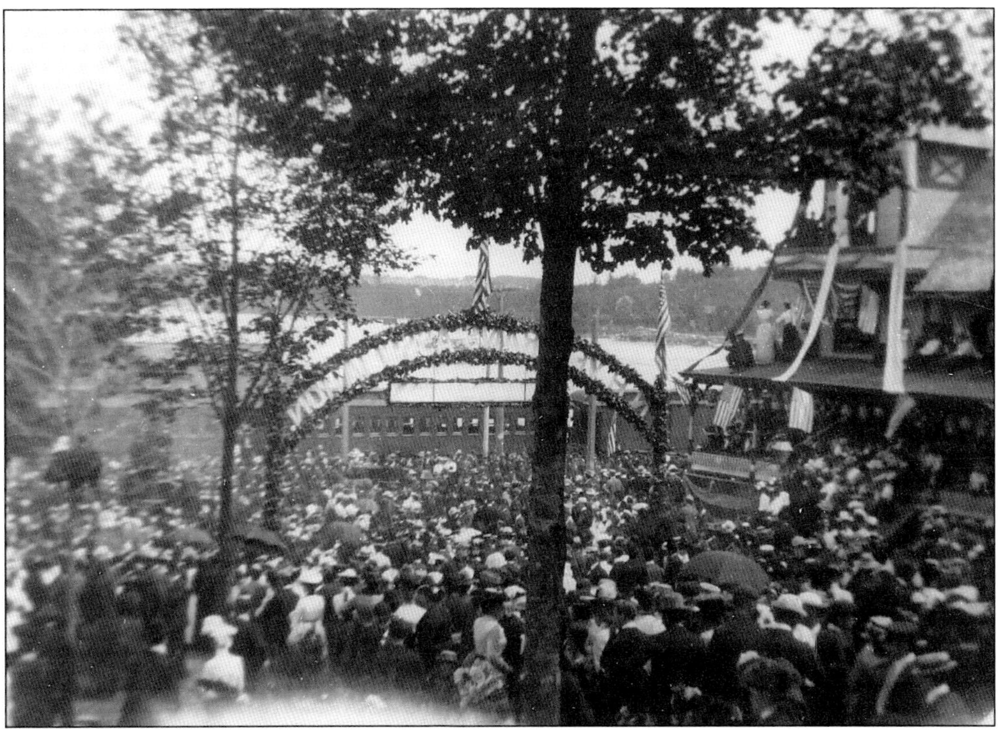

Another view of the crowds present for President Roosevelt's visit, from New Hampshire Avenue. The bunting-draped Headquarters Building of the New Hampshire Veterans Association is on the right.

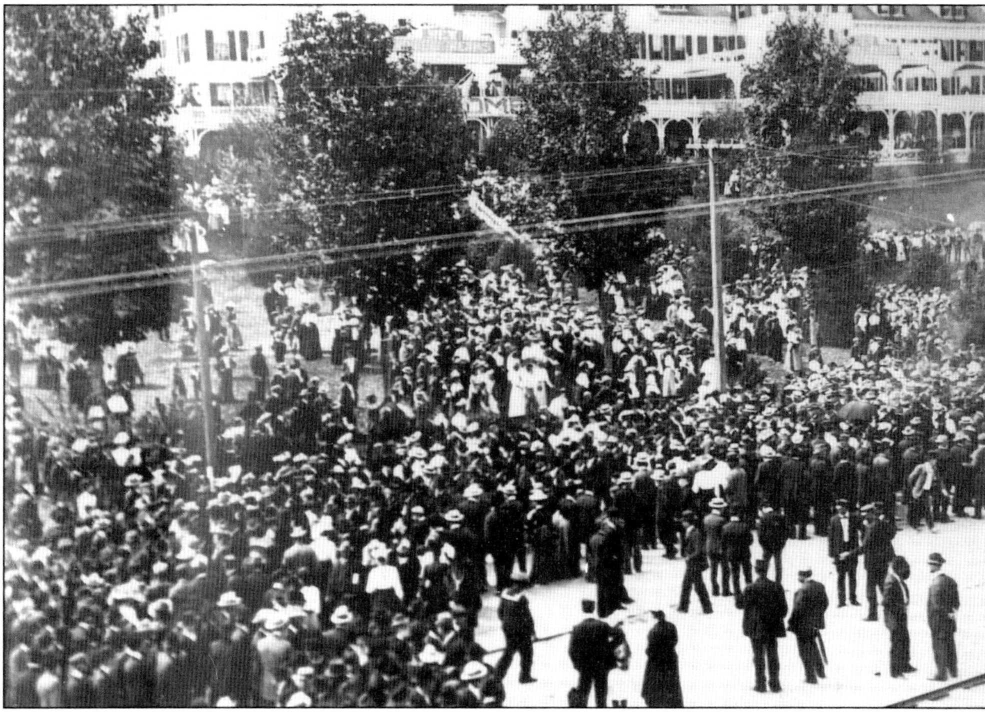

The crowd gathers for President Roosevelt's visit. "The attendance of veterans at the reunion this year has been much larger than for many years past, and on Thursday morning the people within a radius of fifty miles commenced to flock into The Weirs, coming by steam cars, electrics, steamboats, carriages, hay-racks and on foot. Neither the steam cars nor electrics could accommodate the Laconia crowds who tried to get to Weirs."

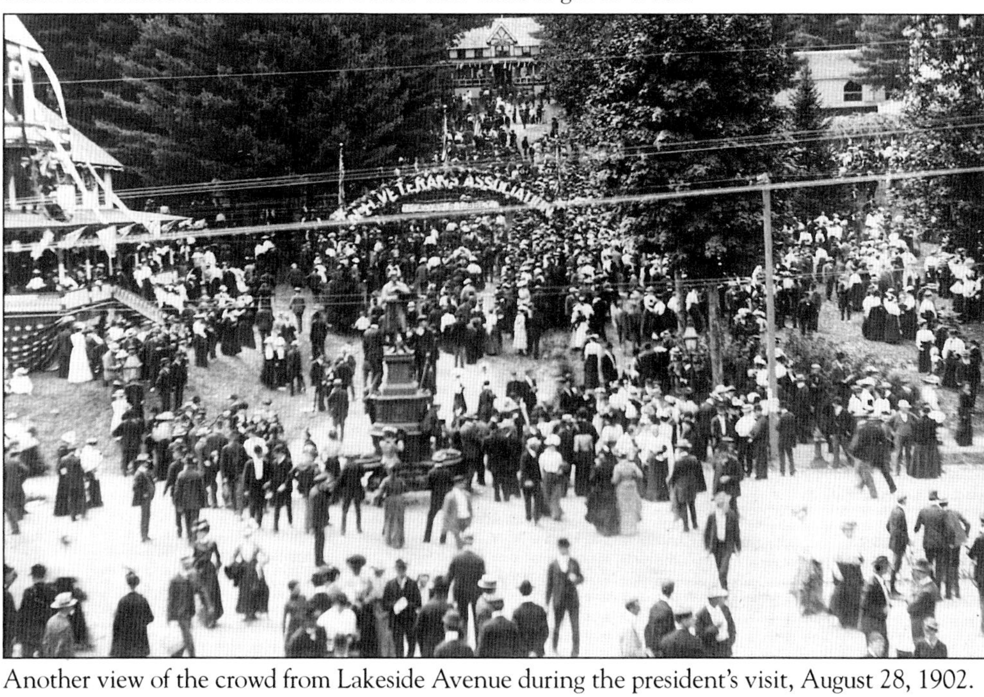

Another view of the crowd from Lakeside Avenue during the president's visit, August 28, 1902.

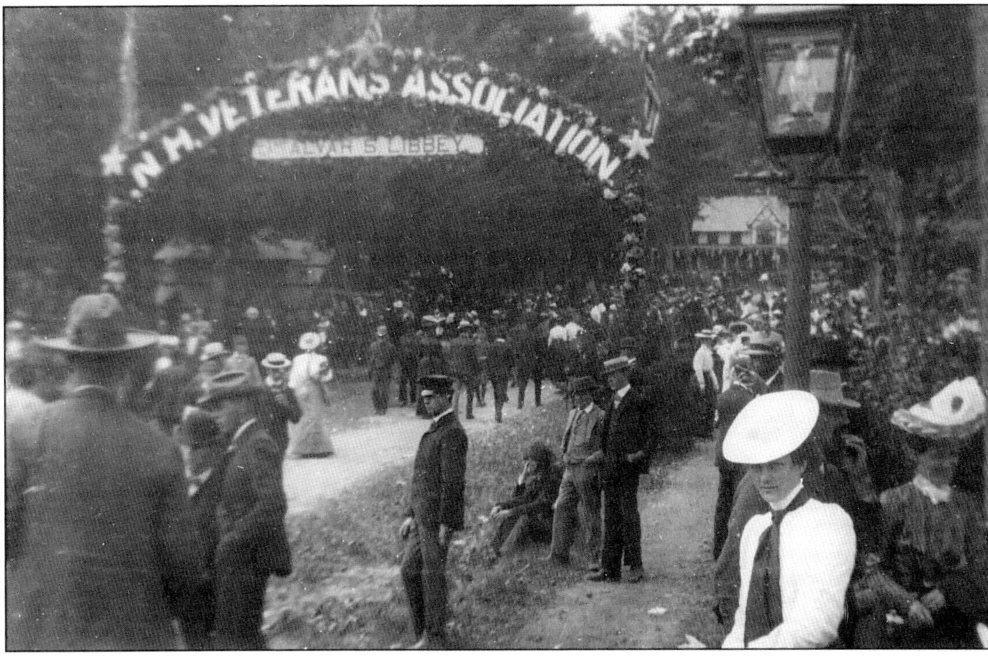

The president's salute of twenty-one guns was fired, from Interlaken Park, by the First New Hampshire Battery, "commencing just as Mr. Roosevelt stepped upon the soil of Laconia." The president then walked from the train to Lakeside Avenue where he reviewed a long line of regimental associations and then was escorted up the hill, through the archway, and thence to Hotel Weirs (off the photograph to the right).

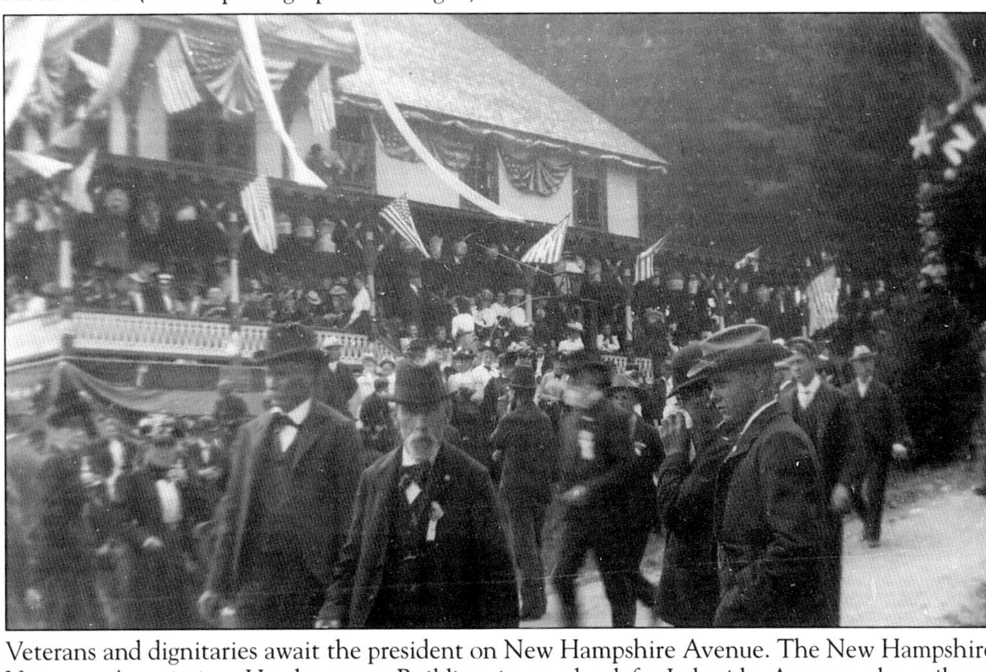

Veterans and dignitaries await the president on New Hampshire Avenue. The New Hampshire Veterans Association Headquarters Building is on the left. Lakeside Avenue, the railroad platform, "and in fact almost every inch of available space surrounding the railroad track was occupied by the veterans and the spectators."

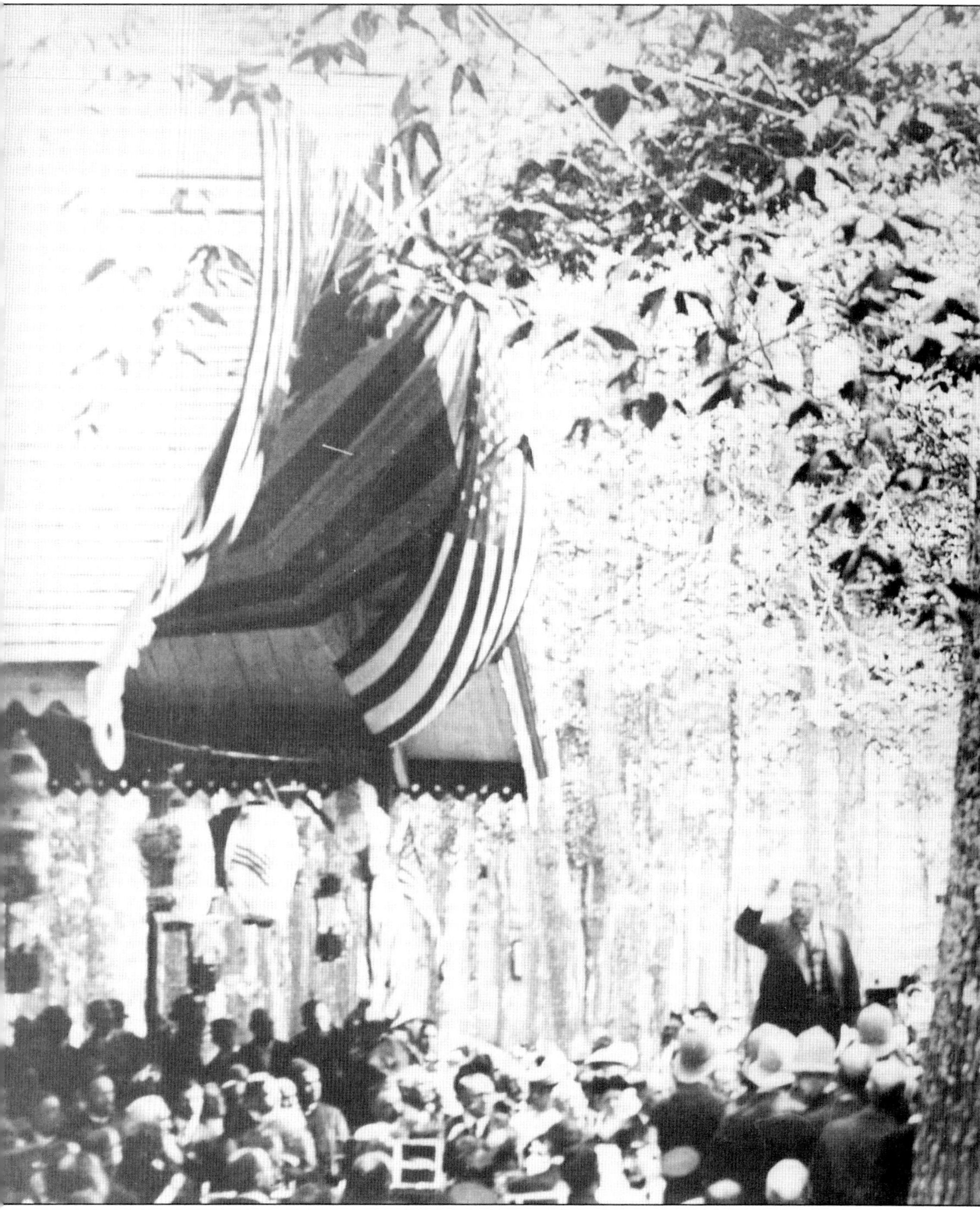

President Theodore Roosevelt delivers his address at Veterans Grove, The Weirs, August 28, 1902. The crowd was "altogether too large for the veterans' grove, and thousands of people could hardly get near enough to the speaker's stand to obtain a glimpse of the President, and comparatively few could get a place where they could hear what he said. Many of the occupants of the seats in the grove came early in the morning and brought their

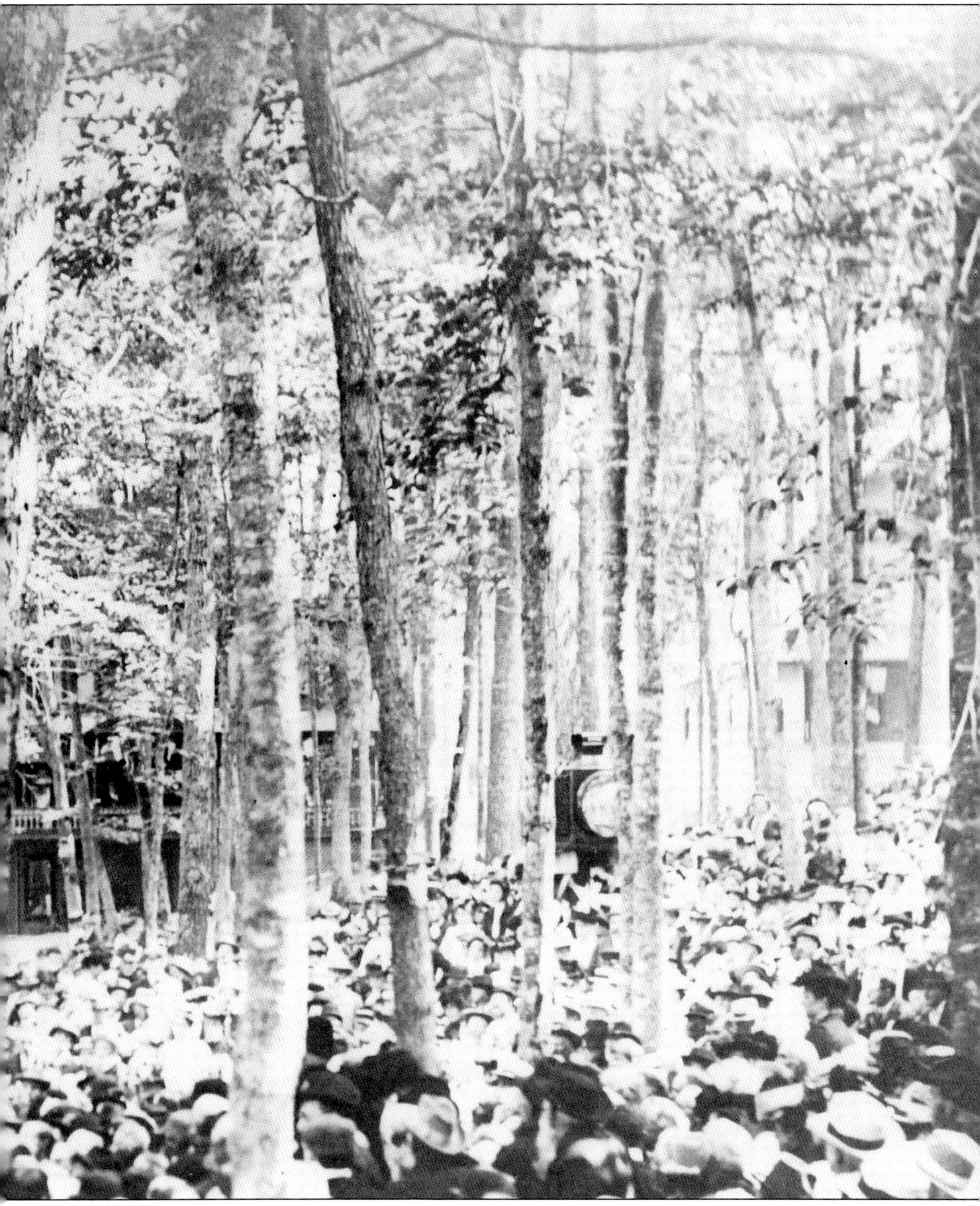

dinners in boxes and baskets, so that late comers were obliged to stand around the outskirts of the grove," reported *The Laconia Democrat*. Six days after the president's visit, he narrowly escaped death or serious injury when his landau was struck by a trolley car near Pittsfield, Massachusetts, on the last day of his New England tour.

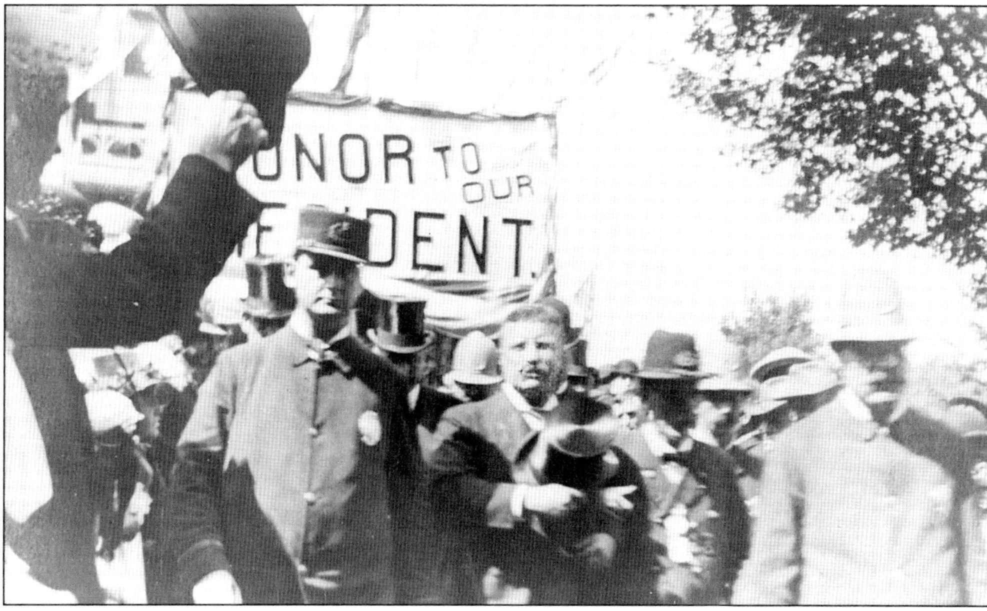

President Roosevelt crosses from the Hotel Weirs to the speaker's stand in the veterans grove, with Assistant Marshal Frank Bailey and Officer Charles Harvell of the Laconia Police Department "close beside him, as a special guard, and followed by Gov. Jordan and staff, Congressman Sulloway and a few other distinguished guests."

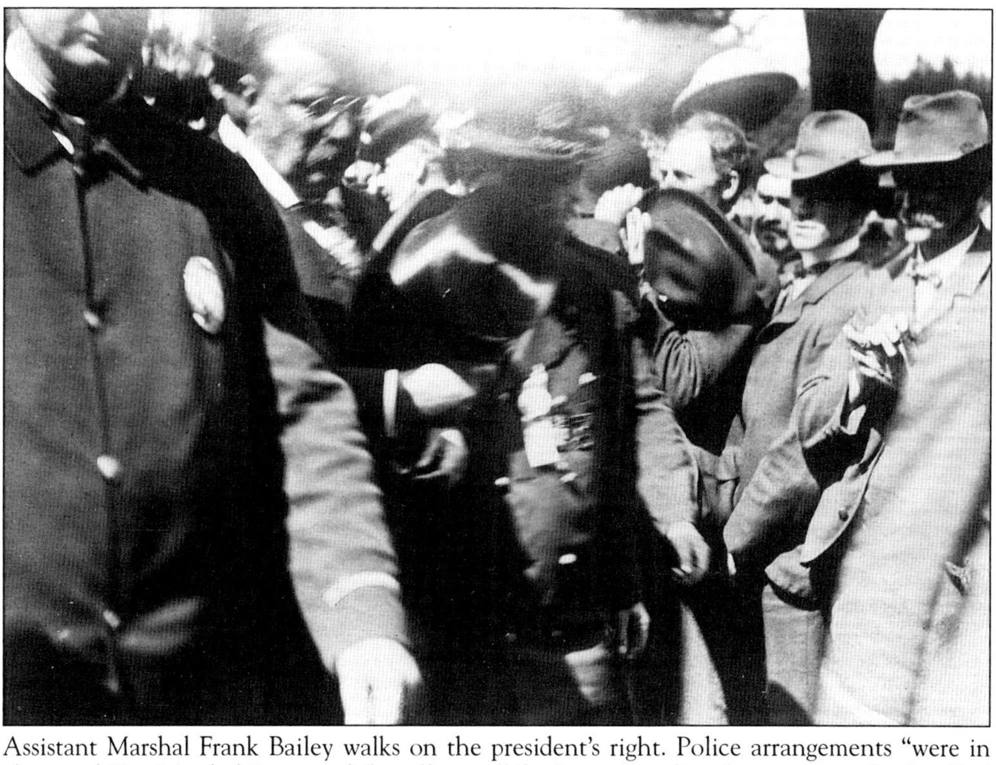

Assistant Marshal Frank Bailey walks on the president's right. Police arrangements "were in charge of City Marshal Scott and the officers of the Laconia police department, who handled the crowd in excellent style."

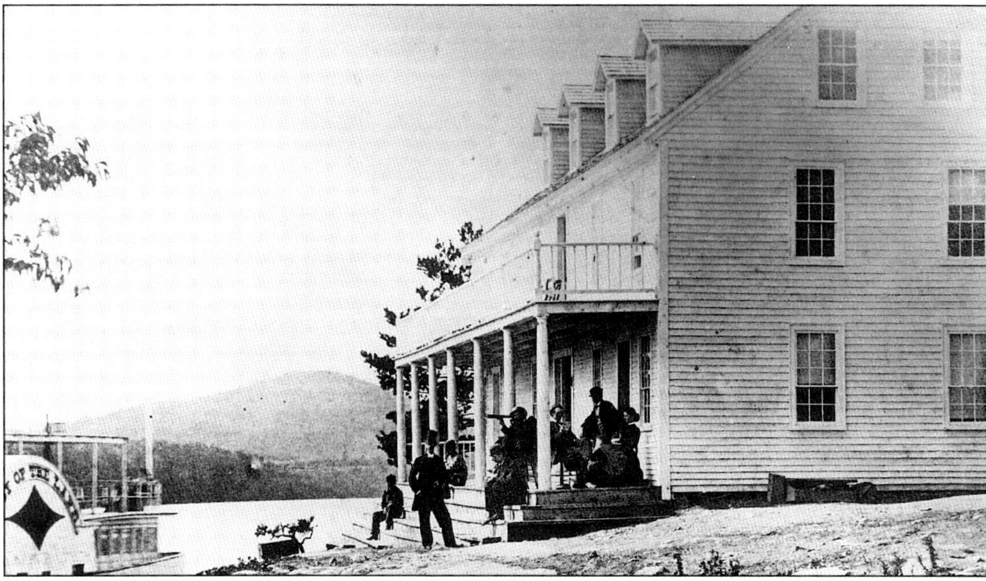

Diamond Island House, *c.* 1865. From the late 1860s into the 1870s, Diamond Island was a popular picnic resort, with its good-sized hotel, a bowling alley, and dancing pavilion. Excursionists would crowd the decks of the *Lady of the Lake* (left) until the craft was fairly top-heavy, and a rush of passengers from one side of the boat to the other to view some object of interest would cause the craft to tip, creating panic for some nervous passengers. On one of these excursions, the *Lady* carried a crowd of 1,280 people from the island to The Weirs. The hotel lost its solid patronage when it became known as a gambling den in the 1870s.

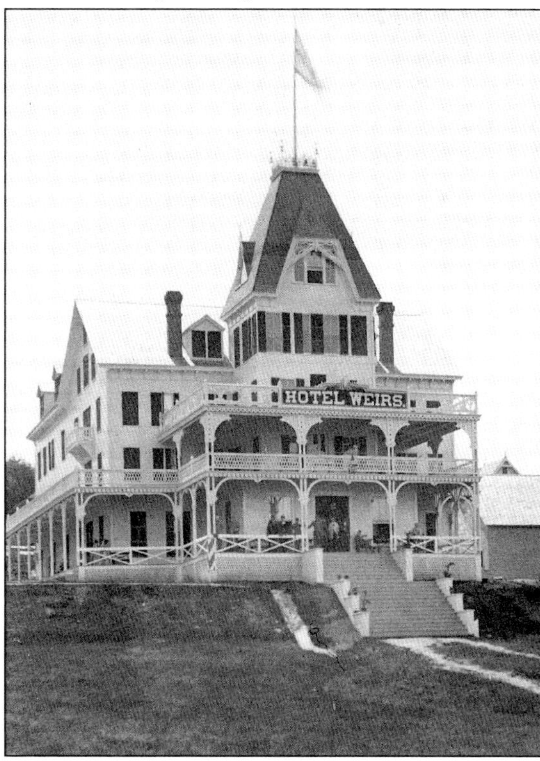

Hotel Weirs, *c.* 1880. The Diamond Island House was cut into sections in 1880, and hauled over the ice to The Weirs where it was reassembled and enlarged as Hotel Weirs. According to tradition, when the final section reached the area of the steamboat landing and was being pulled up the embankment, the heavy structure went through the ice. "Every available pair of oxen in the county" was required to finish the job. The new hotel was later (around 1893) called Sanborn's, after its first owner, but in the late 1890s it reverted to the original name and was finally known as the New Hotel Weirs.

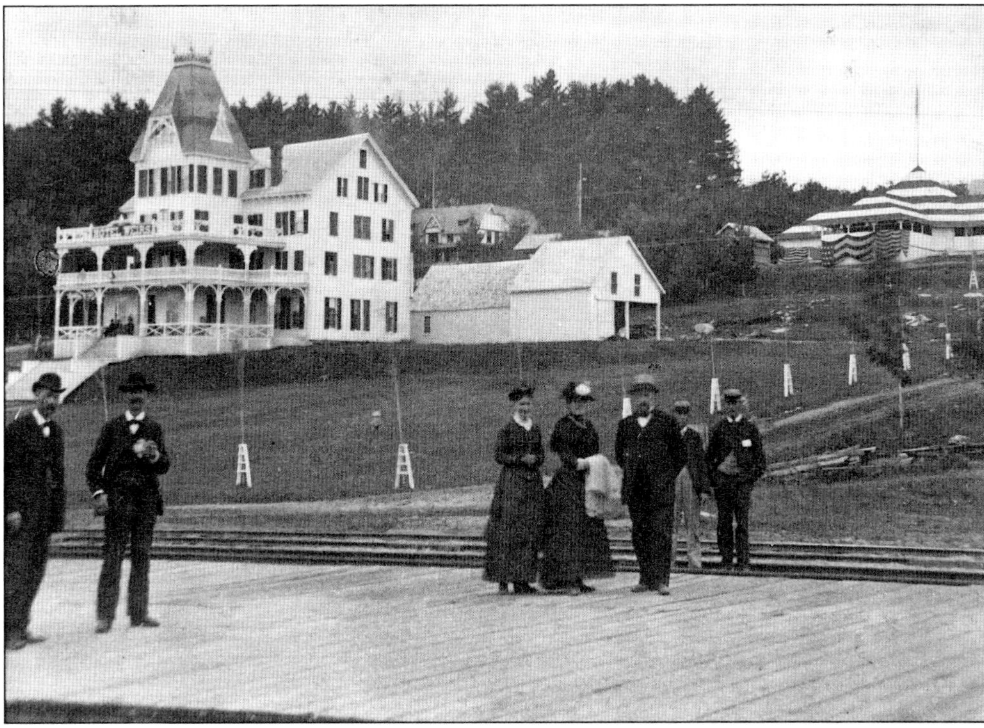

Another early view of the Hotel Weirs, which opened with sixty rooms, with the New Hampshire Veterans Association dining pavilion (also built in 1880) visible on the hillside, above, to the right.

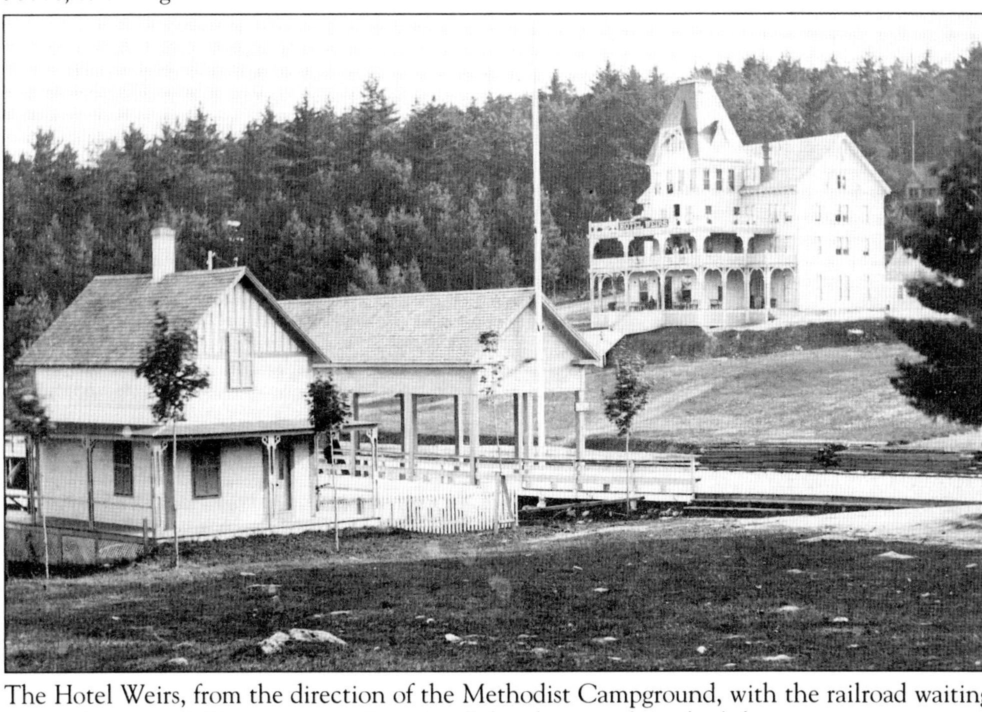

The Hotel Weirs, from the direction of the Methodist Campground, with the railroad waiting area in foreground. The passenger depot is off the photograph to the left.

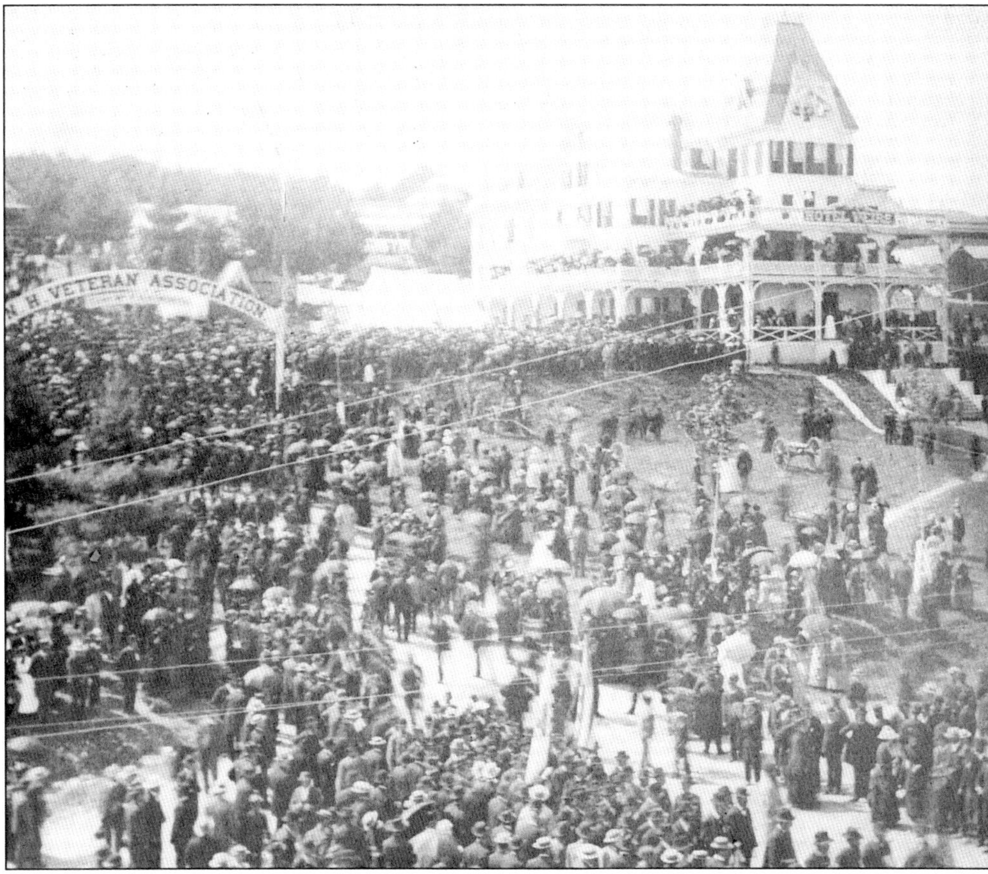

A crowd gathers on Lakeside Avenue, in front of the Hotel Weirs, c. 1880. They may have assembled to greet Union Army General George B. McClellan, who attended the reunion events that year.

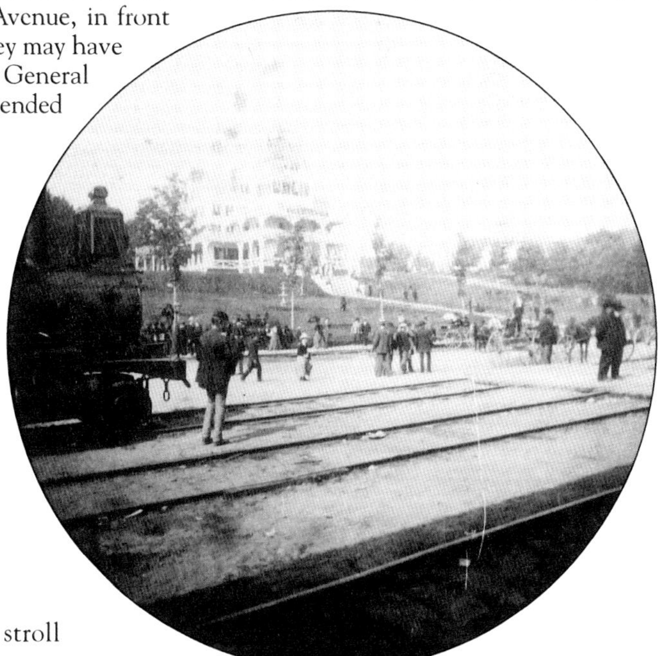

Vacationists, early 1880s, stroll along Lakeside Avenue.

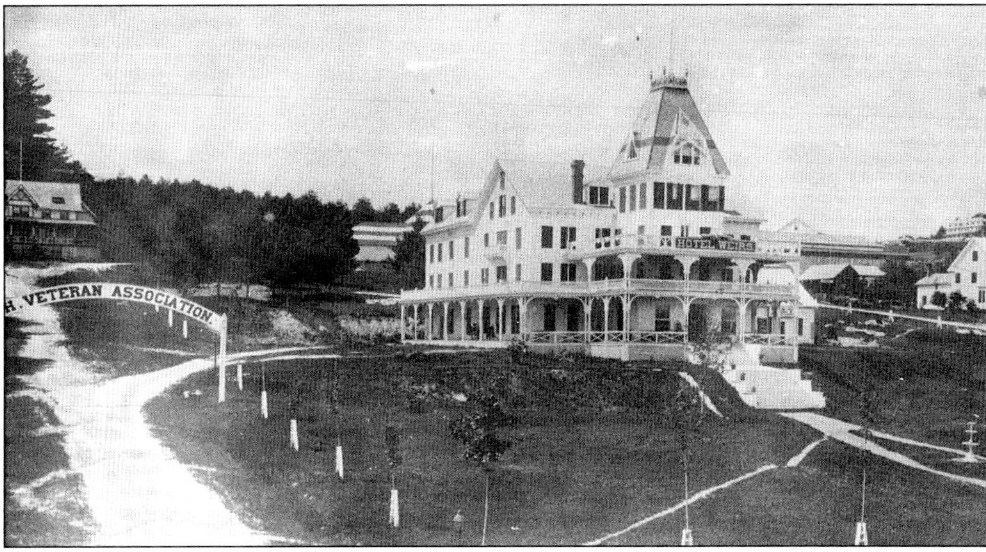

Another view of the Hotel Weirs, *c.* 1880, with the Lowell Building visible at the upper left, on the New Hampshire Veterans Association grounds.

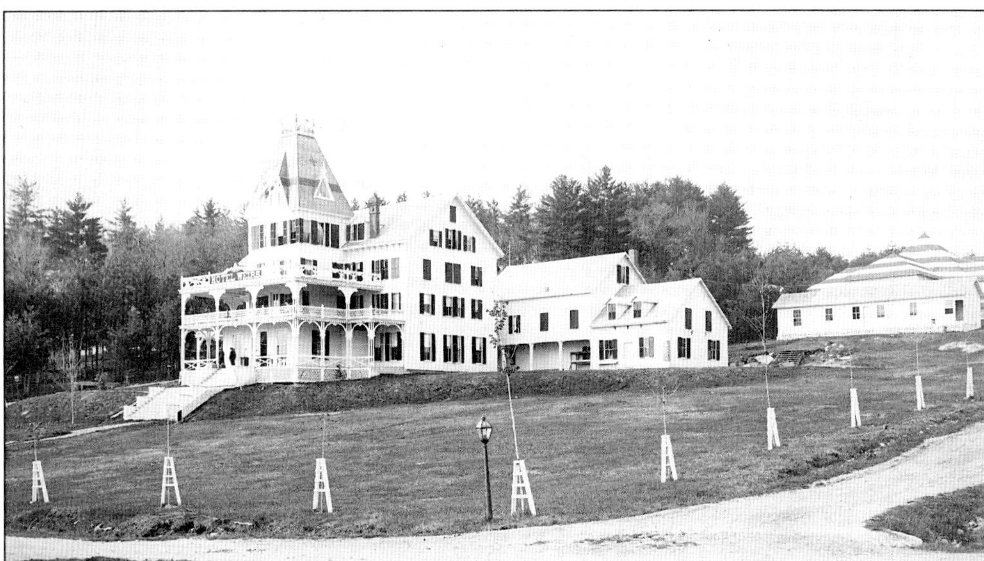

The same view, from a different angle, with the New Hampshire Veterans Association dining pavilion up the hill on the right on Tower Street.

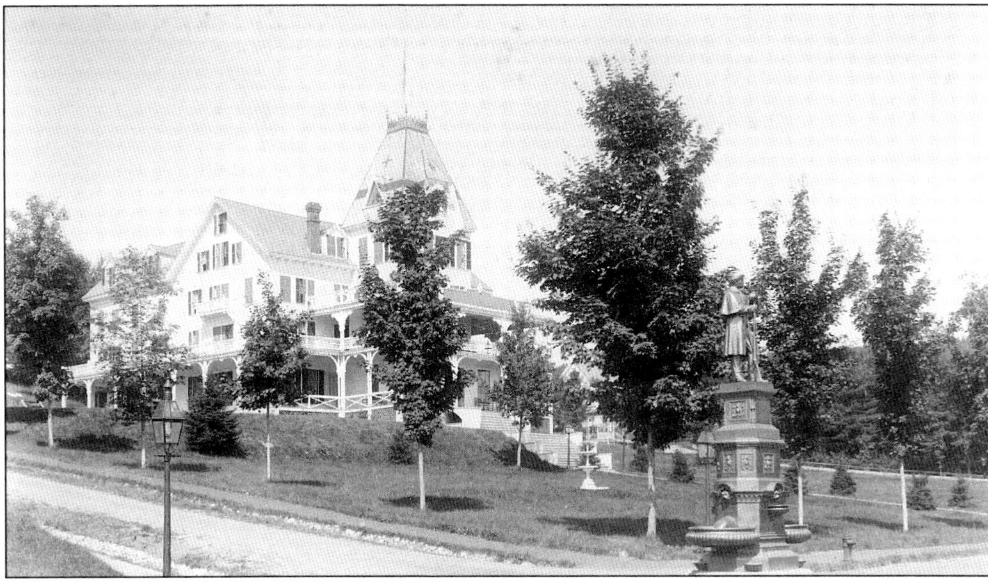

Hotel Weirs, *c.* 1895, with the soldiers' monument in the right foreground.

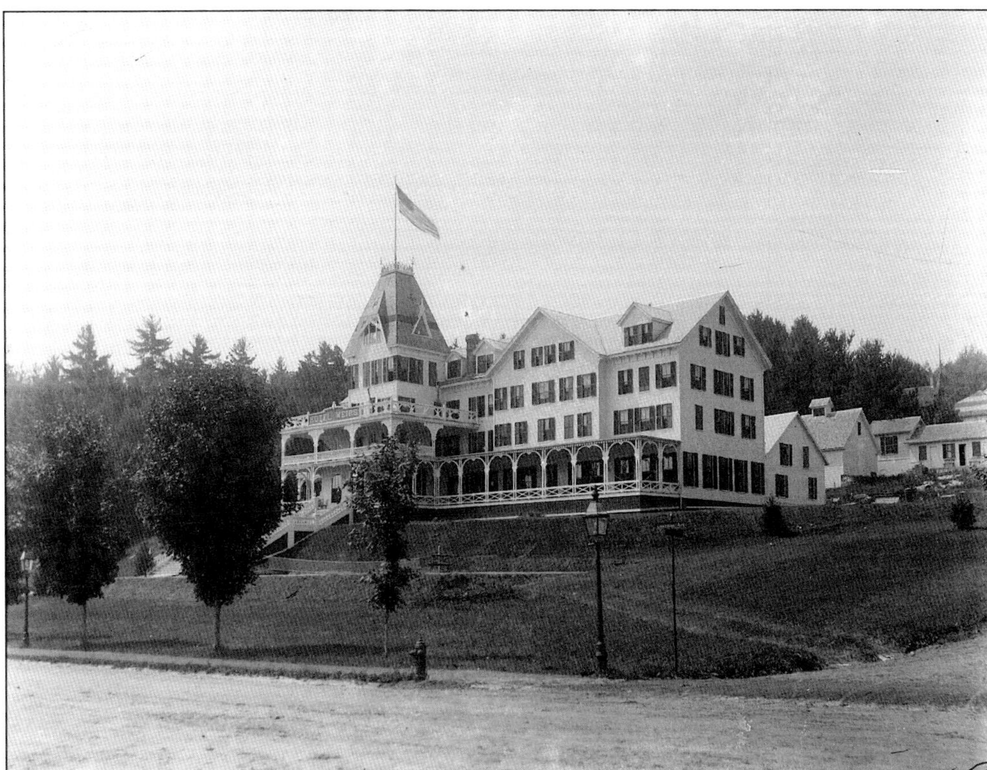

New Hotel Weirs. Considerable further expansion is evident in this view, *c.* 1896. Elaborate porches were provided for viewing the landscape and for promenading.

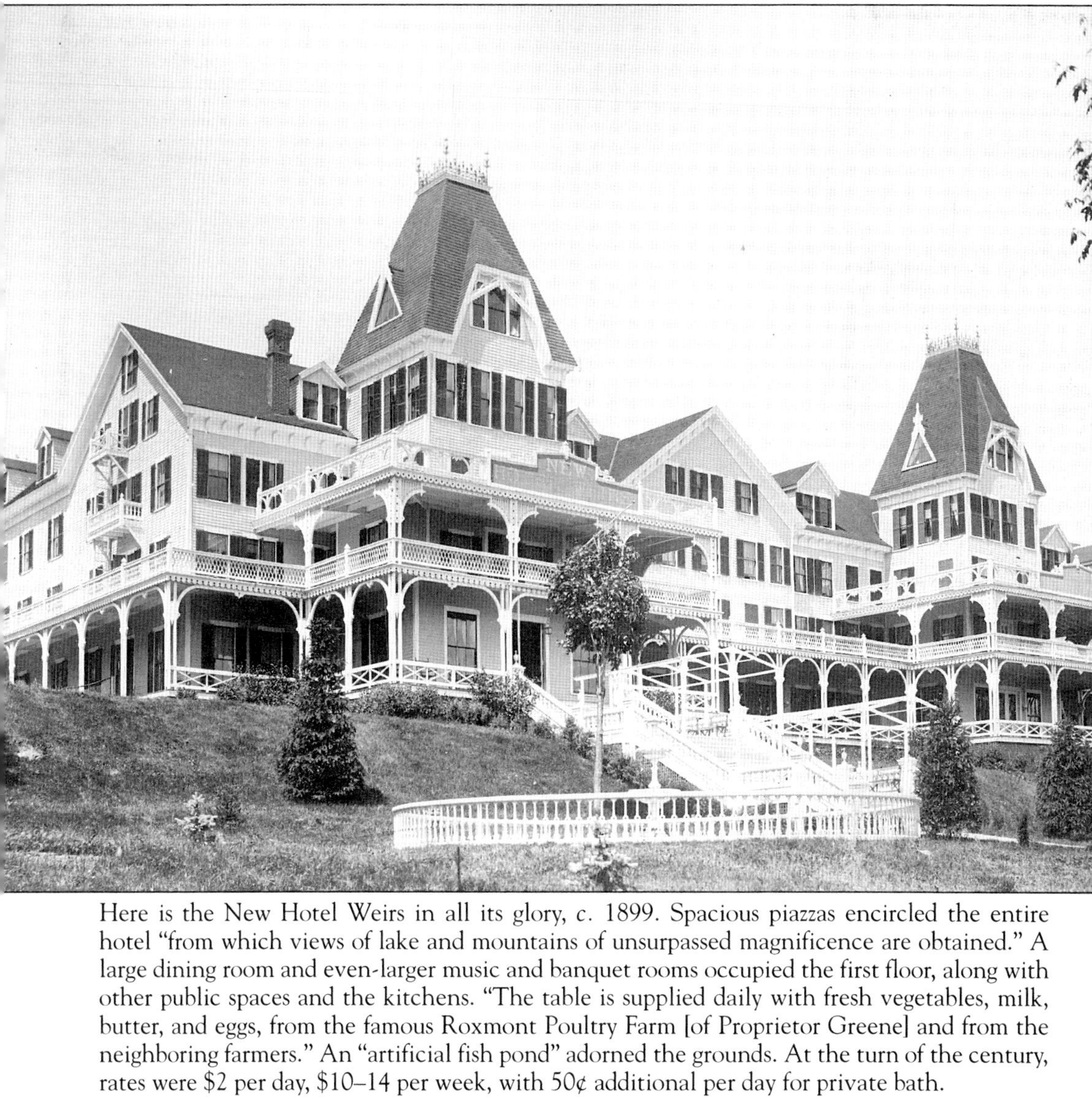

Here is the New Hotel Weirs in all its glory, *c.* 1899. Spacious piazzas encircled the entire hotel "from which views of lake and mountains of unsurpassed magnificence are obtained." A large dining room and even-larger music and banquet rooms occupied the first floor, along with other public spaces and the kitchens. "The table is supplied daily with fresh vegetables, milk, butter, and eggs, from the famous Roxmont Poultry Farm [of Proprietor Greene] and from the neighboring farmers." An "artificial fish pond" adorned the grounds. At the turn of the century, rates were $2 per day, $10–14 per week, with 50¢ additional per day for private bath.

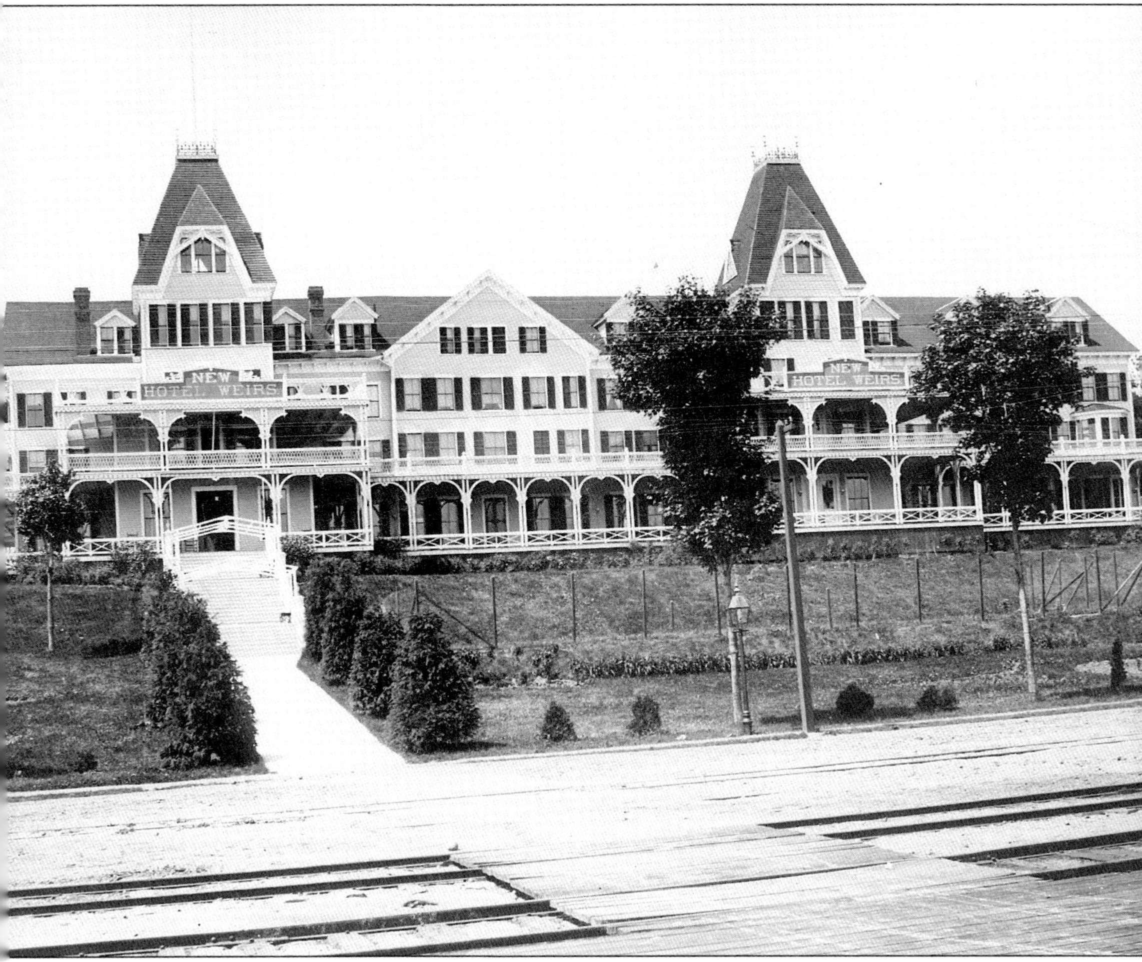

Another view of the imposing structure. The hotel boasted "a fine billiard room and tennis court connected, and an excellent orchestra furnishes good music." The building was "fully equipped with electrical appliances and connected by telephone and telegraph with the direct line to various points." Water was "pure and bright, coming directly from the mountain springs, and a second supply, for sprinkling, bathing, and fire protection, from the lake itself." Four express trains left "the Union station on Causeway street, Boston, every day for The Weirs, with parlor and buffet cars attached, thus ensuring perfect comfort in travel. Steamboats leave The Weirs every few hours for Centre Harbor, Wolfeborough, Alton Bay and all points on the lake, affording many delightful excursions."

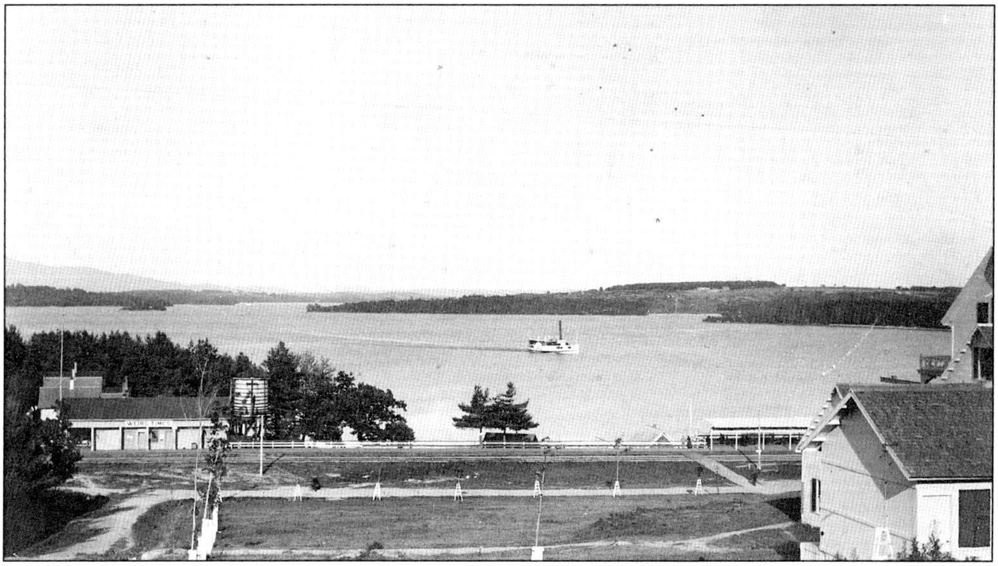

A view of Lake Winnipesaukee from partway up Tower Hill, early 1880s. Part of the Hotel Weirs is visible on the right, and Tower Street is on the left.

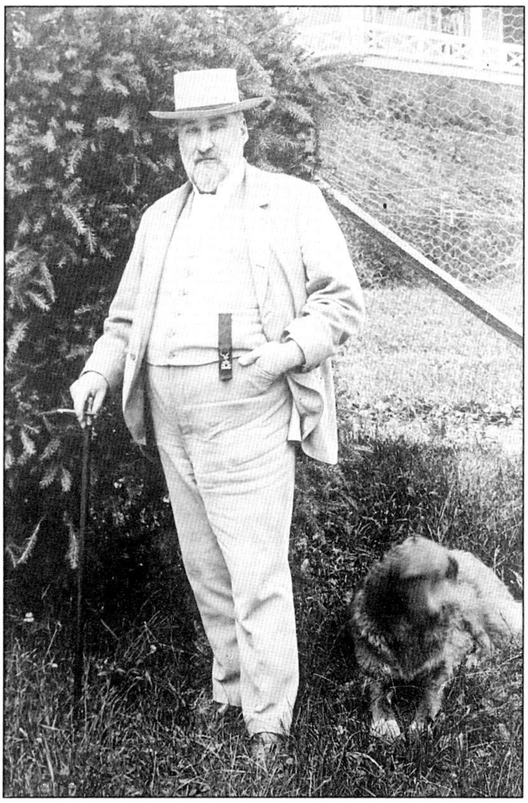

Dr. J. Alonzo Greene (*c.* 1843–1917). Backed by a fortune amassed from the sale of the patent medicine Nervura, he became a principal in the further expansion of the New Hotel Weirs in the mid-1890s. Following three years' service in the Union army during the Civil War, Greene was an 1875 graduate of the Eclectic Medical Institute of Cincinnati. He came to Lake Winnipesaukee around 1892, purchasing a farm on the Moultonboro shore and erecting a fanciful medieval castle on Long Island which he called "Roxmont." Mayor of Laconia from 1901 to 1902, he made unsuccessful runs for governor and for Congress. He was "a genial and companionable man, generous to a fault, ready to invest his money in any enterprise which promised to develop this section of New Hampshire."

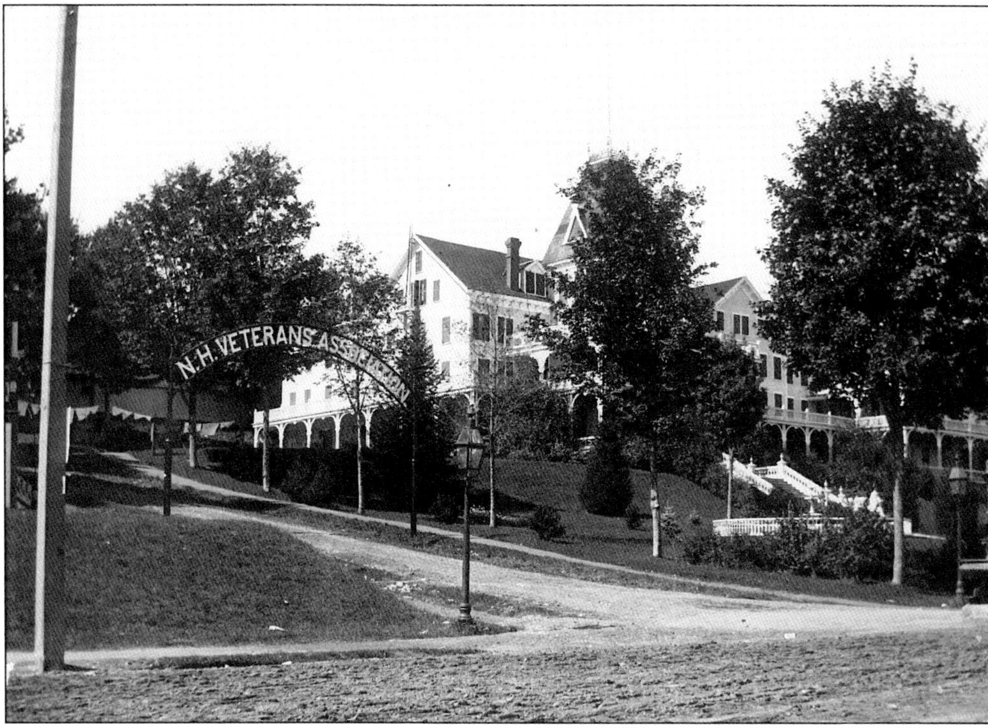

The New Hotel Weirs, late 1890s. With the expansion of the hotel, the trees, which had been planted as saplings in 1880, had grown to considerable height by the time of this photograph.

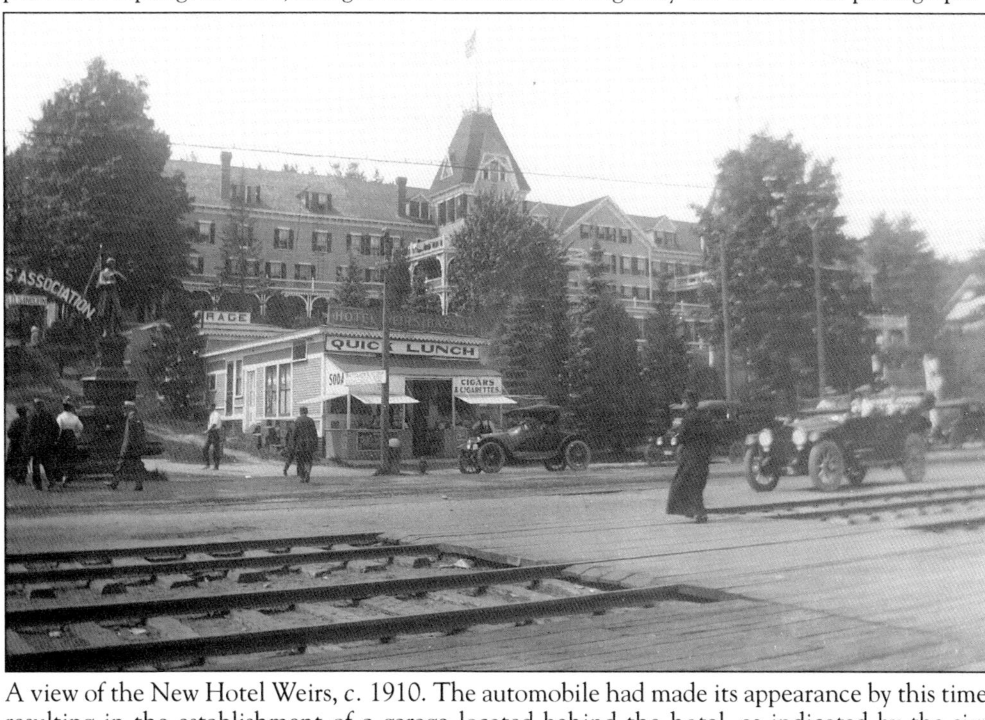

A view of the New Hotel Weirs, *c.* 1910. The automobile had made its appearance by this time, resulting in the establishment of a garage located behind the hotel, as indicated by the sign behind the Quick Lunch building (center left).

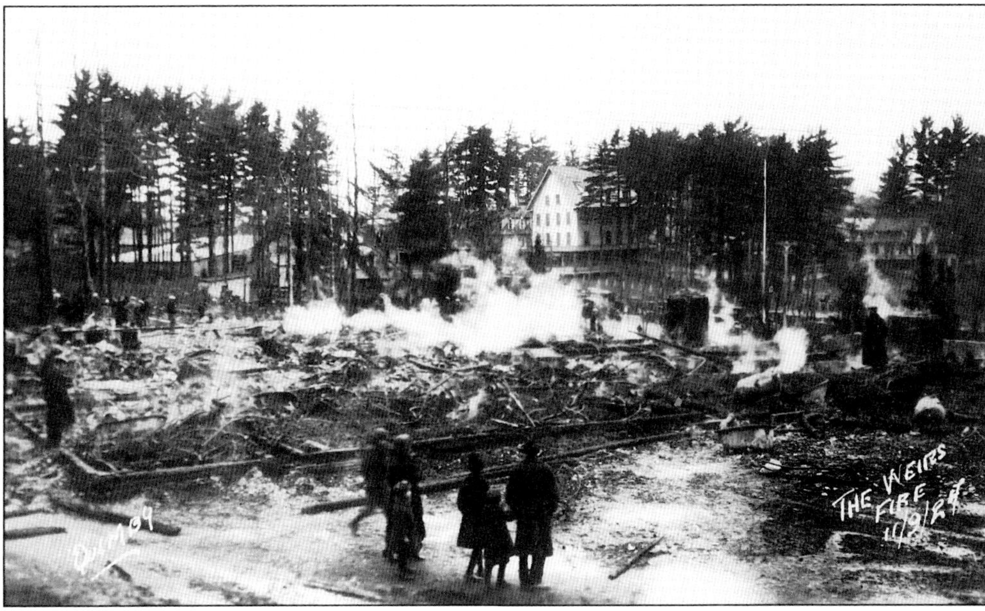

Conflagration and destruction. Late in the evening of November 9, 1924, the New Hotel Weirs and twelve other structures on Lakeside Avenue and Tower Street (including the 1886 Methodist church and the adjacent 1903 Music Hall) burned to the ground. Here is the scene of desolation, with Lakeside Hotel in the distance. The fire started in the Music Hall.

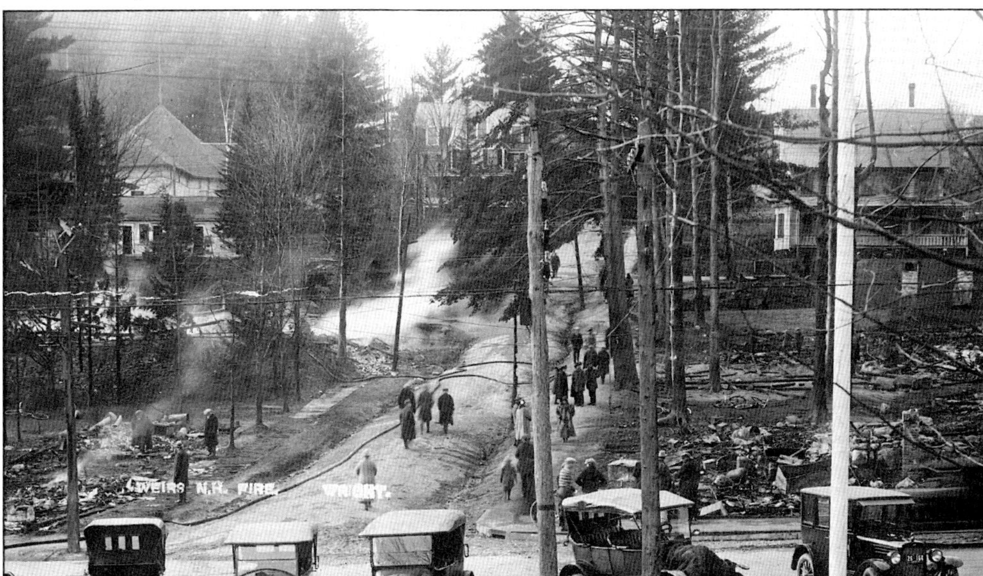

Another view of the fire scene. The heat was so intense that the passenger station was set afire in many places and the steamer *Mount Washington*, tied up at the wharf, was kept under a stream of water. Although the Veterans Association Headquarters Building on Lakeside Avenue was saved, the adjacent Third Regiment Headquarters was lost to the flames. By continuously playing heavy streams of water on the other Association buildings, which were showered with sparks, firefighters quickly extinguished the small fires. That the entire resort area was not destroyed was acknowledged as a tribute to Laconia Fire Chief Arthur W. Spring.

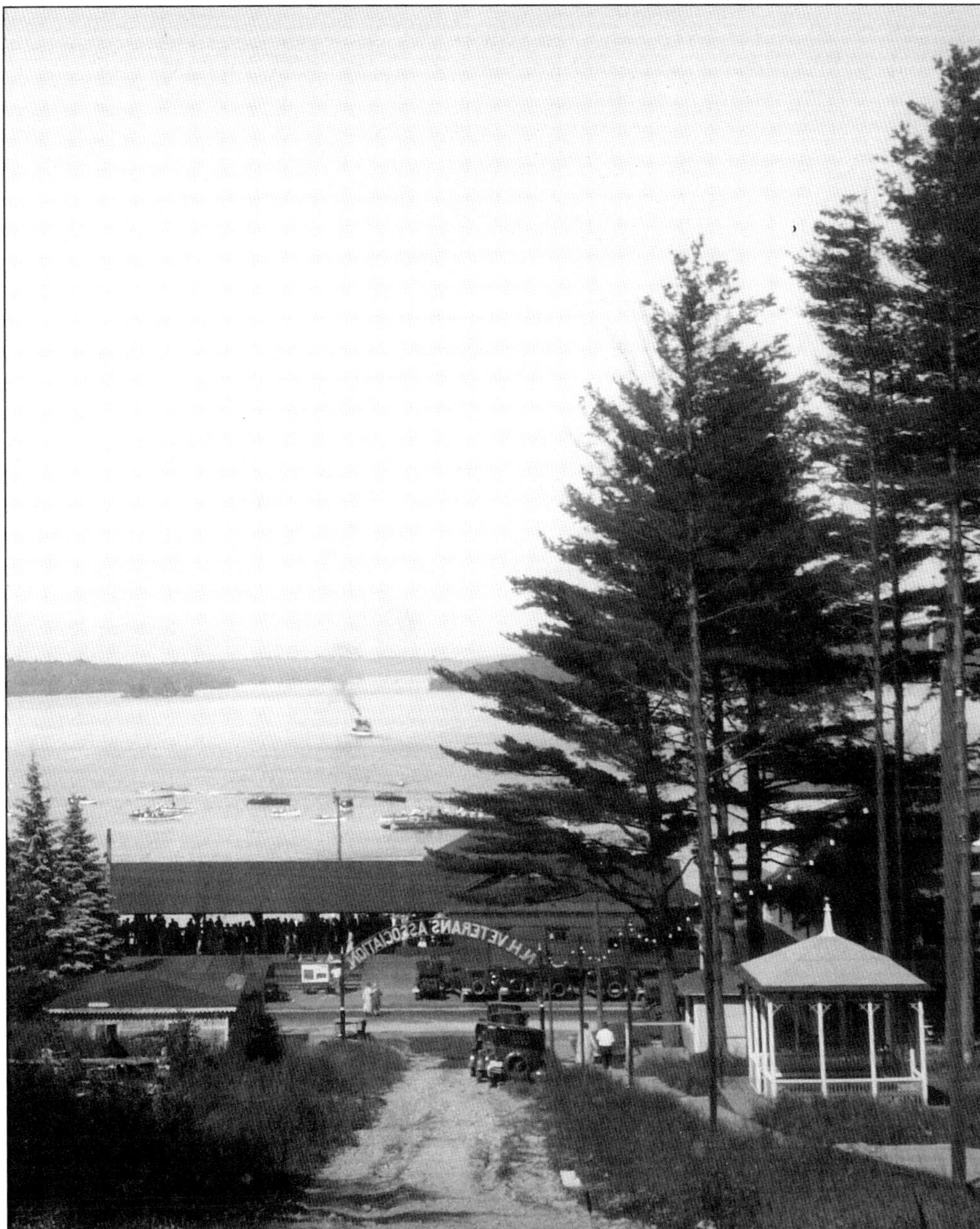

Looking down New Hampshire Avenue (known as Greene Avenue early in the twentieth century) toward the railroad station, from Veterans Avenue on the New Hampshire Veterans Association grounds, c. 1930. By then, the ranks of the Civil War veterans had thinned considerably, though the reunion tradition was still being carried on, with increasing participation by the Sons of Veterans and by those who had fought in the Spanish-American War and World War I.

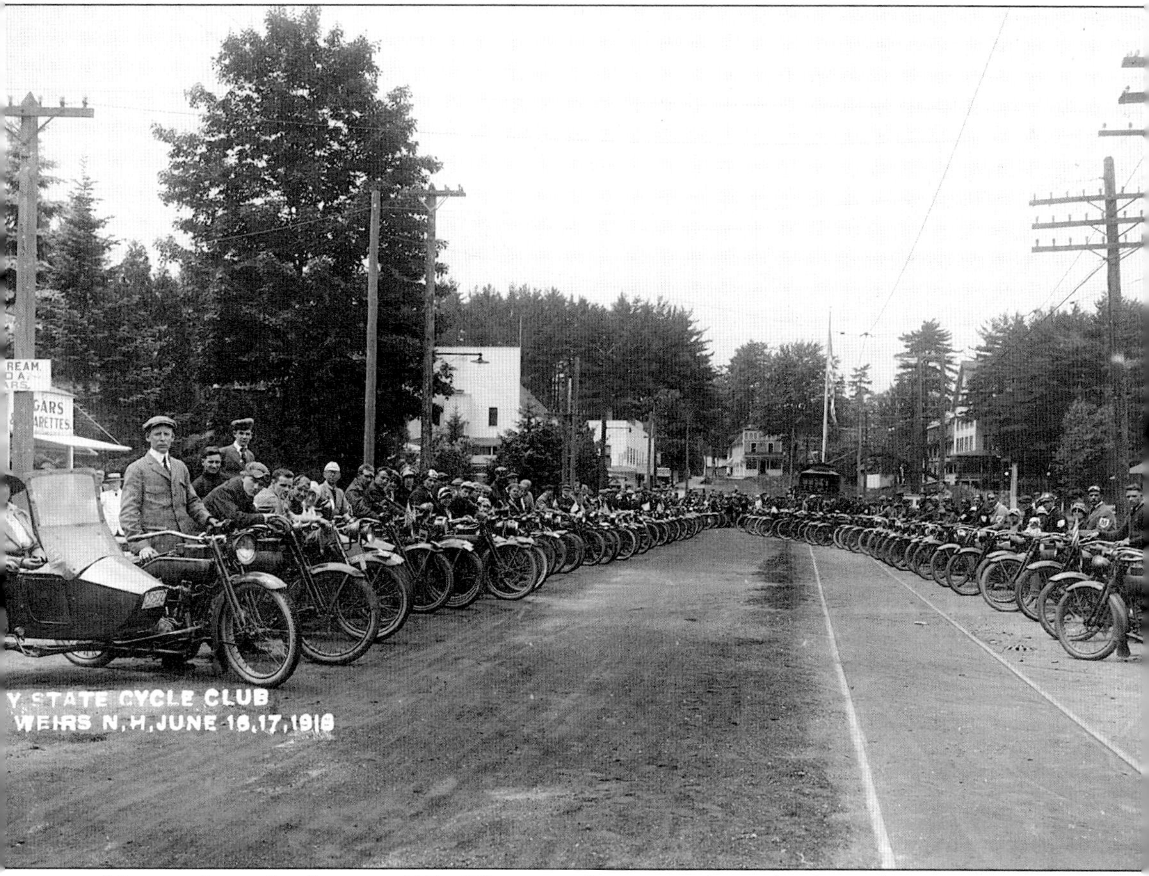

Motorcyclists, who discovered The Weirs as early as 1916. A couple of years later, concerning the gathering depicted here, *The Laconia Democrat* for Friday, June 21, 1918, reported, "The Weirs entertained a big bunch of motorcycle riders last Sunday, the party hailing from Massachusetts, and coming up over the state boulevard [as U.S. Route 3 was then known] from Boston, arriving at The Weirs about the middle of the afternoon, where they enjoyed a ride on the lake, dinner at the hotels and a concert in the evening, returning to Boston the next day. The organization was the Bay State Motorcycle club and the party numbered about 300, many of the cycles having sidecars, occupied by ladies." Tracks of the Laconia Street Railway appear on the right. A feature of early motorcycle gatherings was often a hill-climb up Tower Street.

Four

Railroad and Waterfront

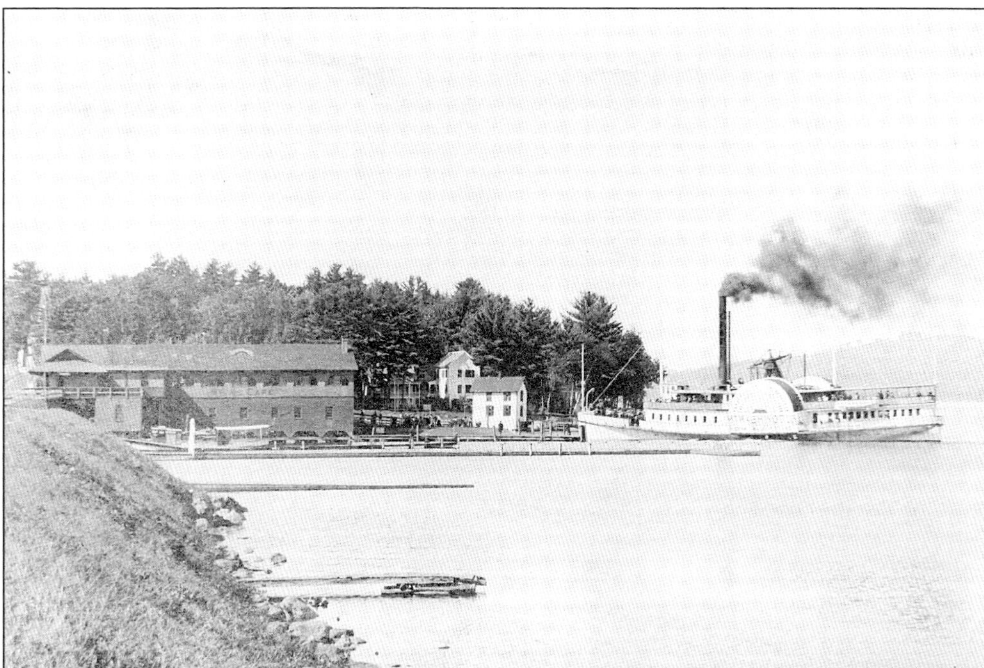

The steamer *Mount Washington* at The Weirs, late 1890s. The 1885 Weirs Cafe and 1893 railroad station can be seen on the left. The deceptively bucolic atmosphere masks the burgeoning Methodist Campground and other residential development in the wooded area

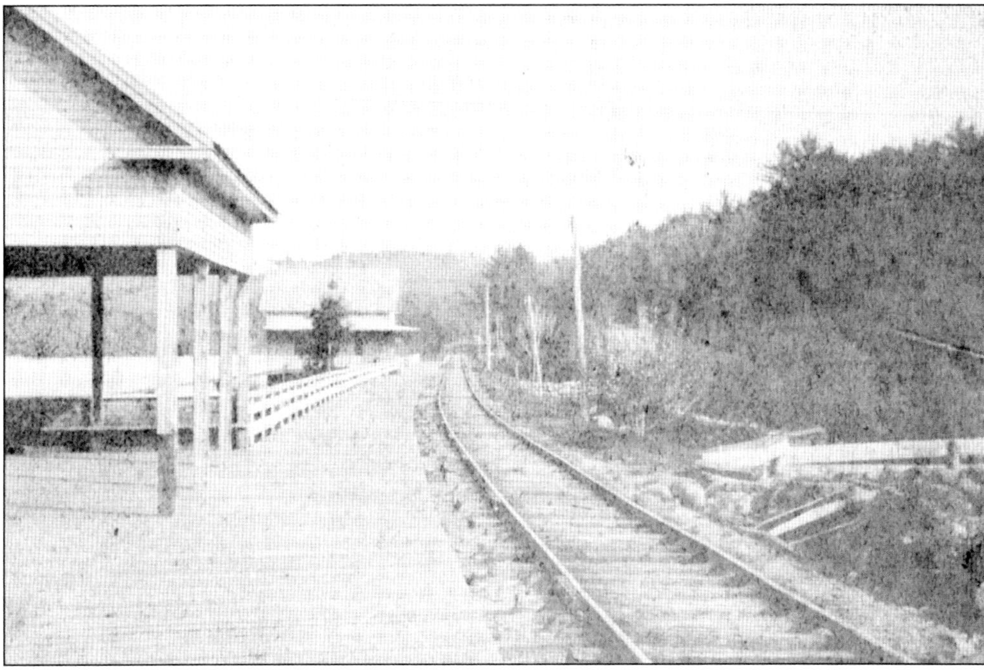

Weirs Boardwalk, early 1870s, with the original *c.* 1848 passenger depot in the distance on the left. Until the mid-1870s, "Weirs Steamboat Landing," despite its impressive boardwalk, was a tiny, sleepy, primarily agricultural community—serving also as a transfer point for the lake steamers. In this rare early view, Lakeside Avenue (in the space at right) hasn't even been thought of.

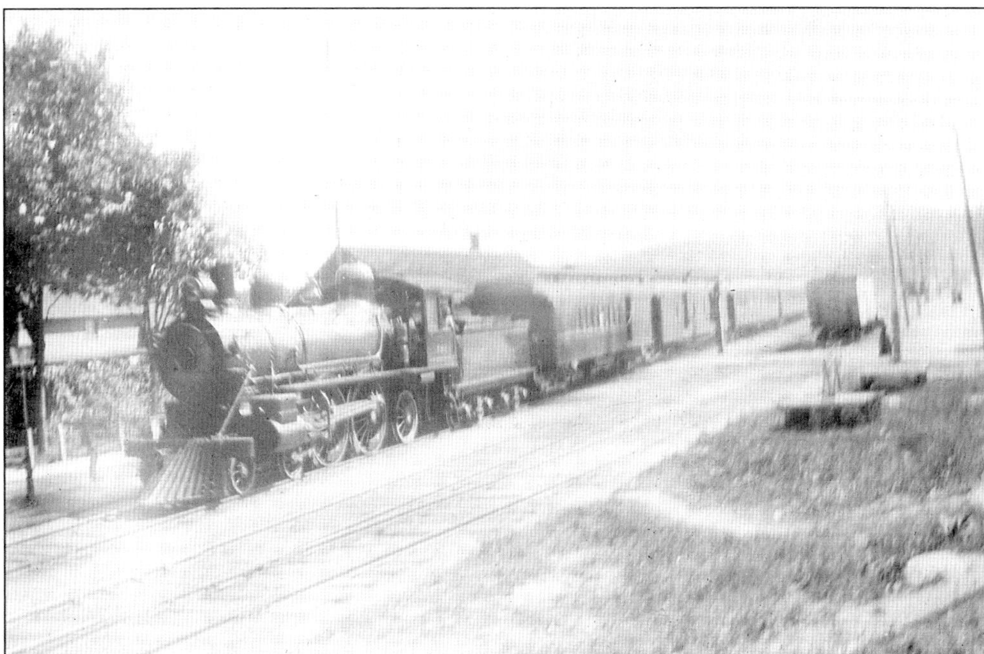

The noon express north, The Weirs, late 1880s. By now, there are additional sidings and a rudimentary Railroad Avenue (later Lakeside Avenue) is visible in the distance on the right.

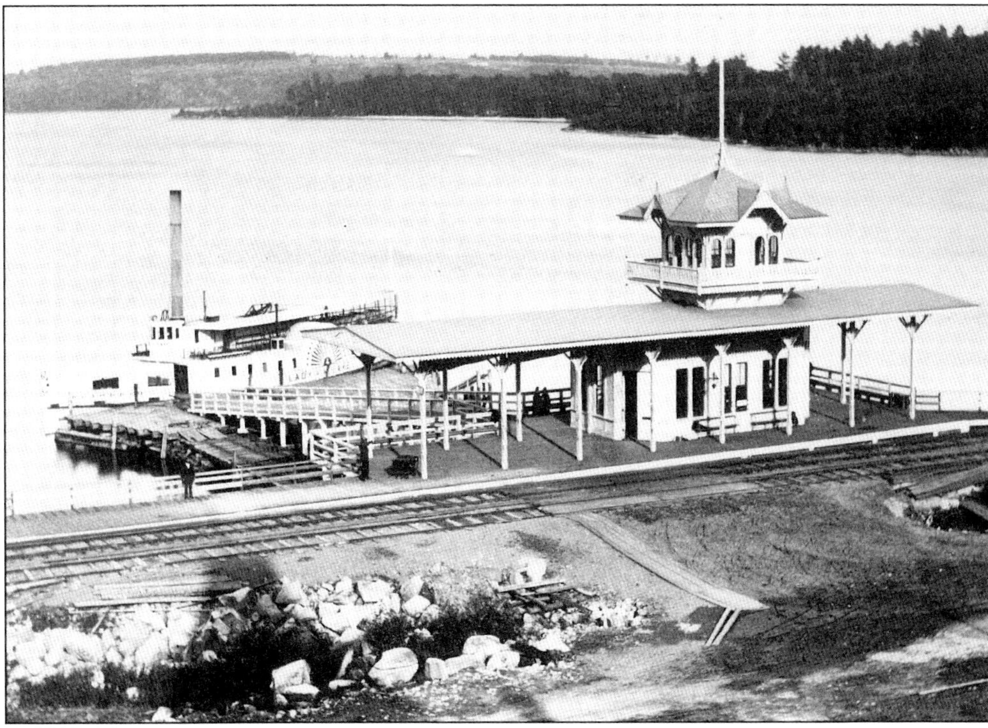

Weirs station and the steamer *Lady of the Lake*, c. 1880.

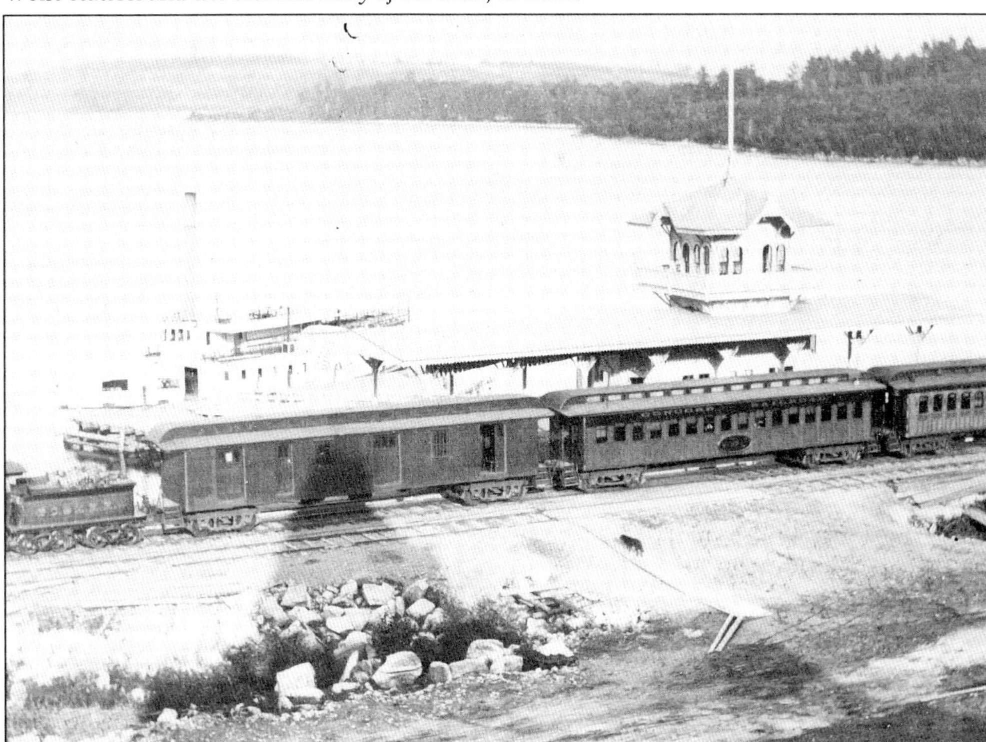

The same view, this time with a passenger train at the station.

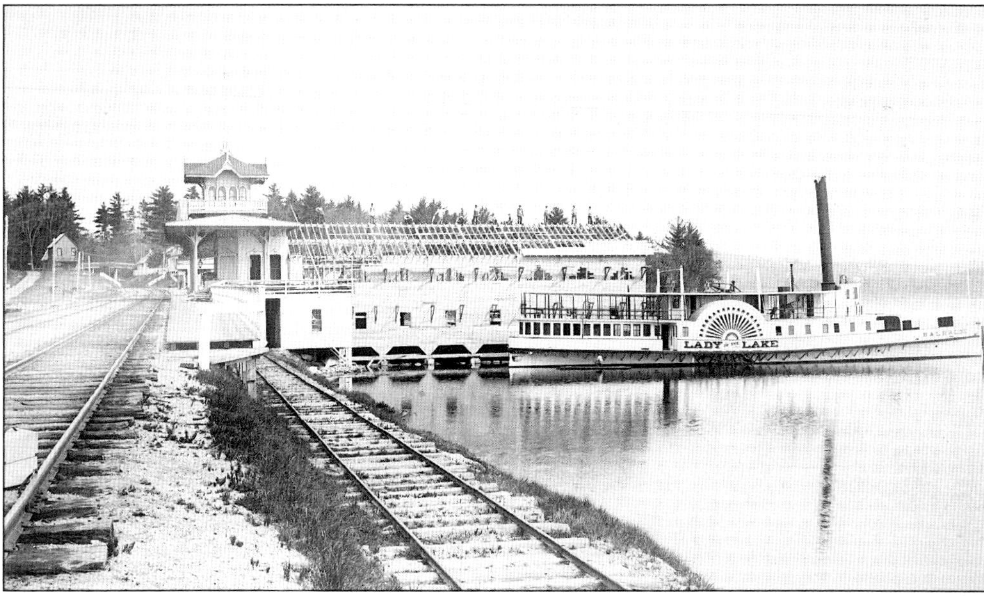

Weirs Cafe under construction, 1885. The sidetrack on the right was used for transferring freight to lake steamers like the *Lady of the Lake* (on the right). A freight house occupied the lower level at the end of the spur.

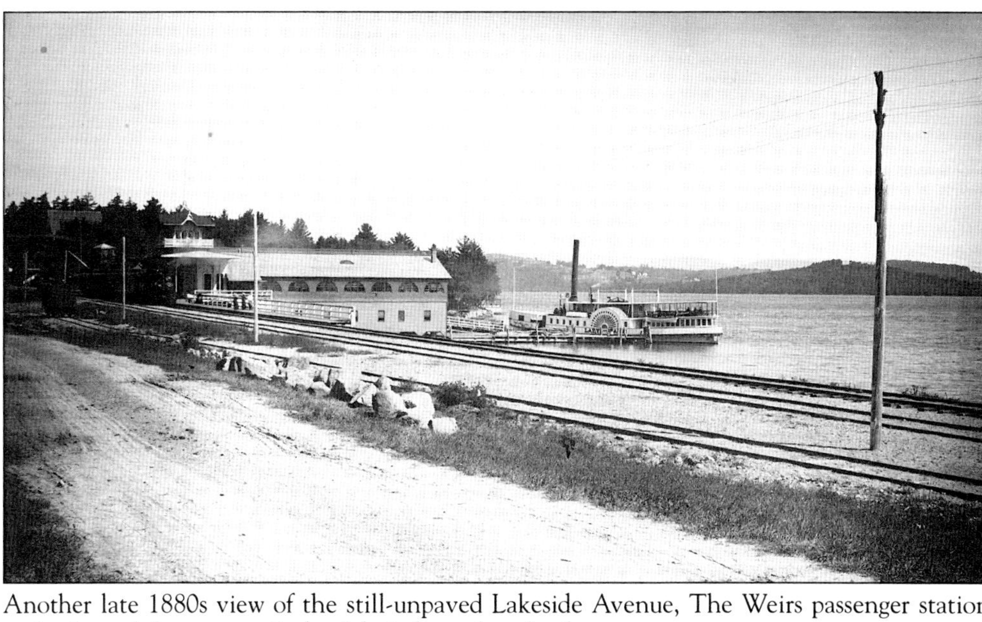

Another late 1880s view of the still-unpaved Lakeside Avenue, The Weirs passenger station and cafe, and the steamer *Lady of the Lake* at the wharf.

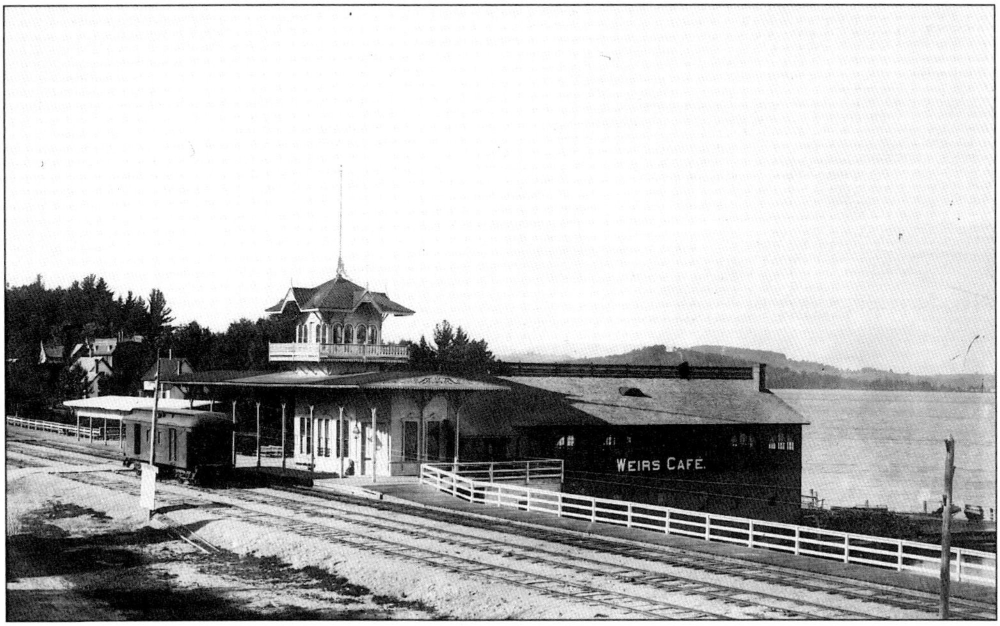

The Weirs station and cafe, late 1880s.

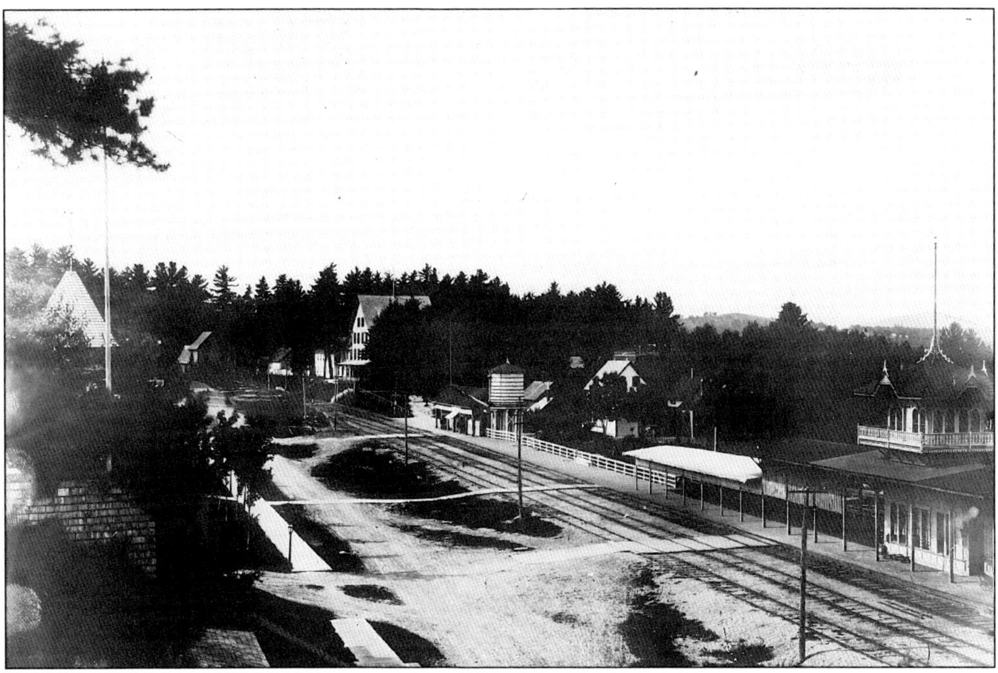

The view north along Lakeside Avenue, late 1880s. Lakeside House is visible in the distance at the center, along with the Headquarters Building (on the left) of the New Hampshire Veterans Association. The water tower (at the center) served steam locomotives of the Concord & Montreal Railroad until 1893, when standpipes were installed at the same time the depot was remodeled to add the long canopy over the boardwalk.

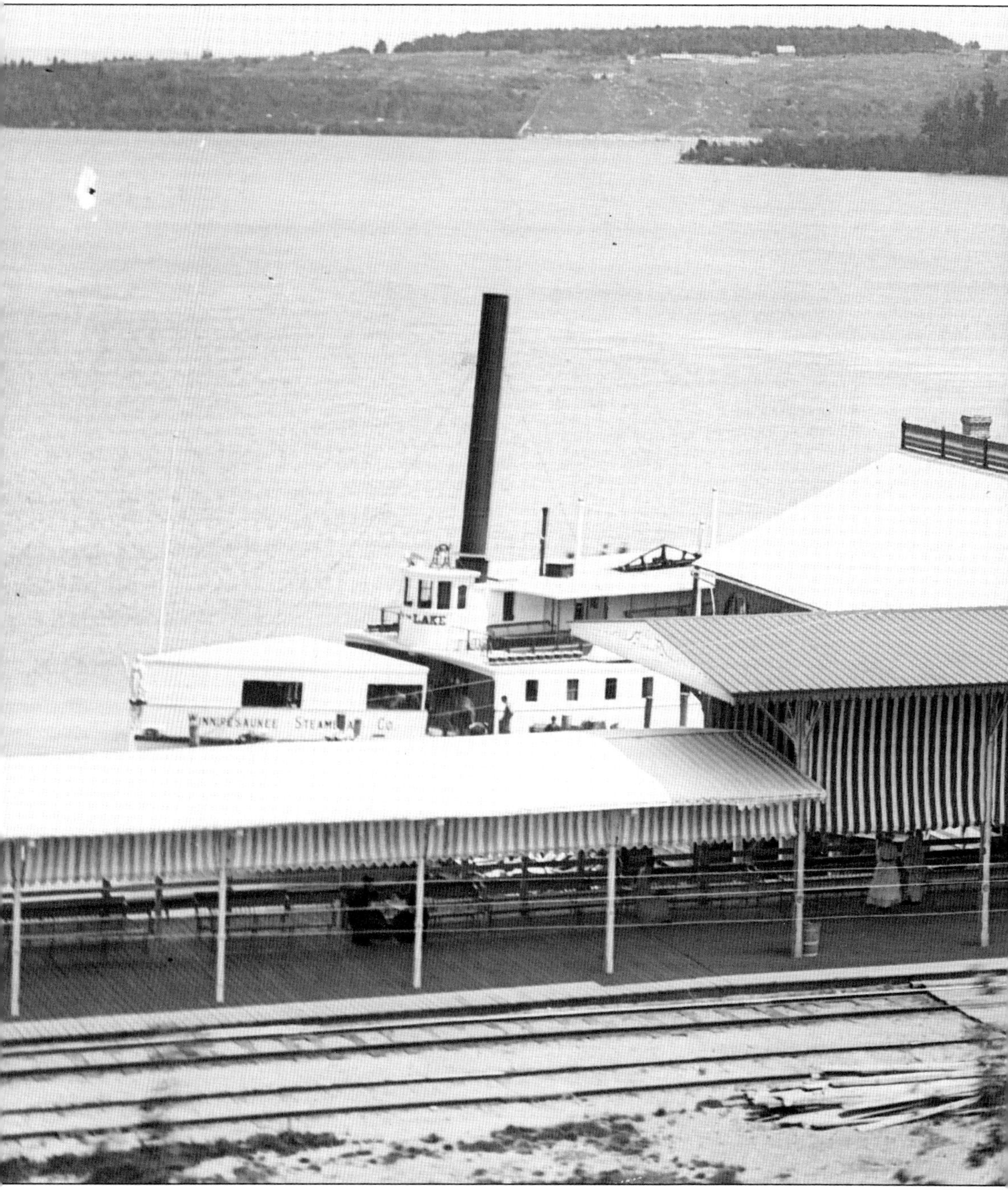

The Weirs station, with the steamer *Lady of the Lake*, late 1880s. The architect for the 1880 passenger depot had been A.L. Davis of Laconia. (Designer of the New Hampshire Building at the Philadelphia Centennial Exhibition in 1876, Davis had designed the Hotel Weirs, also in 1880, and, in Laconia, he would eventually have a dozen or more major buildings to his credit.) The Weirs Cafe building, extending 100 feet from the boardwalk out into the lake behind the depot, was built in 1885. At the time of this photograph, Railroad Avenue was still a pretty rough affair; yet, within fifteen years, a much improved thoroughfare—with its name changed

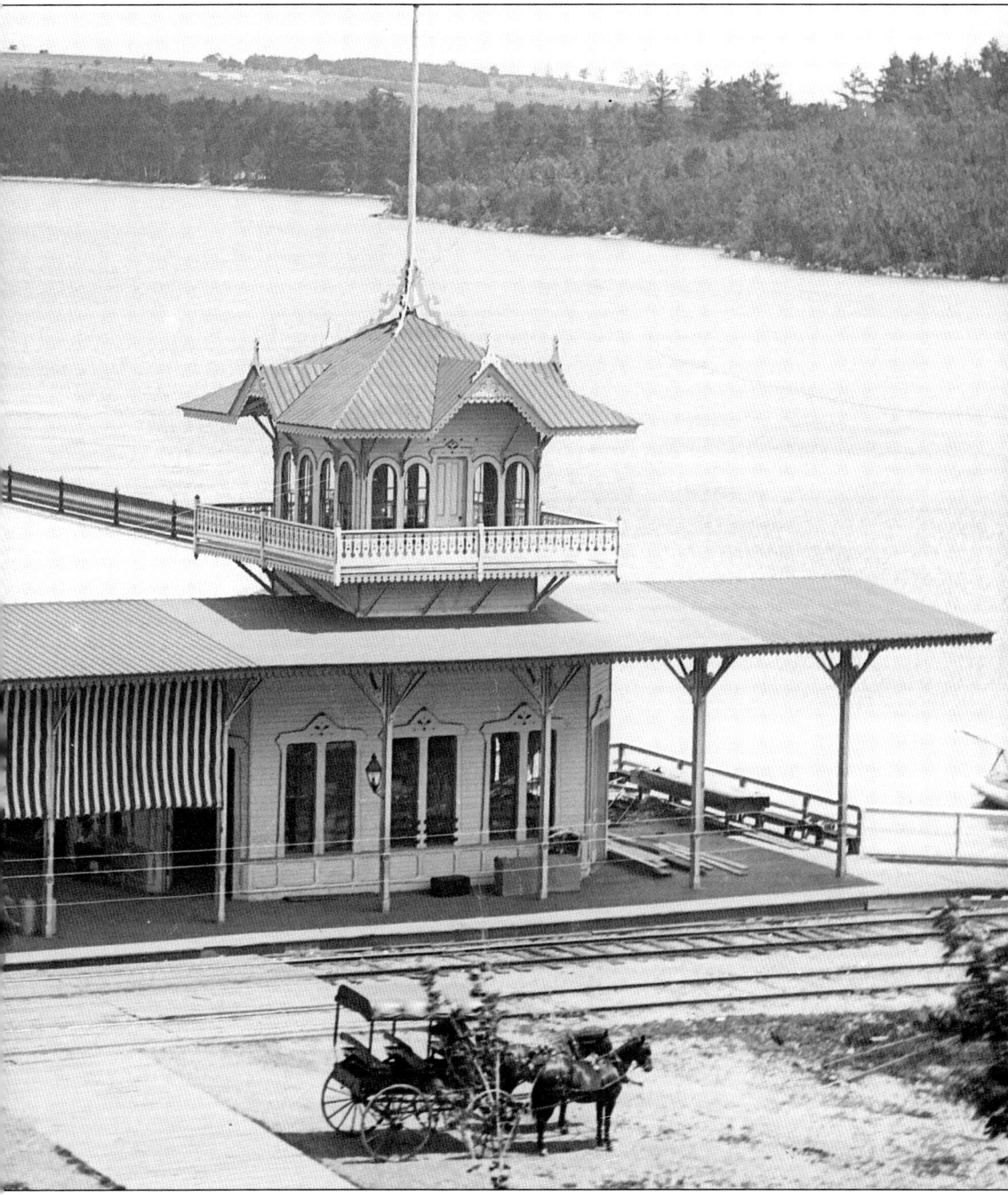

to Lakeside Avenue—would boast the trolley tracks of the Laconia Street Railway, which began service all the way to Lakeside House (off the photograph to the left) in June 1899. This image gives an idea of the scene which greeted veterans at their reunions, music teachers at their festivals, Methodists and other religious groups at their camp meetings, as well as an ever-increasing number of summer residents and tourists during the eight years before construction of the 1893 long canopy over the boardwalk (see p. 75).

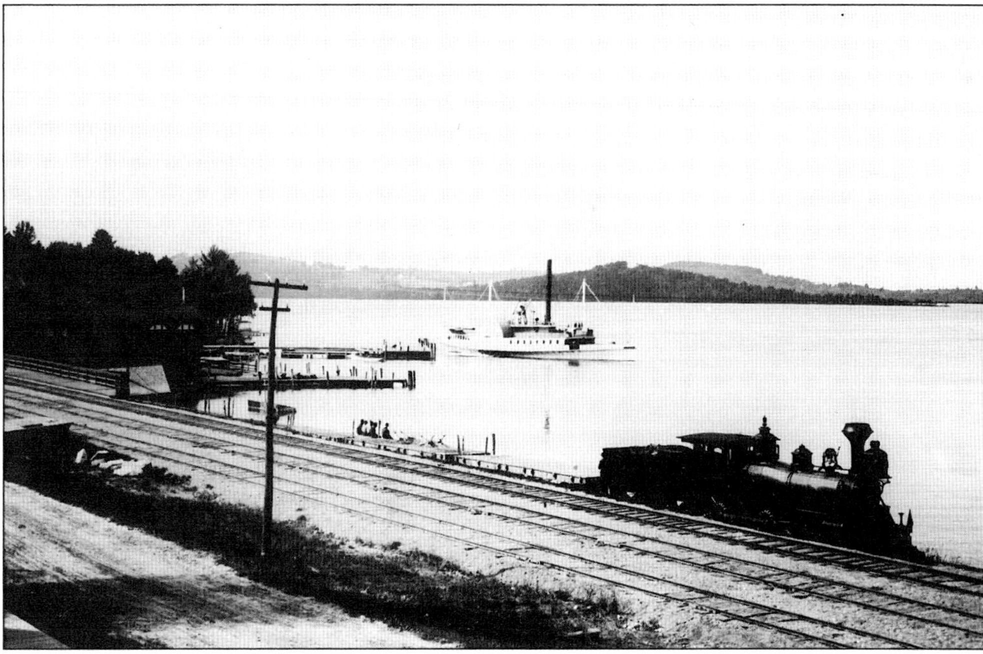

Freight service, late 1880s. The wood-burning locomotive and flatcars of the Boston, Concord & Montreal Railroad, on the waterside siding, head toward the main line.

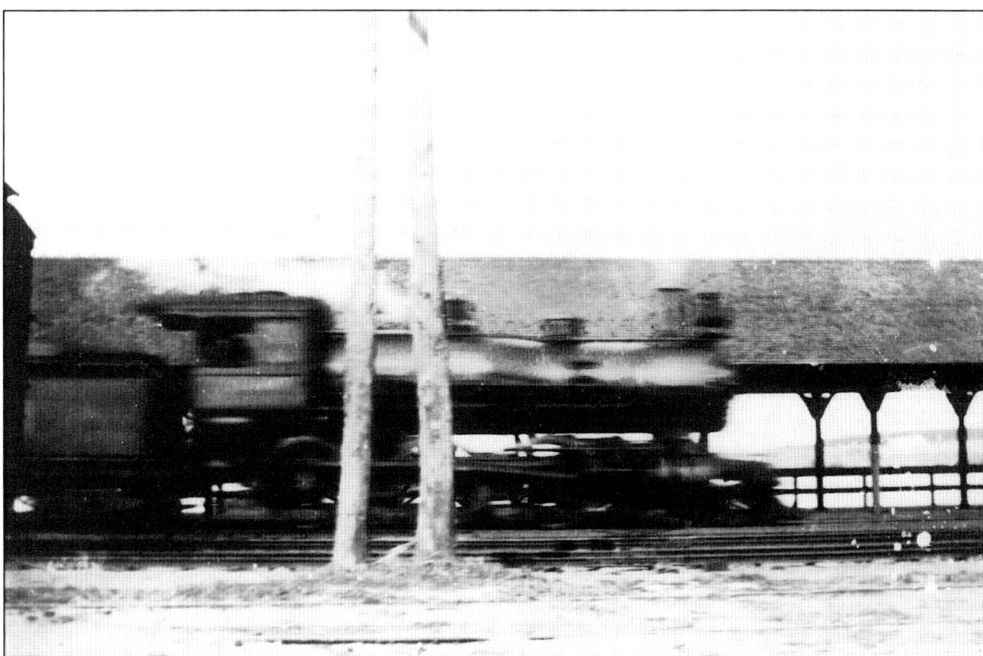

A locomotive heading south, late 1890s. In addition to regularly scheduled passenger and freight service, the railroad operated numerous excursion trains between Boston and the White Mountains.

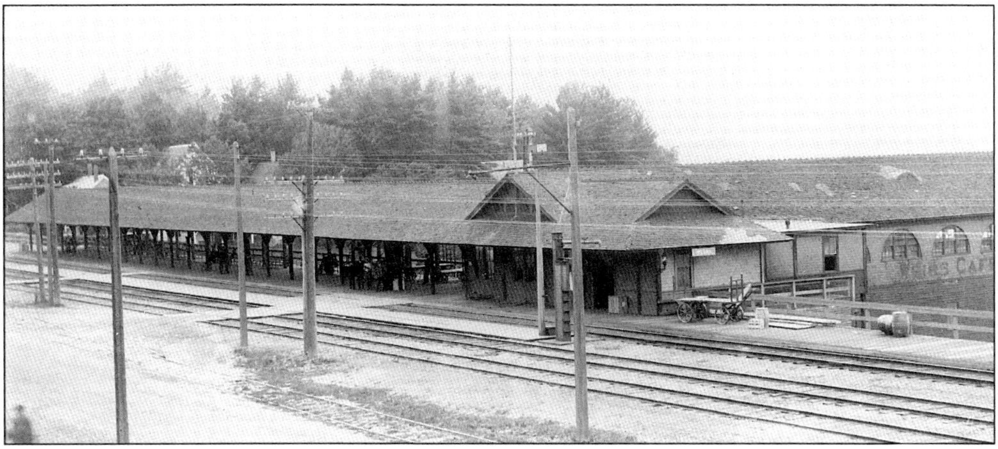

The Weirs passenger station, early 1890s. By 1893, it had become apparent to the Concord & Montreal Railroad that The Weirs was an important summer tourist destination. The veterans reunions, camp meetings, and music festivals were attracting as many as 10,000 people on a regular basis and three or four times that number on occasion. The new station provided an improved ticket office, waiting room, and baggage space, as well as a canopy, 30-by-500 feet, over the boardwalk to shield travelers from sun and rain.

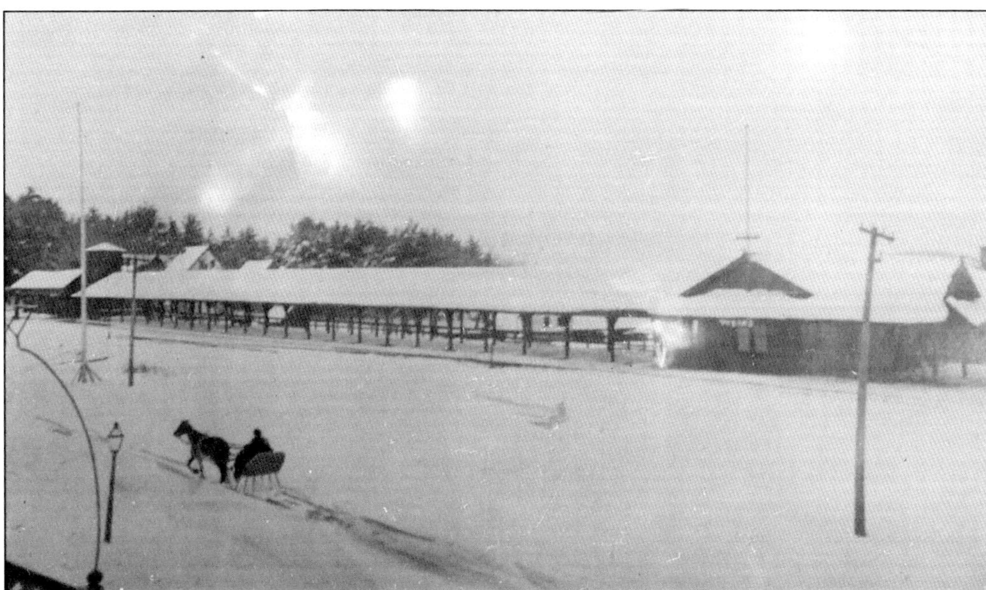

Winter scene, 1893. This photograph was one of the illustrations in a souvenir booklet published to mark the incorporation, in March of that year, of the new City of Laconia.

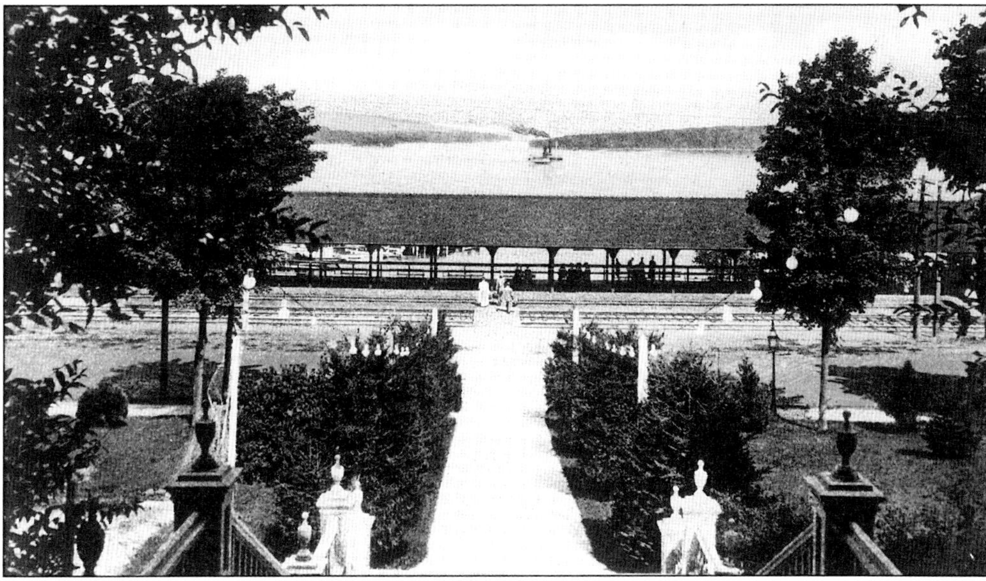

Lake view from the steps of the Hotel Weirs, about 1905. In its advertising and promotional literature, the hotel capitalized on its proximity to the station and steamer wharf.

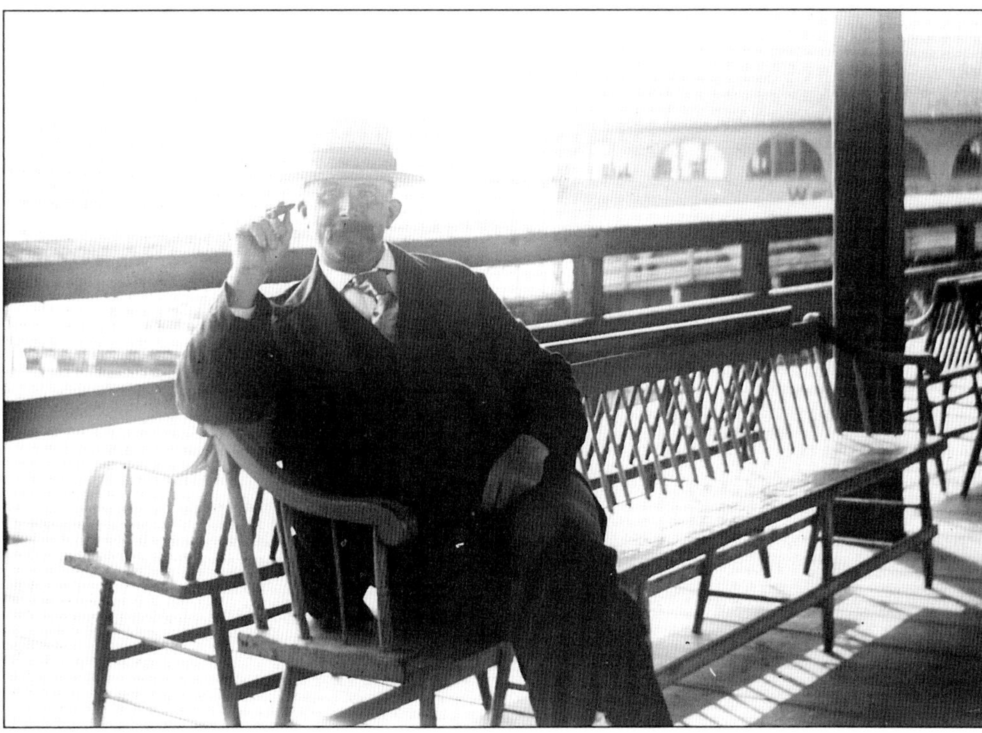

Julian F. Trask, at The Weirs, late 1890s. The private secretary to Governor Charles A. Busiel of Laconia, Trask later served as state labor commissioner and as Laconia city clerk and postmaster among a host of other appointments. In addition, he was an enterprising newspaperman, writing for the *Manchester Union* as well as for the Associated Press.

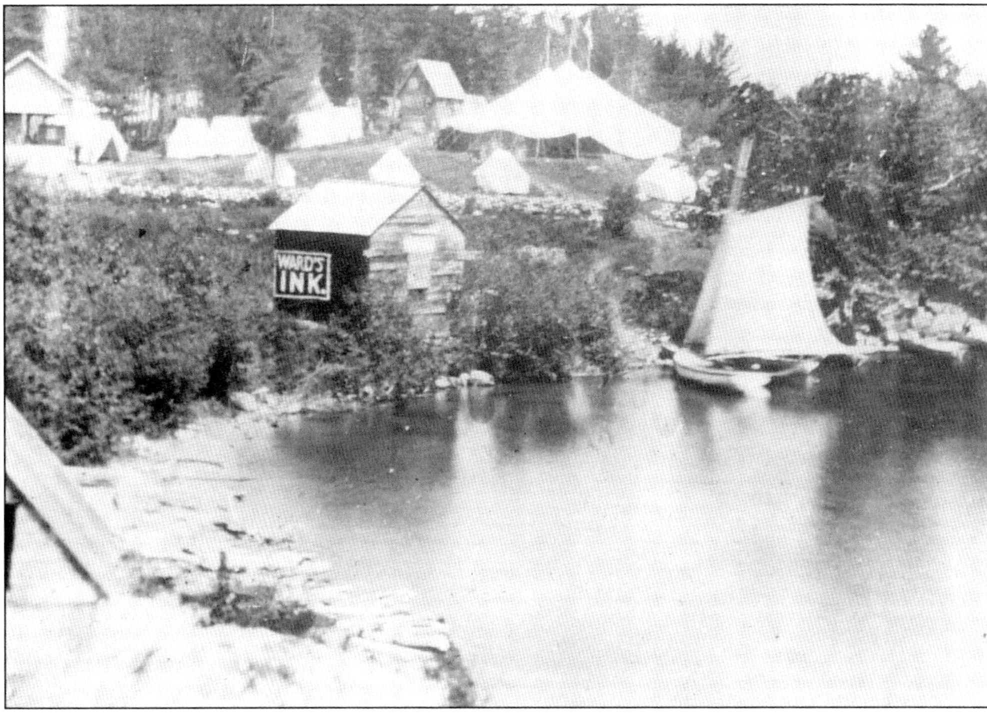

Early days at The Weirs waterfront, with the first veterans encampment set up in tents, 1878. Tents were used until 1880, when a new Veterans Association campground was established on the hillside to the west of Lakeside Avenue.

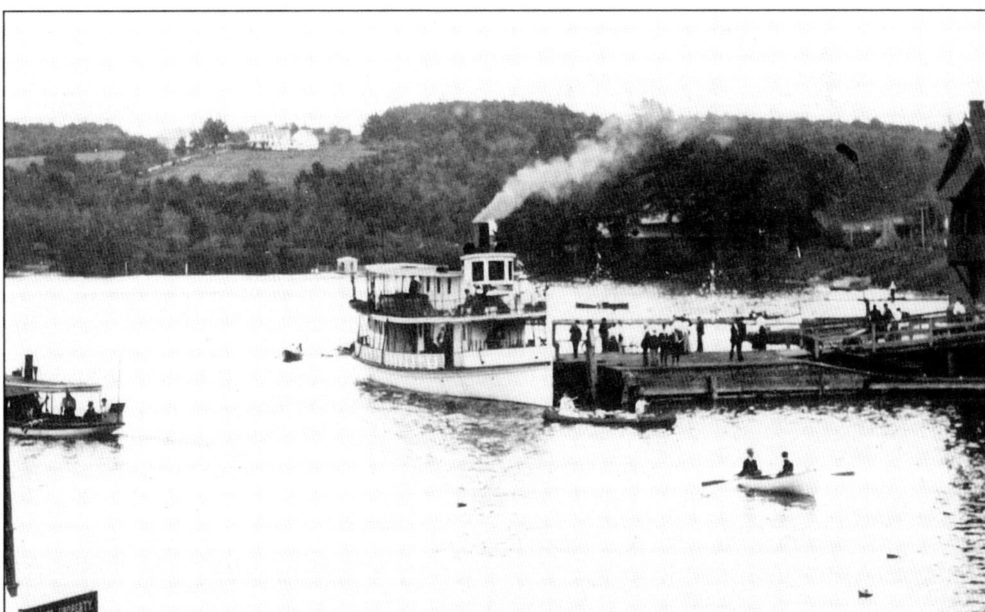

The steamer *Maid of the Isles* at Weirs wharf, 1900.

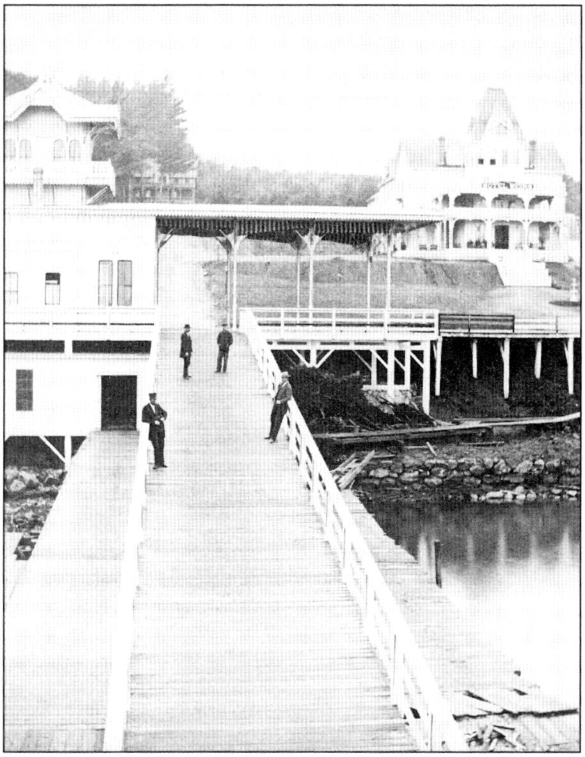

Weirs Landing, with the Hotel Weirs in the background, c. 1880. This scene appears to have been framed deliberately with a view toward capturing the new depot, ramp, and hotel.

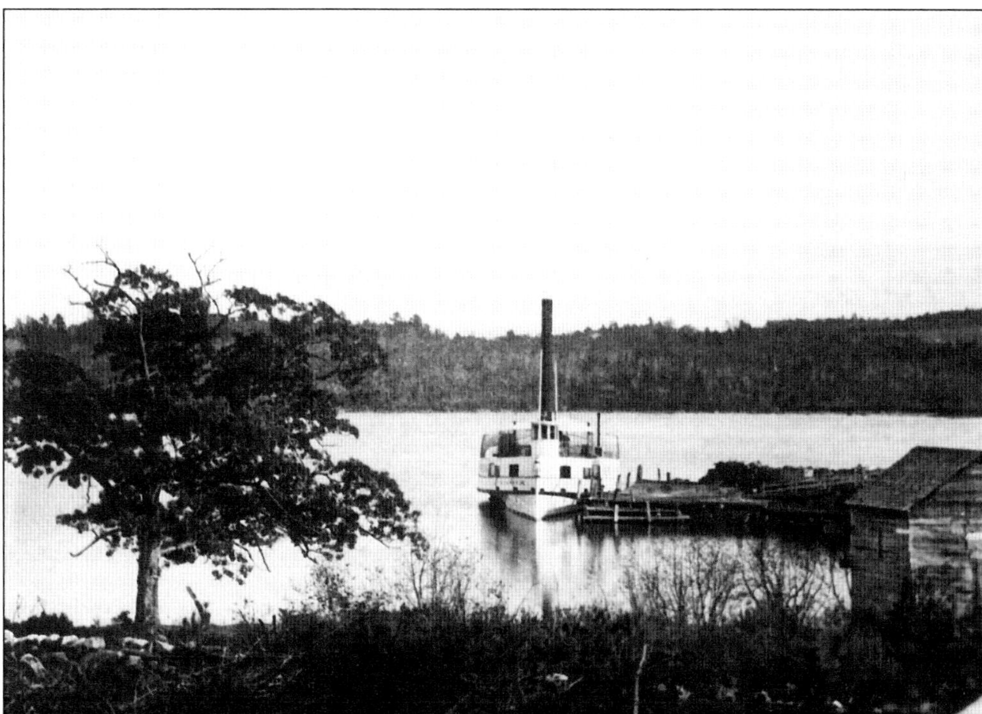

The steamer *Lady of the Lake* at Weirs Landing, c. 1870. The venerable *Lady* served the summer resort trade from 1849 to 1894.

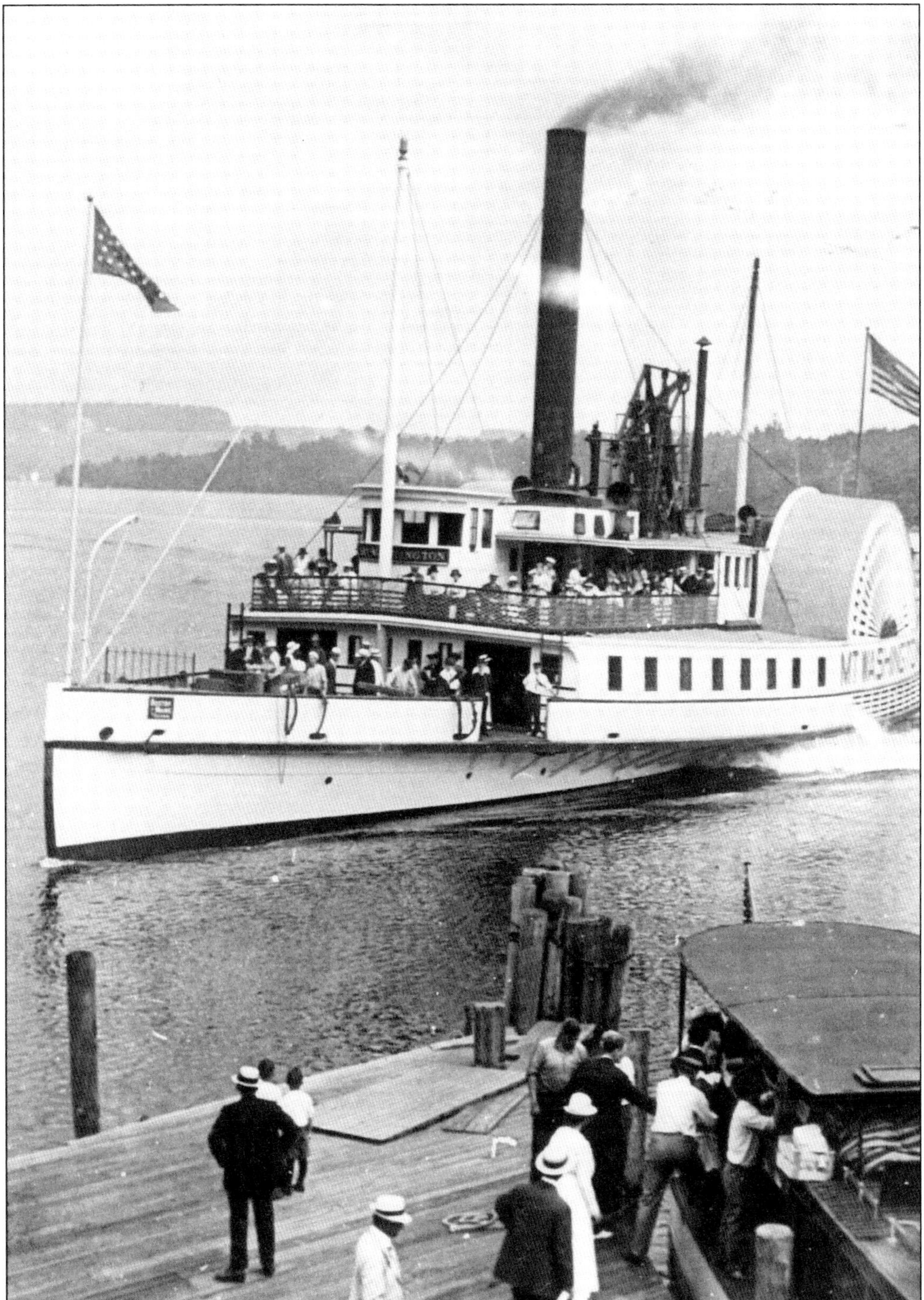

The steamer *Mount Washington* puts in at Weirs landing, *c.* 1900. Built in 1872, she plied the waters of the Big Lake until December 22, 1939, when she was destroyed in a raging inferno which also consumed the 1885 Weirs Cafe, 1893 railroad station, and at least one seaplane.

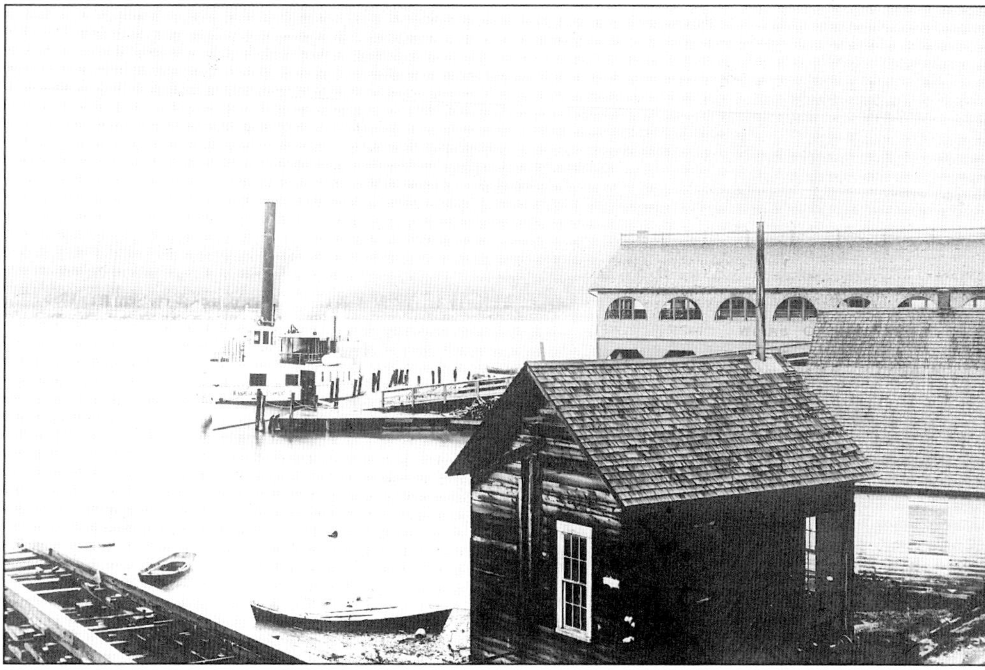

The steamer *Lady of the Lake* at Weirs Landing, *c.* 1890, with the Weirs Cafe on the right. The small building in the foreground may or may not be the later *Weirs Times* office.

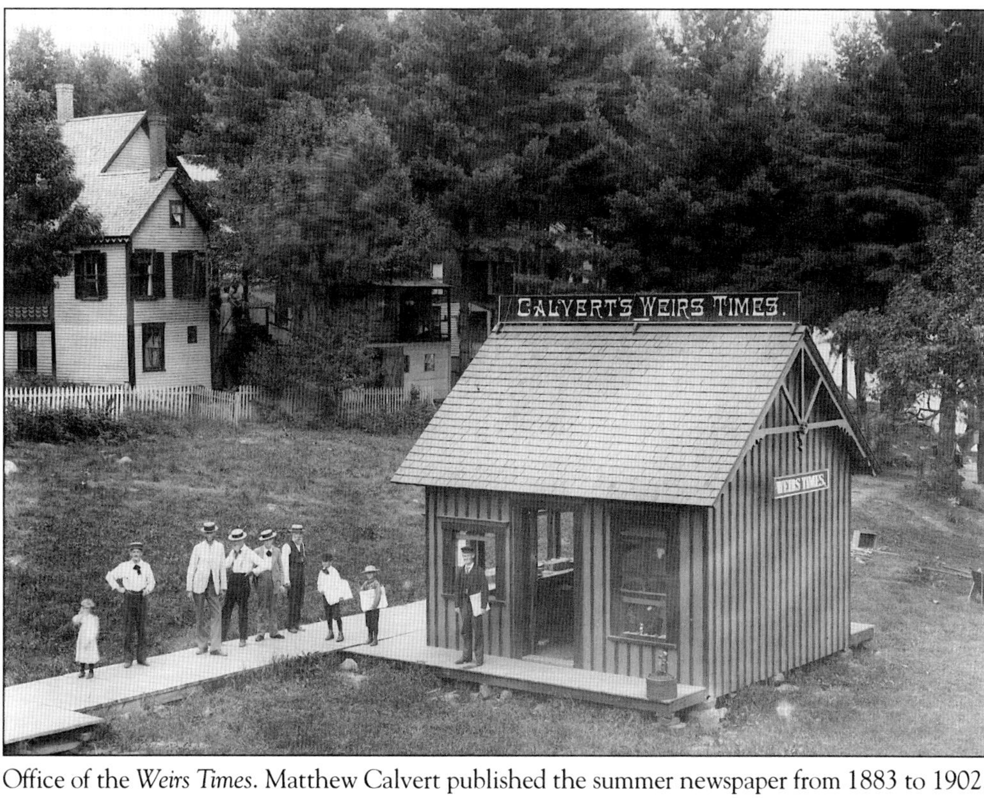

Office of the *Weirs Times*. Matthew Calvert published the summer newspaper from 1883 to 1902.

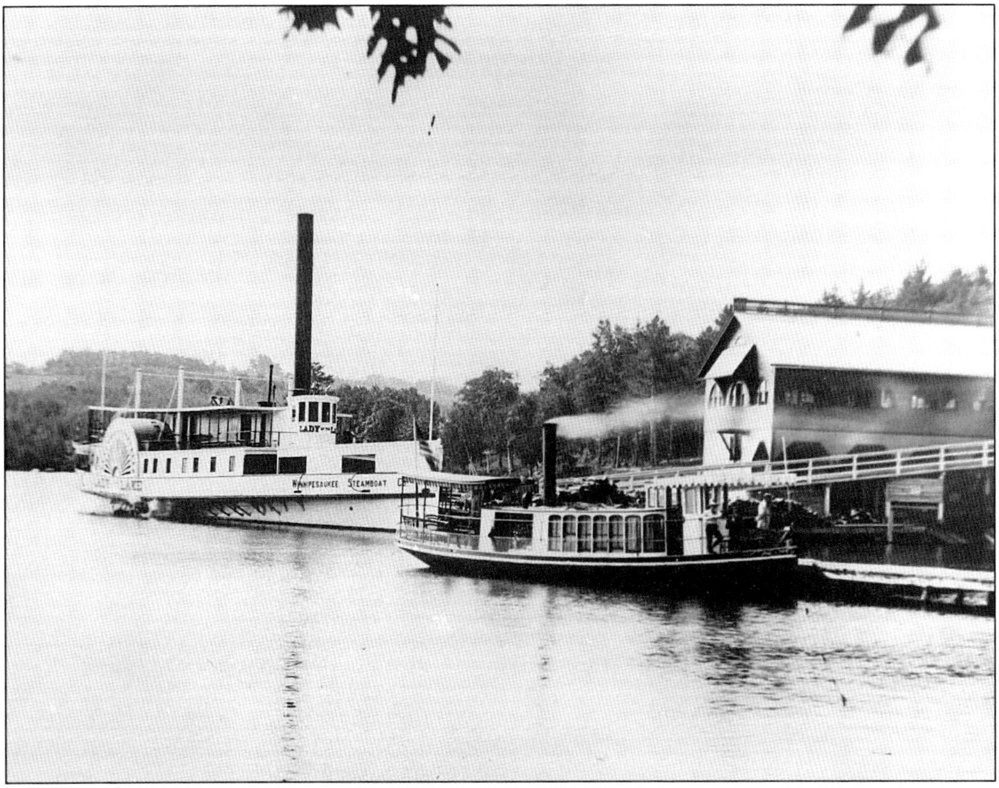

The steamer *Lady of the Lake* (left) and James Worrall's *Gracie*, at Weirs Wharf, late 1880s.

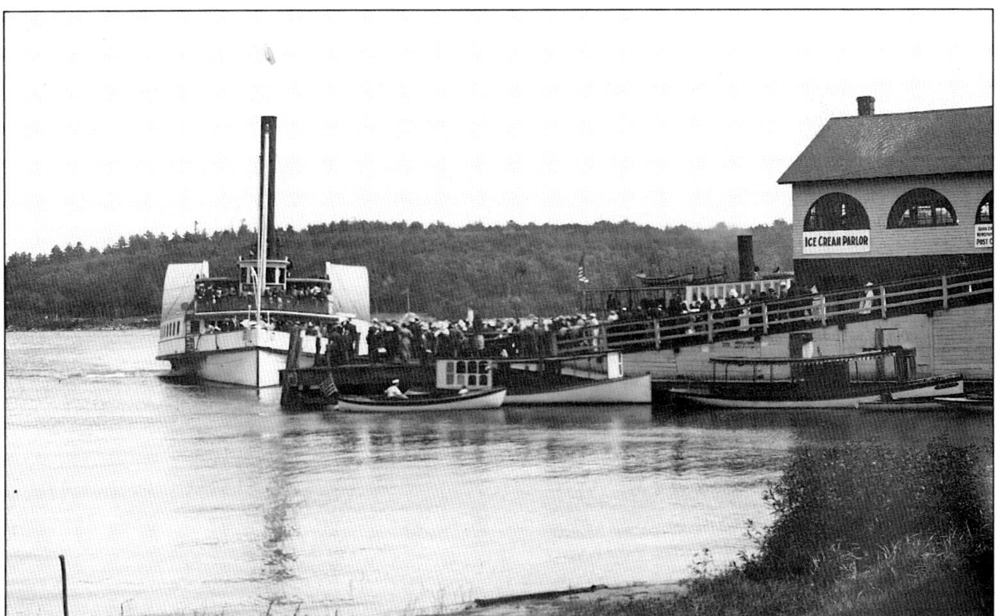

The steamers *Mount Washington* (left) and *Governor Endicott* (beyond ramp) at Weirs Wharf, *c.* 1906, along with numerous smaller vessels.

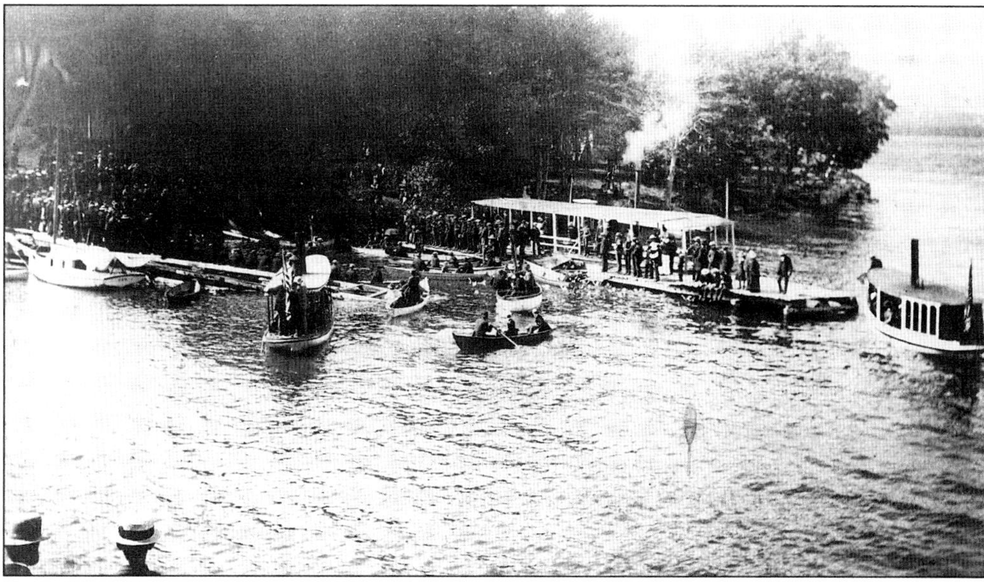

Early Weirs docks. A "recreation pier" was built in 1908 but was replaced two years later, in 1910, by H.H. Buffum's Winnipesaukee Pier (see next page).

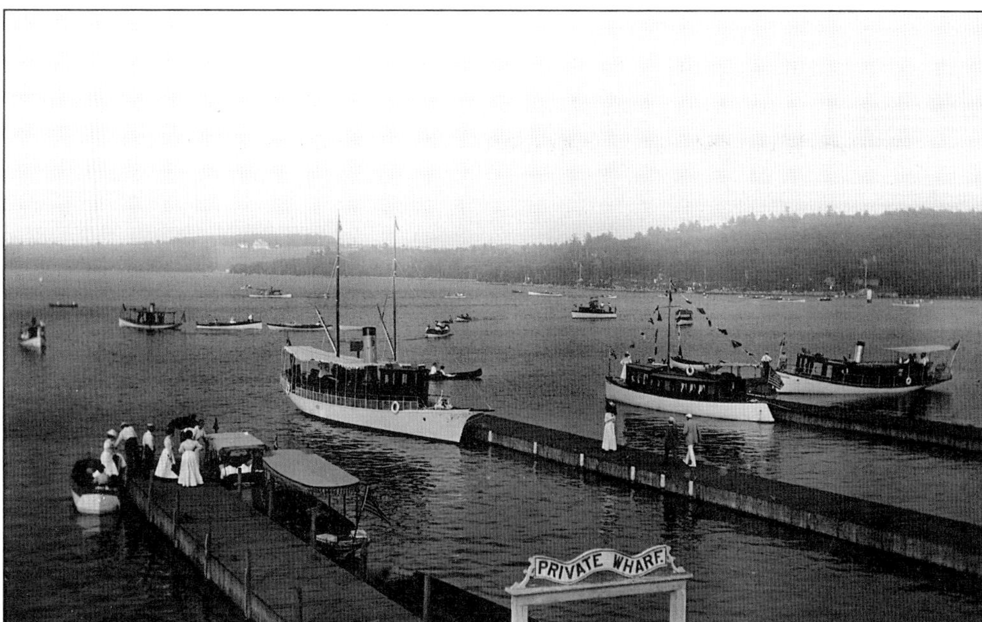

An 1890s summer scene, with Governors Island in the distance (upper left) and Interlaken Park (right). Many smaller steamboats such as the clipper-bowed *Swallow* (third from right) supplemented the Big Lake behemoths like the *Lady of the Lake* and the *Mount Washington*.

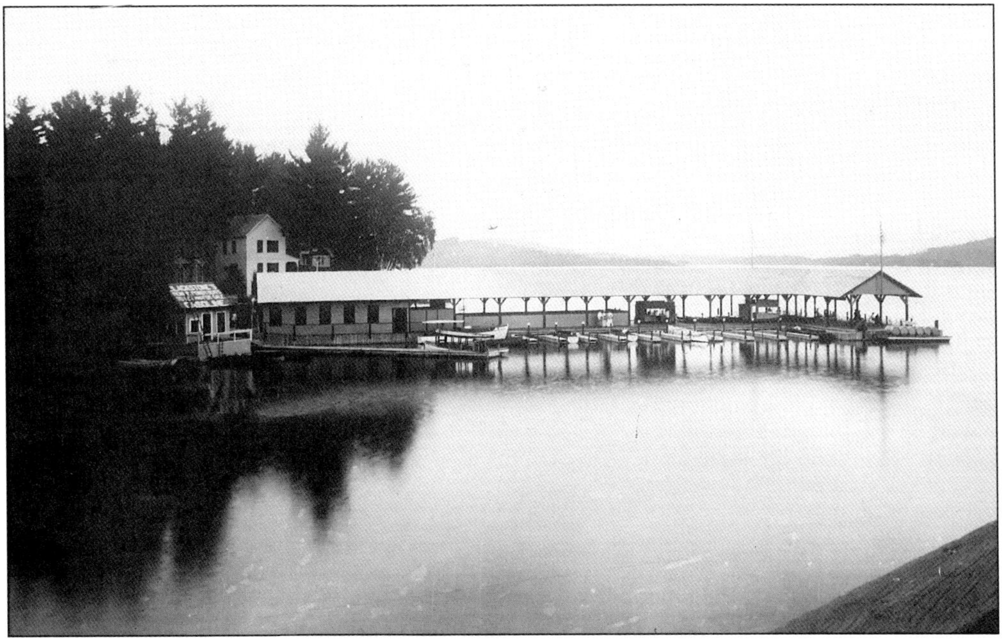

Winnipesaukee Pier, around 1911. In 1925, after having been burned out of the 1903 Music Hall on Tower Street (see p. 101) a year earlier, James Irwin Sr. built his Winnipesaukee Gardens at this location (see p. 127).

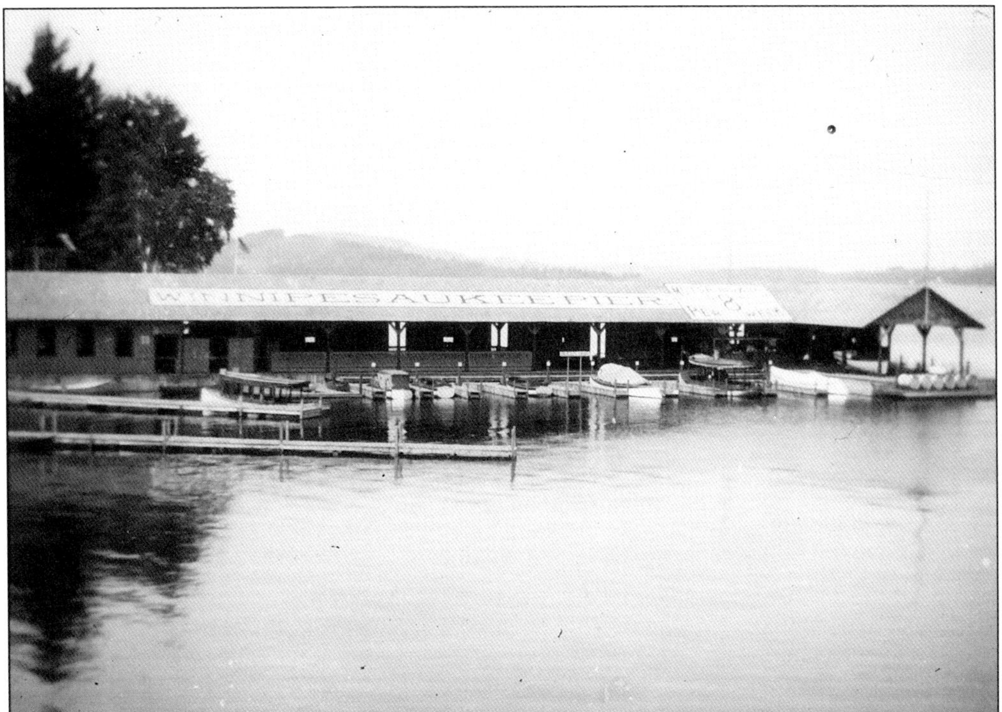

Another view of the pier. By the early years of this century, private pleasure boats had multiplied. This and other public and private wharves catered to their needs.

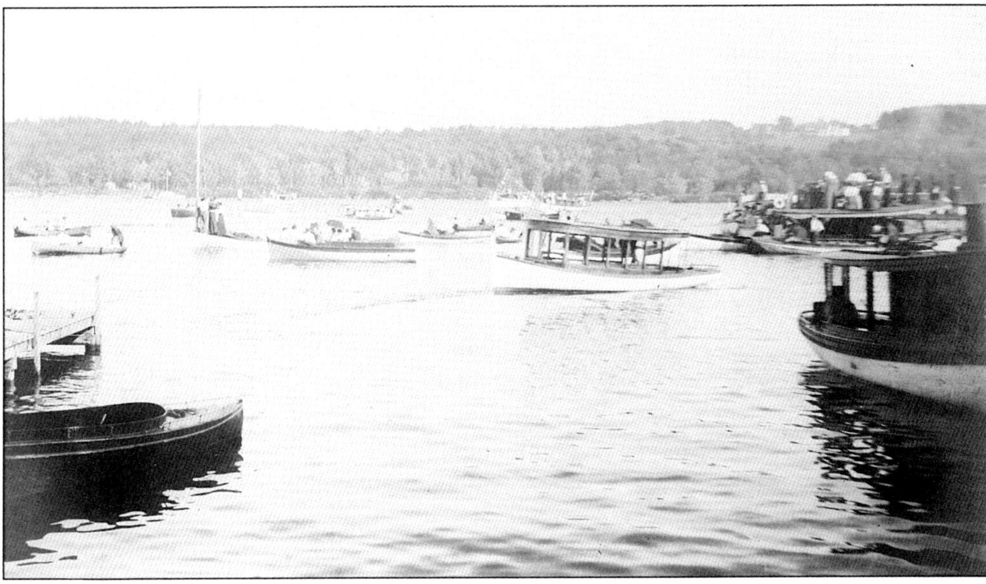

Weirs water carnival, 1908. There were, in fact, two water carnivals staged in August 1908. These featured powerboat races, balloon ascensions and parachute jumps, a parade of illuminated boats in the evening, dancing, and other attractions.

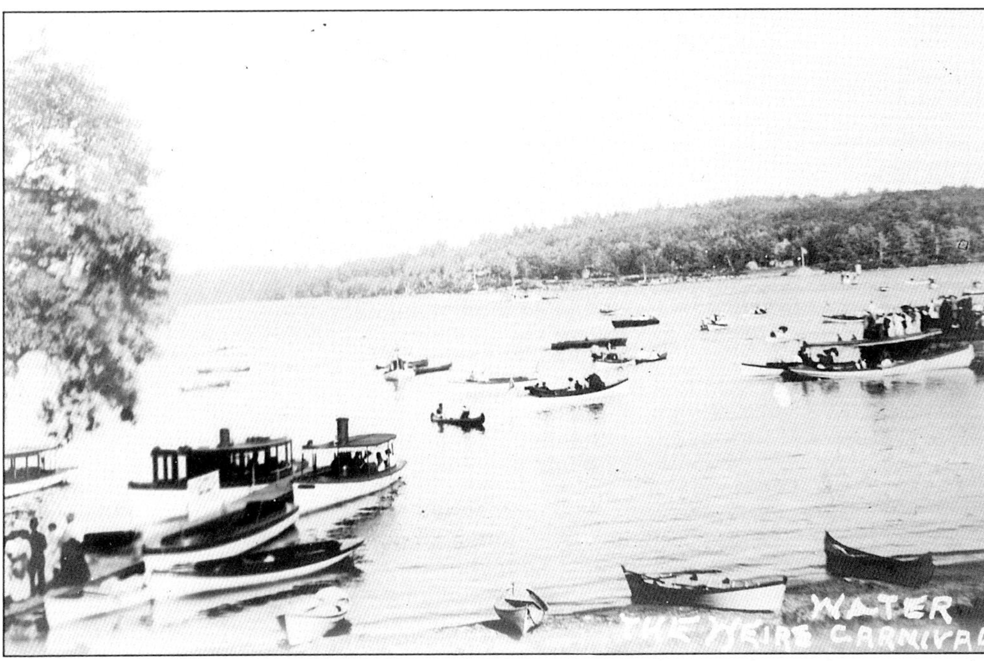

Weirs water carnival, 1908. Among the events were canoe, rowboat, and motorboat races and a swimming race. So successful were the two weeks' activities that plans were announced to make the water carnival an annual event.

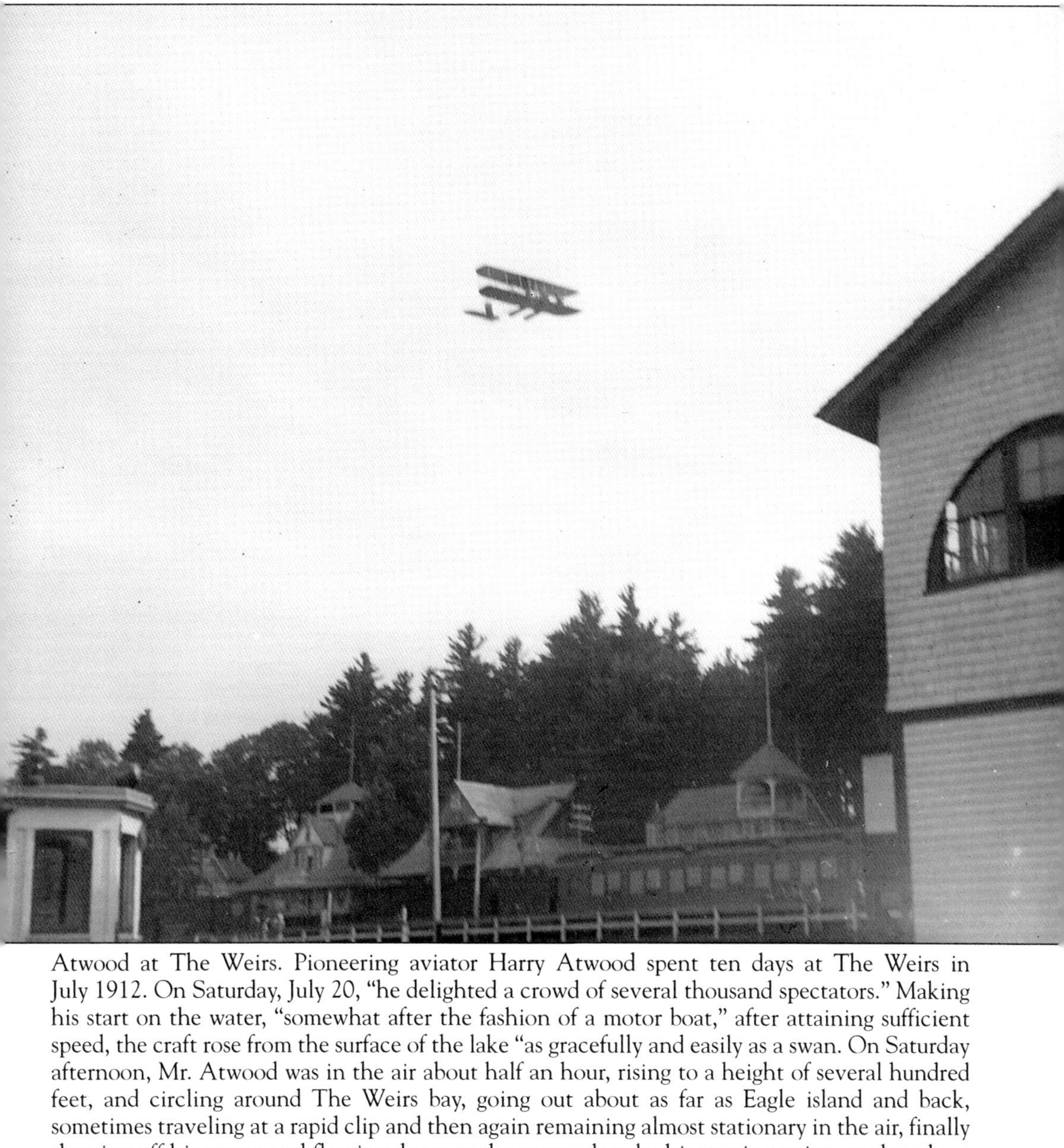

Atwood at The Weirs. Pioneering aviator Harry Atwood spent ten days at The Weirs in July 1912. On Saturday, July 20, "he delighted a crowd of several thousand spectators." Making his start on the water, "somewhat after the fashion of a motor boat," after attaining sufficient speed, the craft rose from the surface of the lake "as gracefully and easily as a swan. On Saturday afternoon, Mr. Atwood was in the air about half an hour, rising to a height of several hundred feet, and circling around The Weirs bay, going out about as far as Eagle island and back, sometimes traveling at a rapid clip and then again remaining almost stationary in the air, finally shutting off his power and floating down to the water close by his starting point, as cleverly as a duck would alight in a pond." In this view from the steamer wharf, Atwood gains altitude, with the Weirs Cafe at right and the headquarters buildings of the New Hampshire Veterans Association, on Lakeside Avenue, visible at the bottom of the photograph.

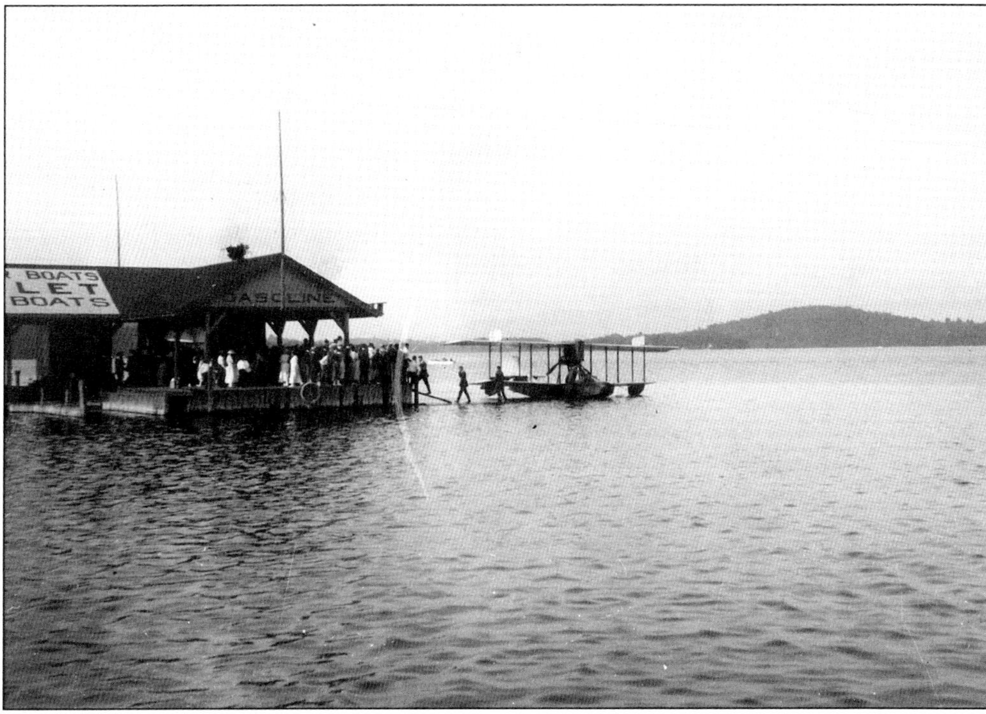

Seaplane at Winnipesaukee Pier. In 1912 Harry Atwood's week of exhibition flights and rides marked the first time most residents of the area had witnessed a flying machine.

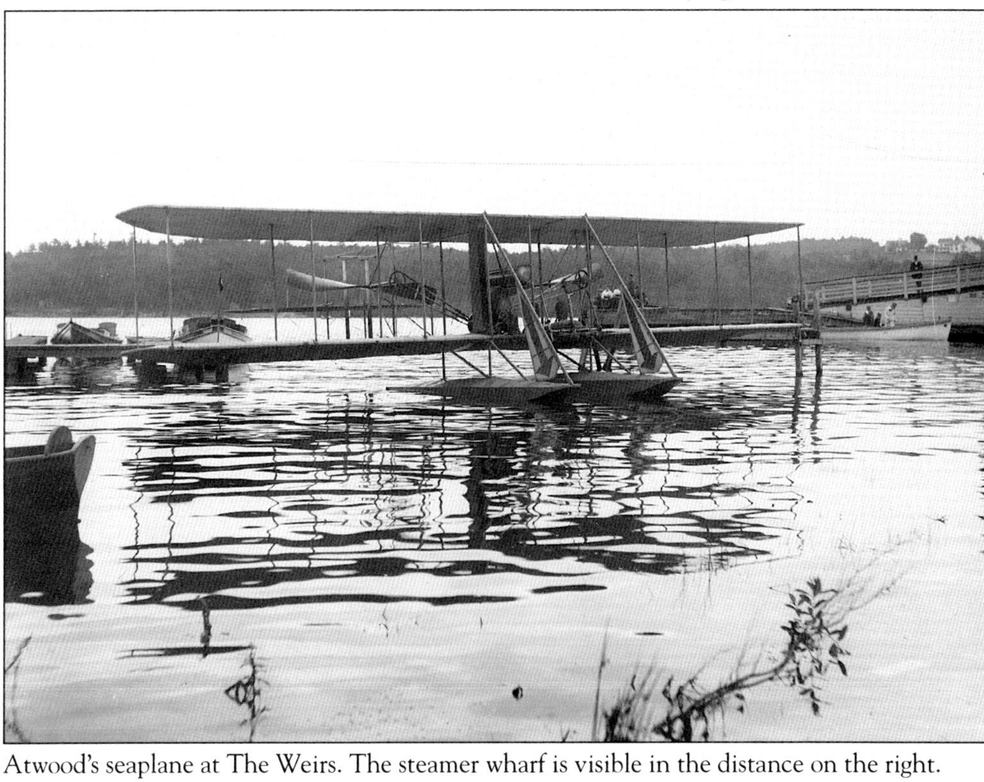

Atwood's seaplane at The Weirs. The steamer wharf is visible in the distance on the right.

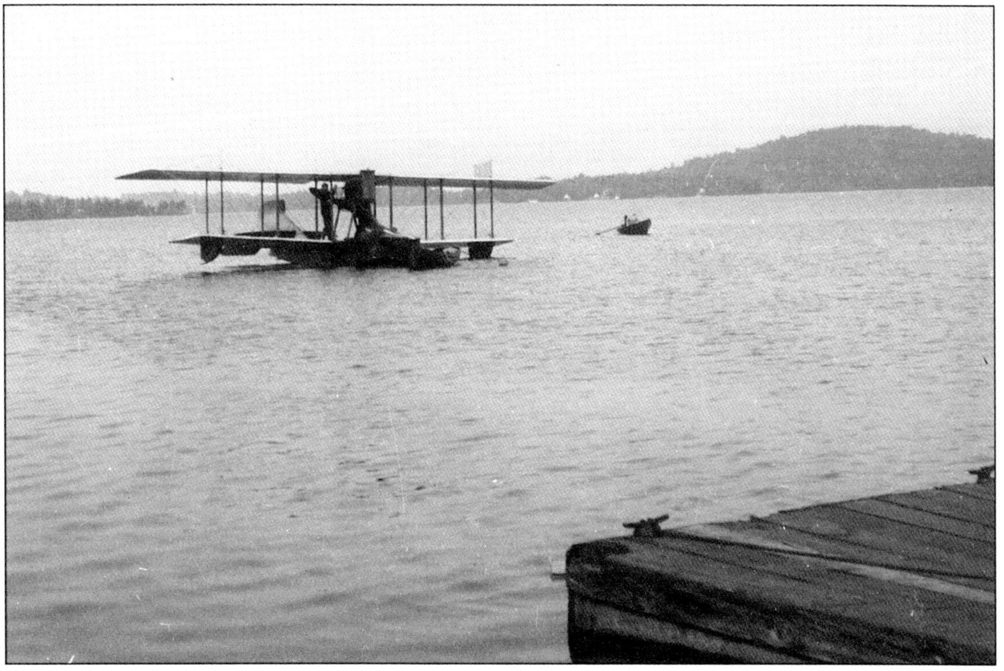

Seaplane, with the steamer wharf visible on the right. In 1912, Harry Atwood "took up passengers on quite a number of flights and all of them reported themselves well satisfied with the novel experience."

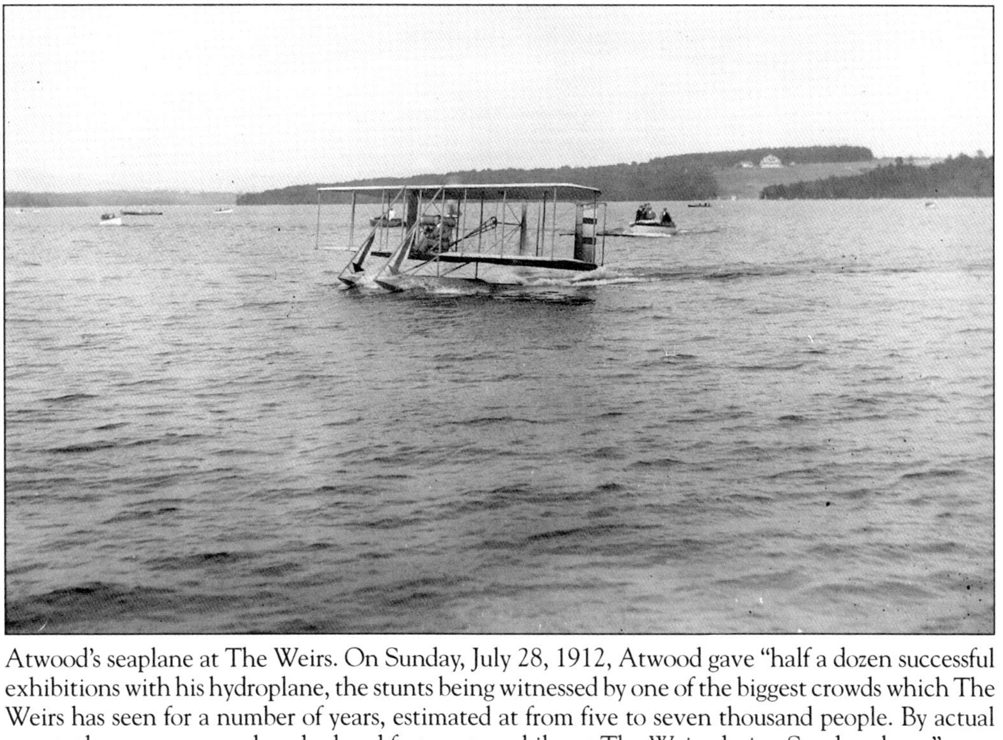

Atwood's seaplane at The Weirs. On Sunday, July 28, 1912, Atwood gave "half a dozen successful exhibitions with his hydroplane, the stunts being witnessed by one of the biggest crowds which The Weirs has seen for a number of years, estimated at from five to seven thousand people. By actual count, there were seven hundred and forty automobiles at The Weirs during Sunday alone."

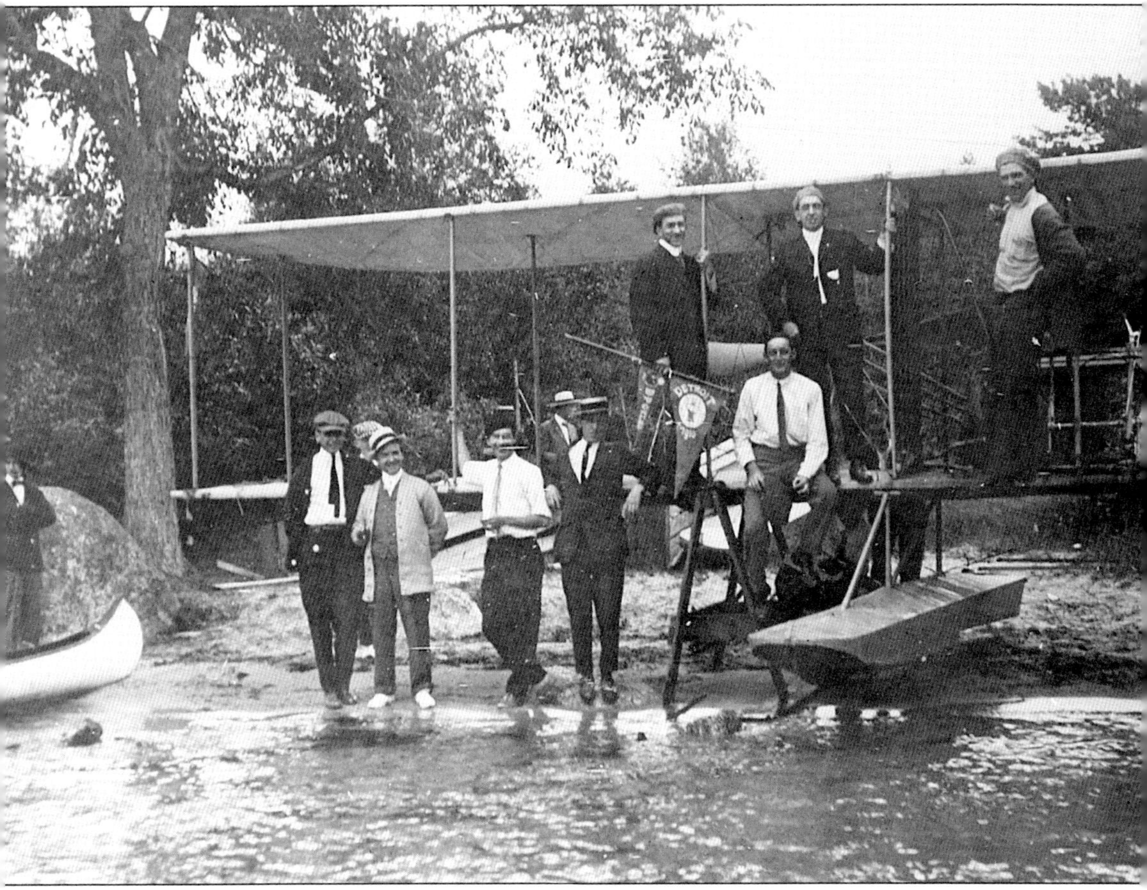

Harry Atwood's "aeroplane" at The Weirs, July 1912. The previous year, in June, Atwood had attempted this visit, but had been unsuccessful due to weather conditions. On that occasion, he had taken off from Waltham, Massachusetts, late in the afternoon of June 19, 1911, "making Concord before dark." The next day, he started again, flying over Penacook and landing in Tilton, after which he attempted to reach Laconia and Lake Winnipesaukee, but "strong winds were encountered just about East Tilton and, when the machine reached Ladd Hill, just south of Laconia, the breeze was so strong that Atwood abandoned the project of going further north and sailed away to the east, passing over Belmont, Gilmanton and Pittsfield, and thence back to Massachusetts. The telephone service along the Merrimack Valley kept the people along the route posted as to the progress of the navigator and thousands of New Hampshire people got their first glimpse of a flying machine."

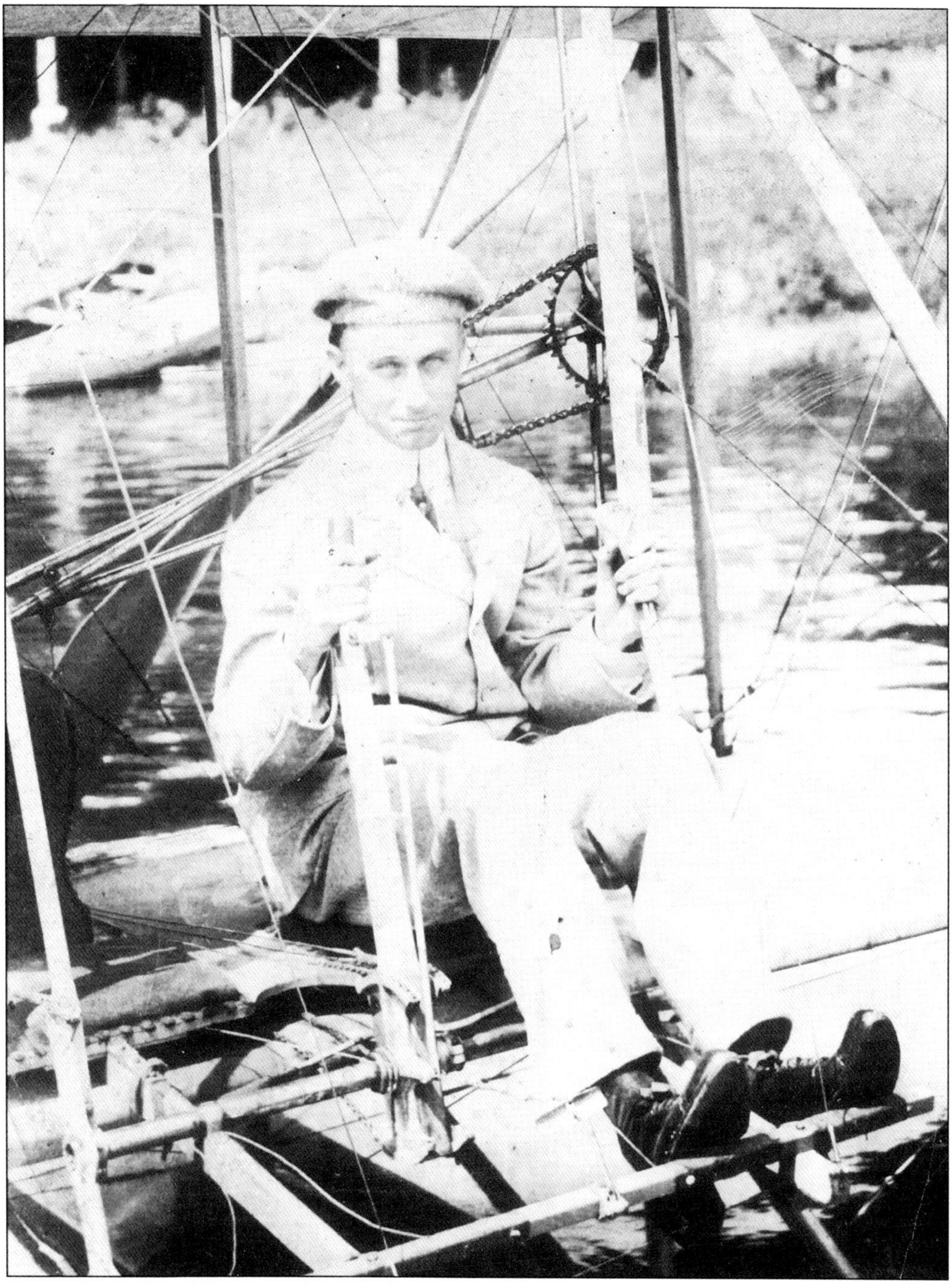

Harry Atwood and his "aeroplane," The Weirs, July 1912. Atwood gave "from three to half a dozen exhibitions daily and visited various sections of Lake Winnipesaukee so that hundreds of the cottagers on the islands and shores enjoyed the novel experience of seeing a flying machine sailing over the islands and swooping down to exchange greetings with the occupants of pleasure boats." Contemporary newspaper accounts described the hydro-aeroplane as a biplane weighing 1,100 pounds, with a 35-horsepower motor. Atwood's visit was sponsored by transportation companies, hotels, and other business interests at The Weirs.

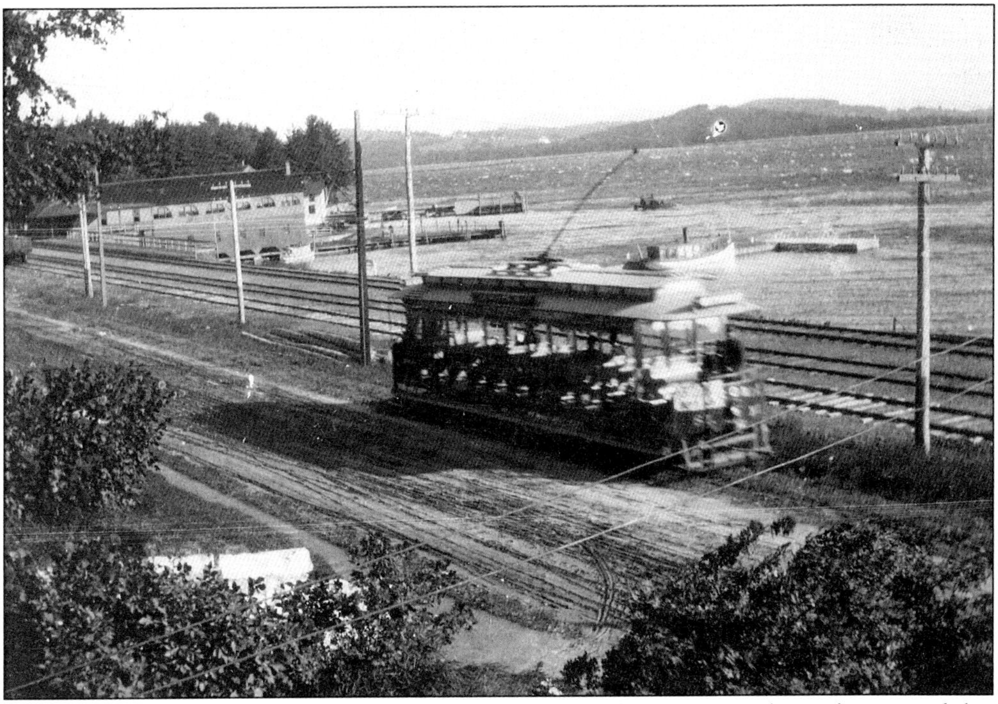

An open car of the Laconia Street Railway heads into The Weirs, in the early years of this century. From June 1899, through the summer of 1925, the trolleys provided a scenic 6-mile ride between Downtown Laconia and The Weirs.

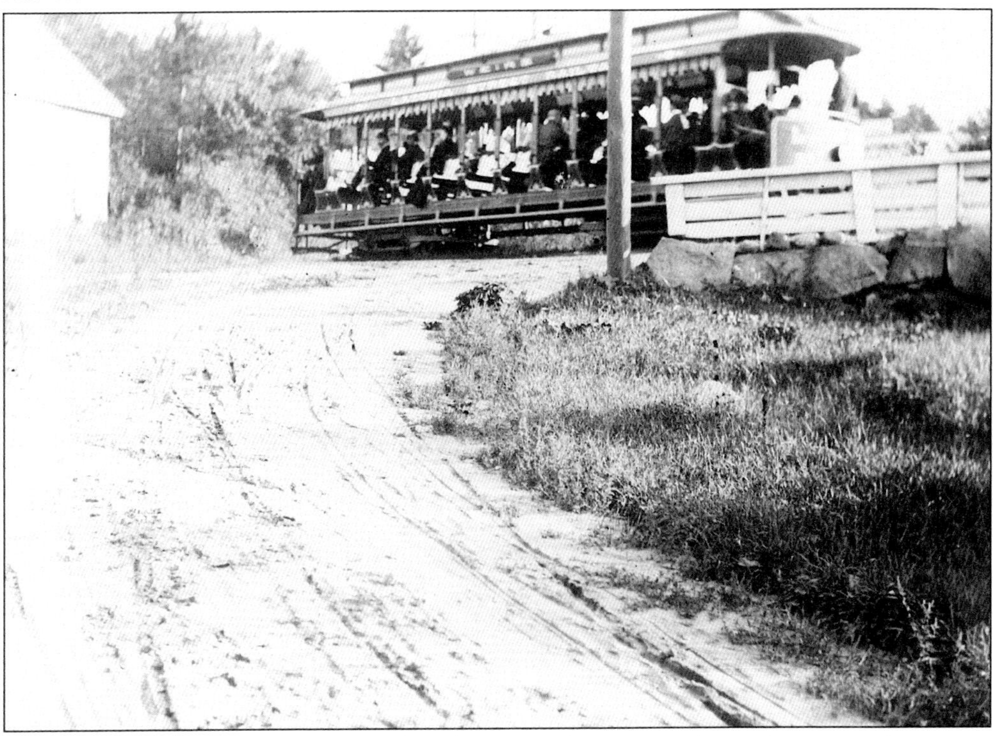

An open car of the Laconia Street Railway heads north across the bridge into The Weirs.

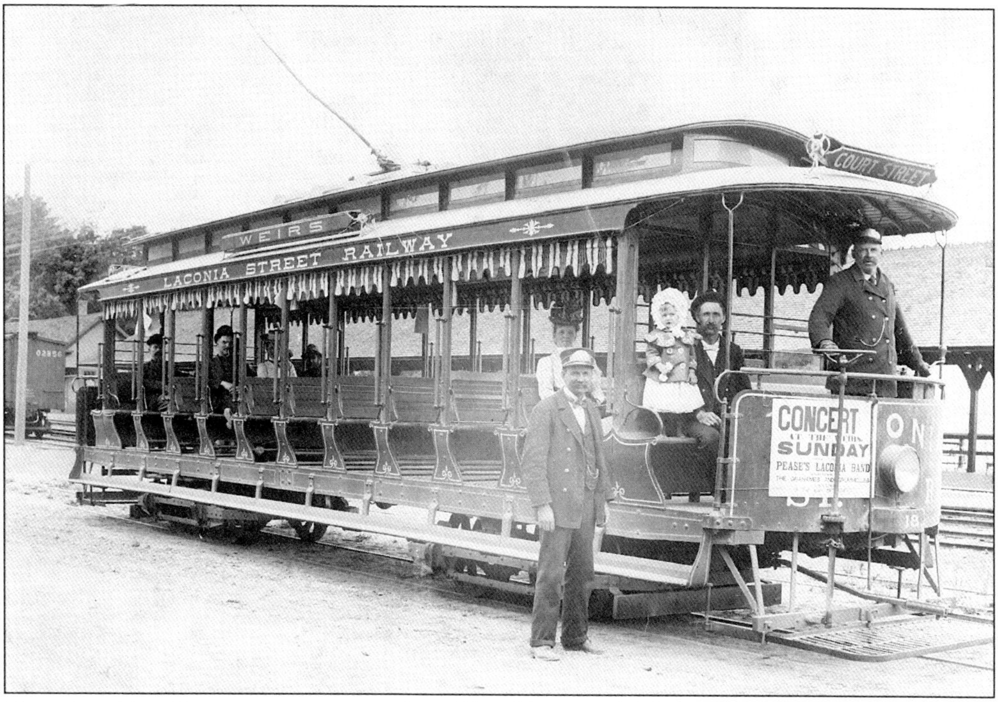

Open Car No. 18 prepares to depart from The Weirs, with Horace "Ed" Rowen (1854–1934) at the controls.

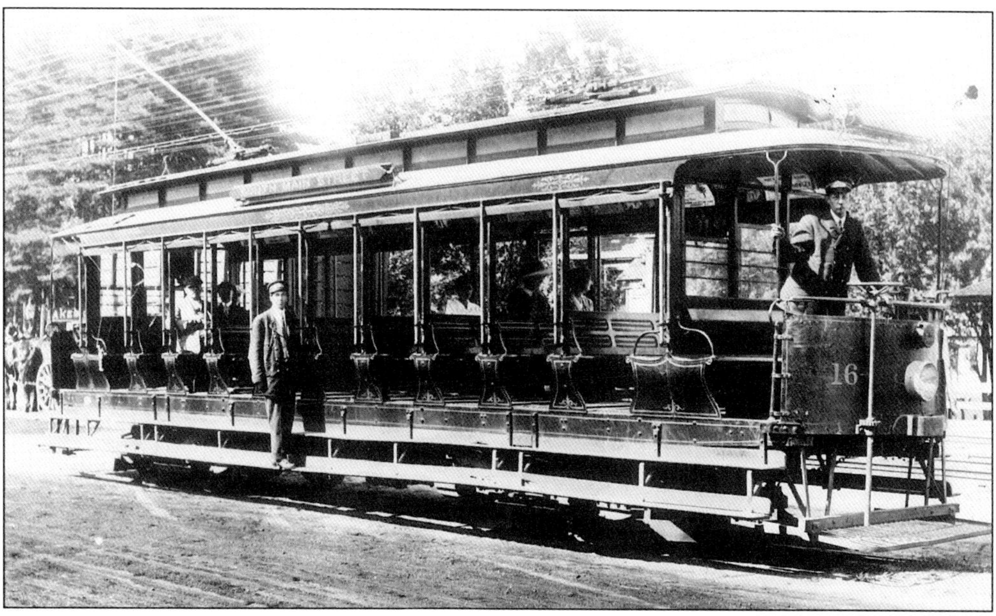

Open Car No. 16, also ready to head for Laconia, *c.* 1913. The conductor may have been Ray C. Young, whose younger brother, Harold H. Young, later wrote a history of the Laconia Street Railway. The motorman may have been Al Pierce, president of the road.

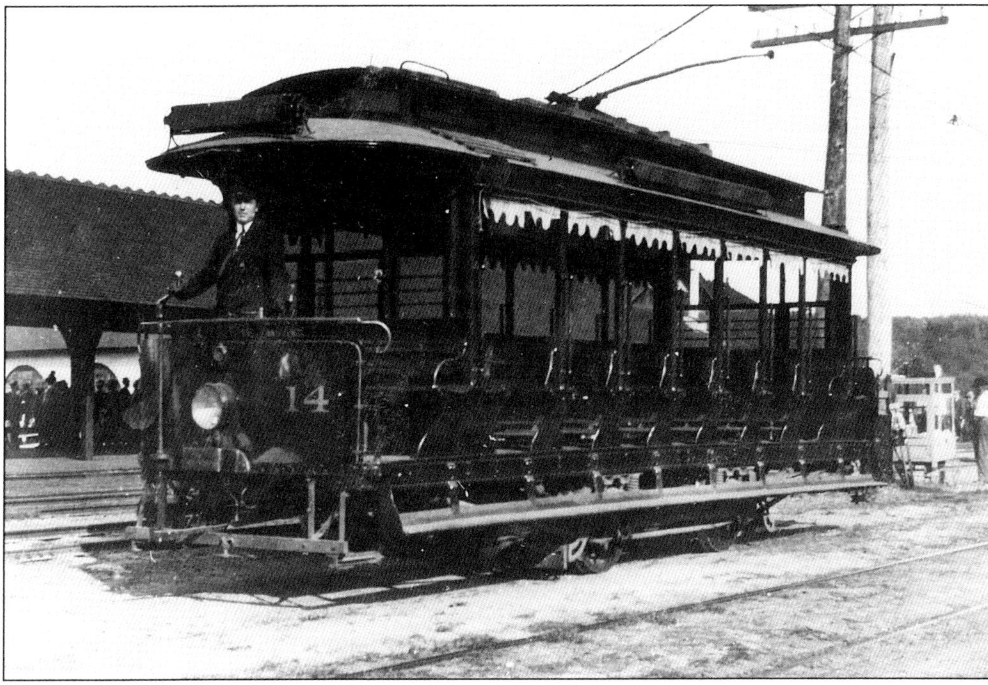

Open Car No. 14 pulls into The Weirs.

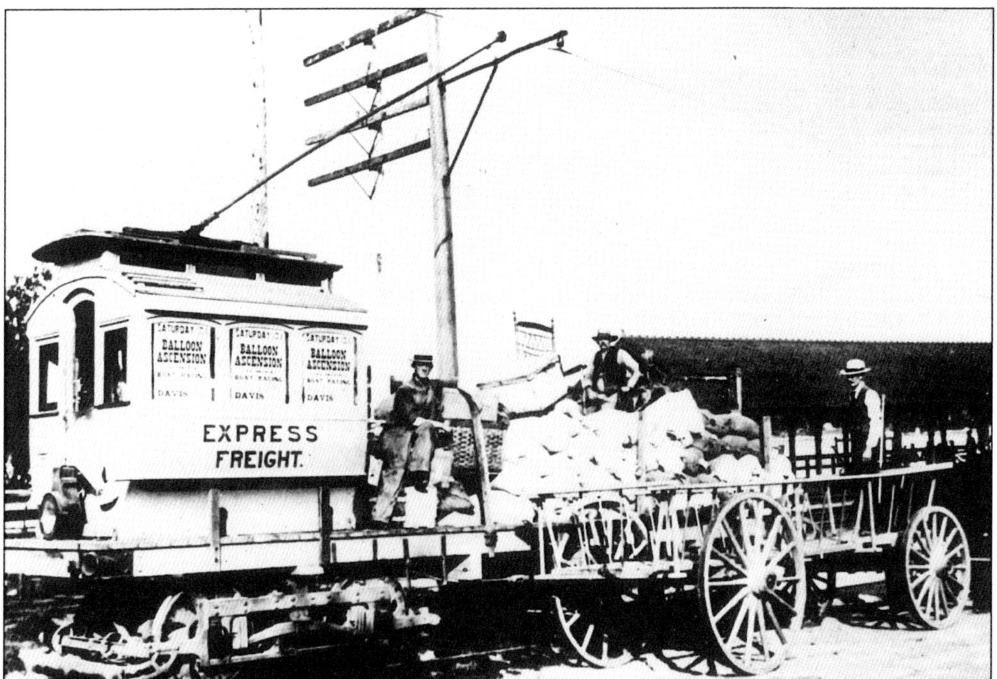

The freight car of the Laconia Street Railway unloads at The Weirs. The "express-freight" car was acquired around 1906. The cab had been salvaged from the line's earlier narrow-gauge fleet.

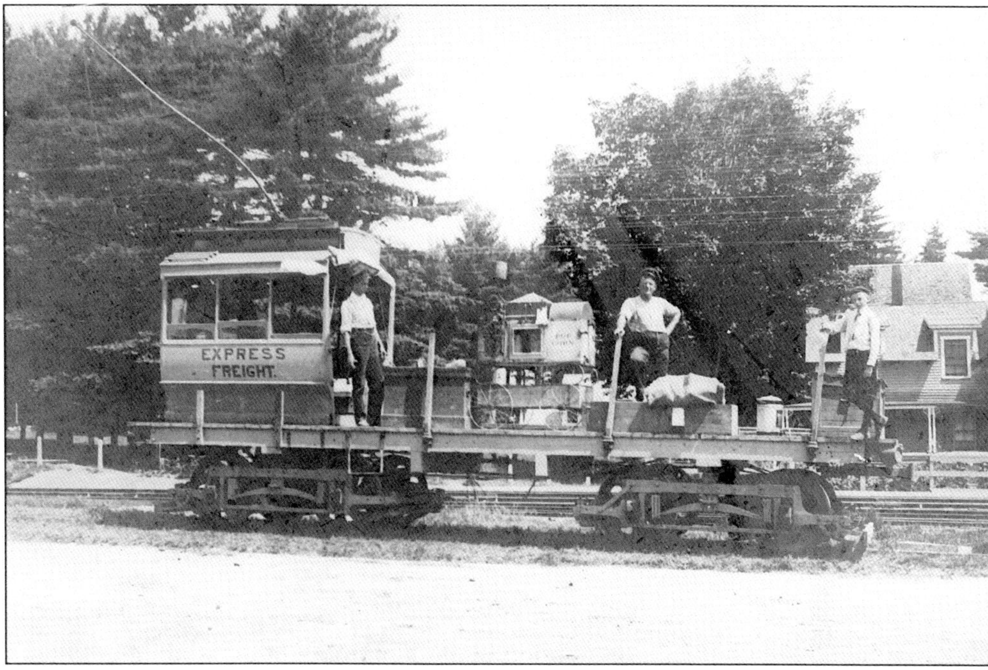

The freight car of the Laconia Street Railway delivers a popcorn cart and other items to The Weirs.

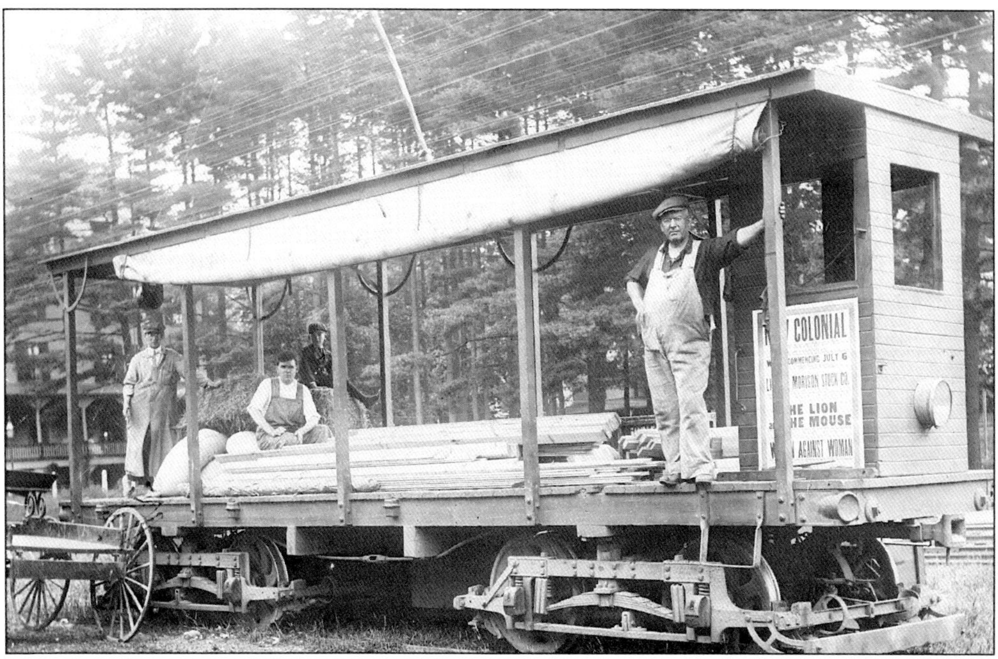

The same freight car, following remodeling, at The Weirs. The man seated at the left was Oscar Hall who, at one time, operated the store pictured on p. 108.

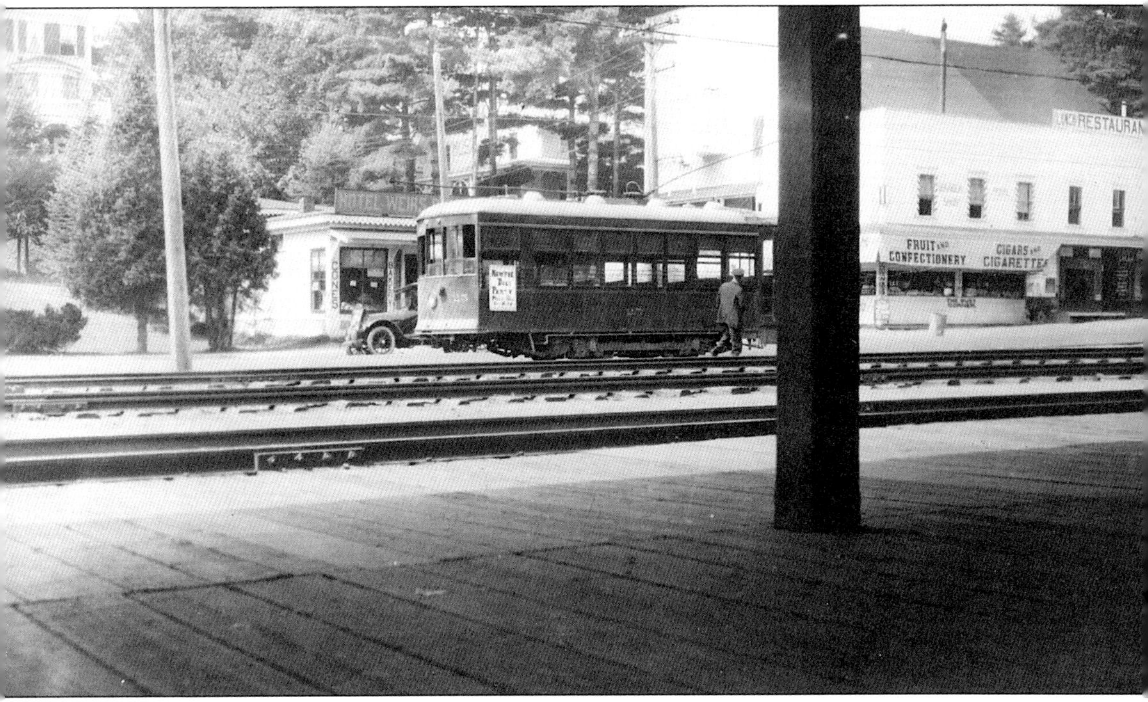

A late-model (Birney) car of the Laconia Street Railway makes the last run of the 1920 season from The Weirs. Part of the Hotel Weirs is visible (upper left), with the hotel market (center left, just beyond the trolley car) at the corner of Tower Street. The restaurant and confectionary (right) occupy the north corner of Tower Street and Lakeside Avenue.

Five

Tower Hill

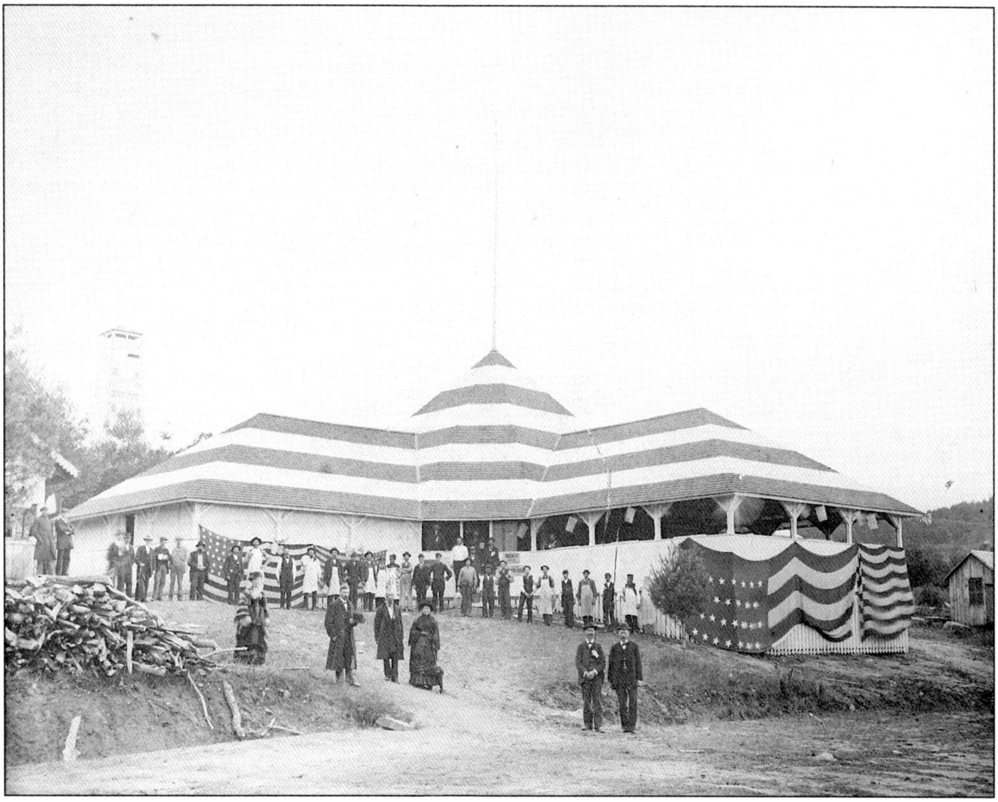

The dining pavilion of the New Hampshire Veterans Association, Tower Hill, The Weirs, with the Orchard View observation tower on the left, about 1883. The 1880 pavilion was one of the first buildings erected for the New Hampshire Veterans Association.

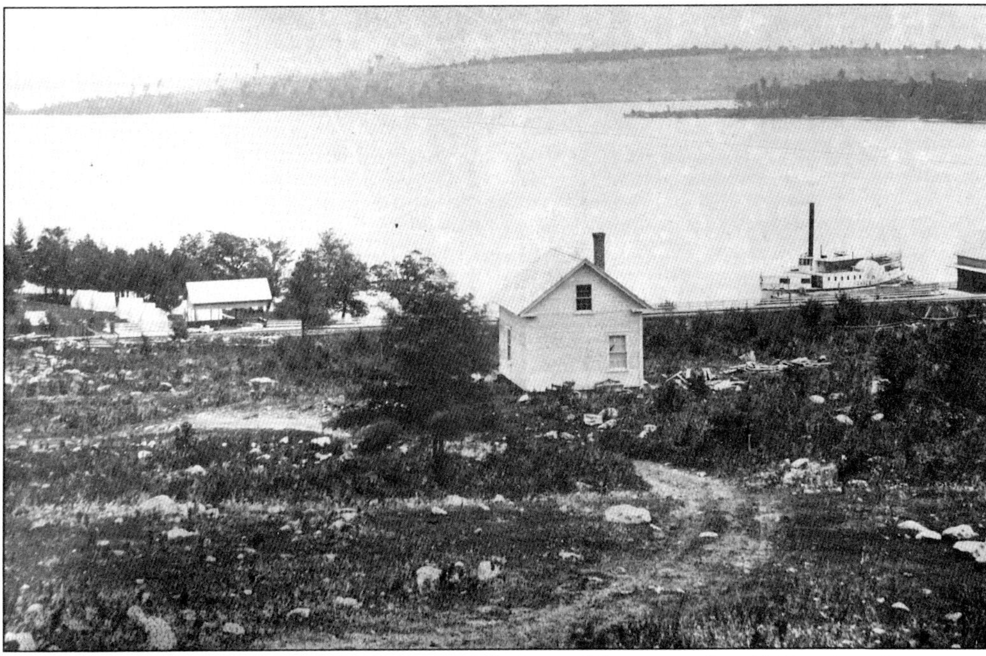

A very early view of The Weirs from Tower Hill. Part of the original *c.* 1848 railroad passenger station is visible on the right. The rails probably did not reach The Weirs until 1849, but the railroad's report for 1848 indicated that the station buildings had been completed. Initially, a second station was located near the bridge over the channel.

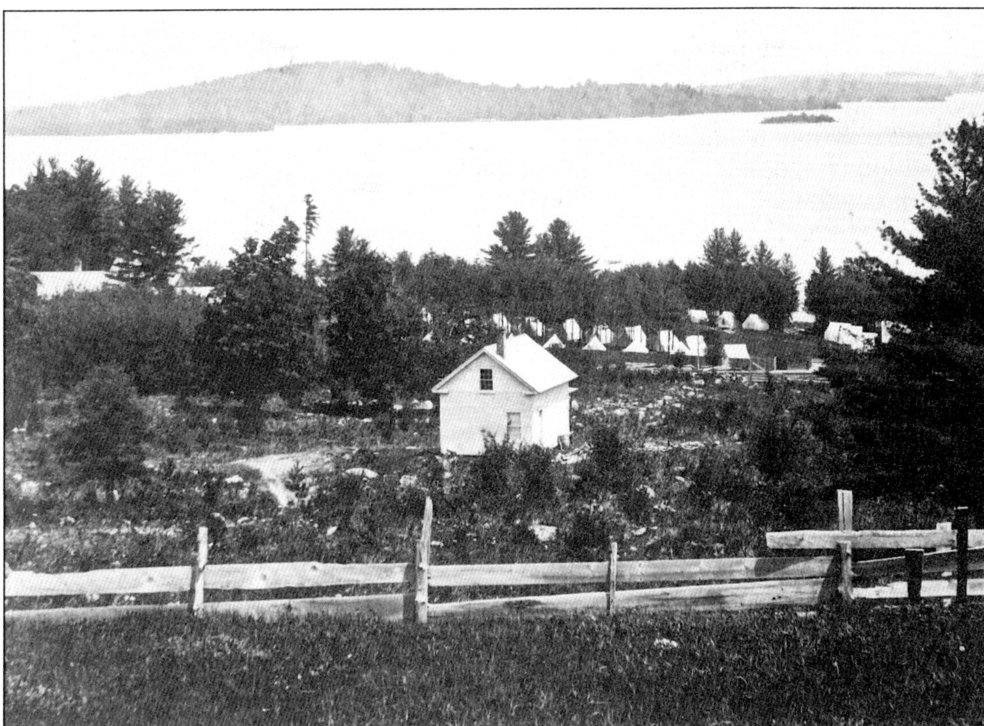

Another view of The Weirs from Tower Hill before the "boom" of the late 1870s.

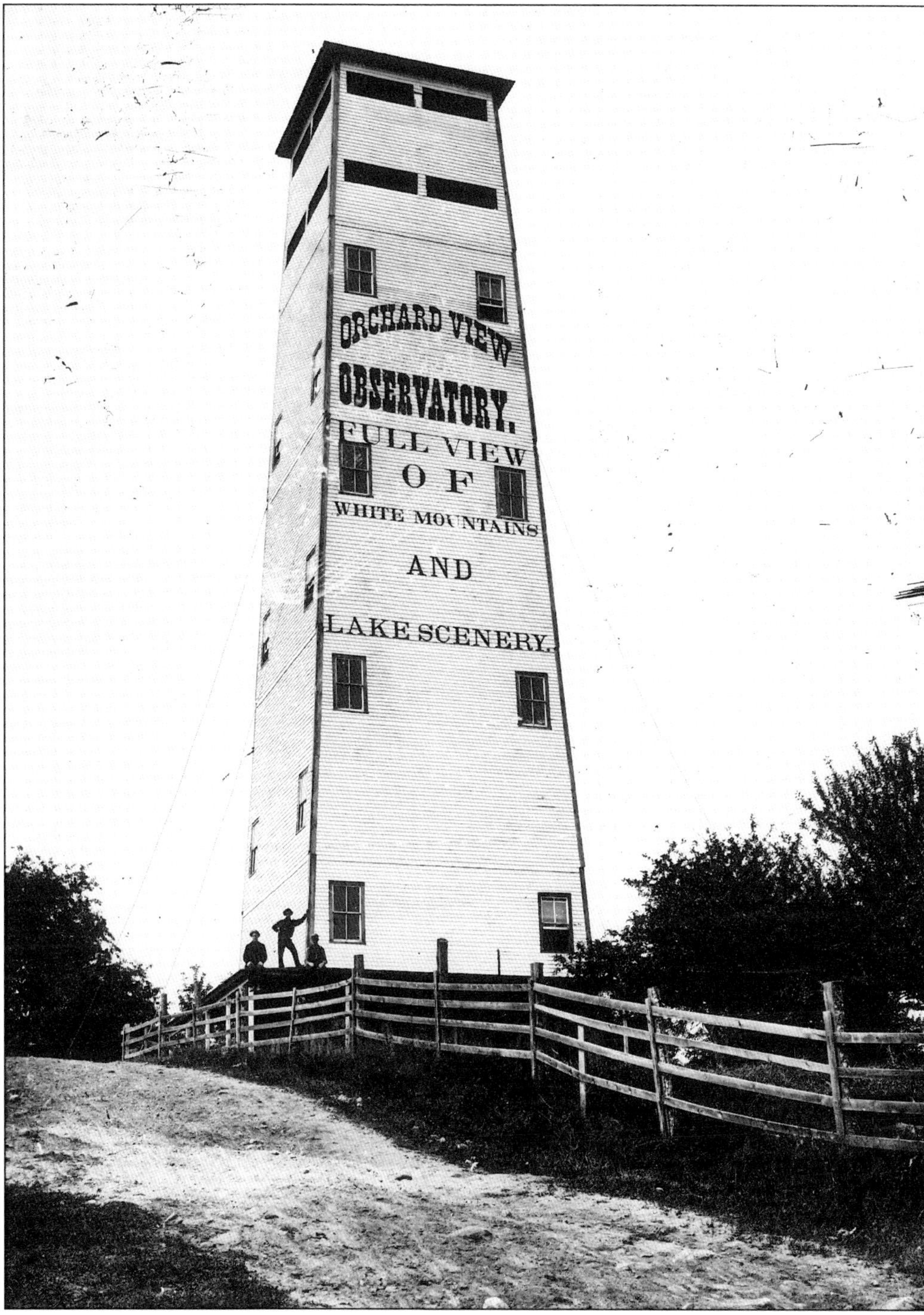

The tower, for which both the hill and street were named, built by Alvah Foster in 1881 and called Orchard View Observatory. The 100-foot-high structure had rooms for rent on the way up the seemingly endless flights of stairs. A restaurant occupied the ground floor. Admission was charged to go to the top where, on a clear day, one could see all over the lake and the White Mountains. The tower burned in 1885.

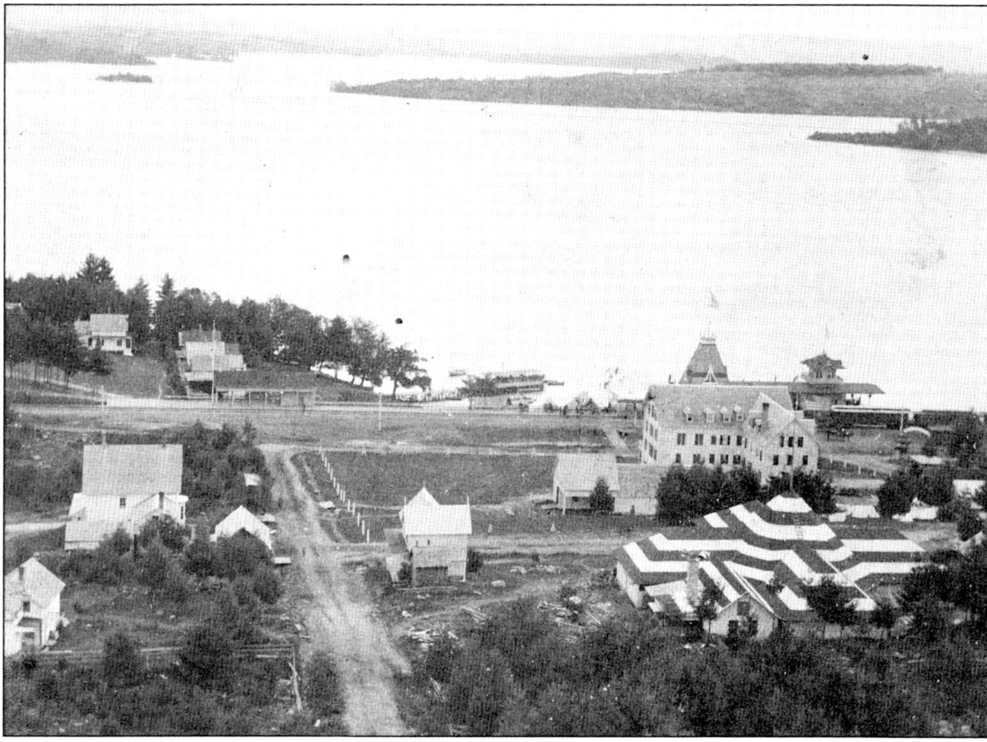

An early 1880s view, probably from observation tower on Tower Hill, with the Veterans Association pavilion at right, and the Hotel Weirs and railroad station in the distance.

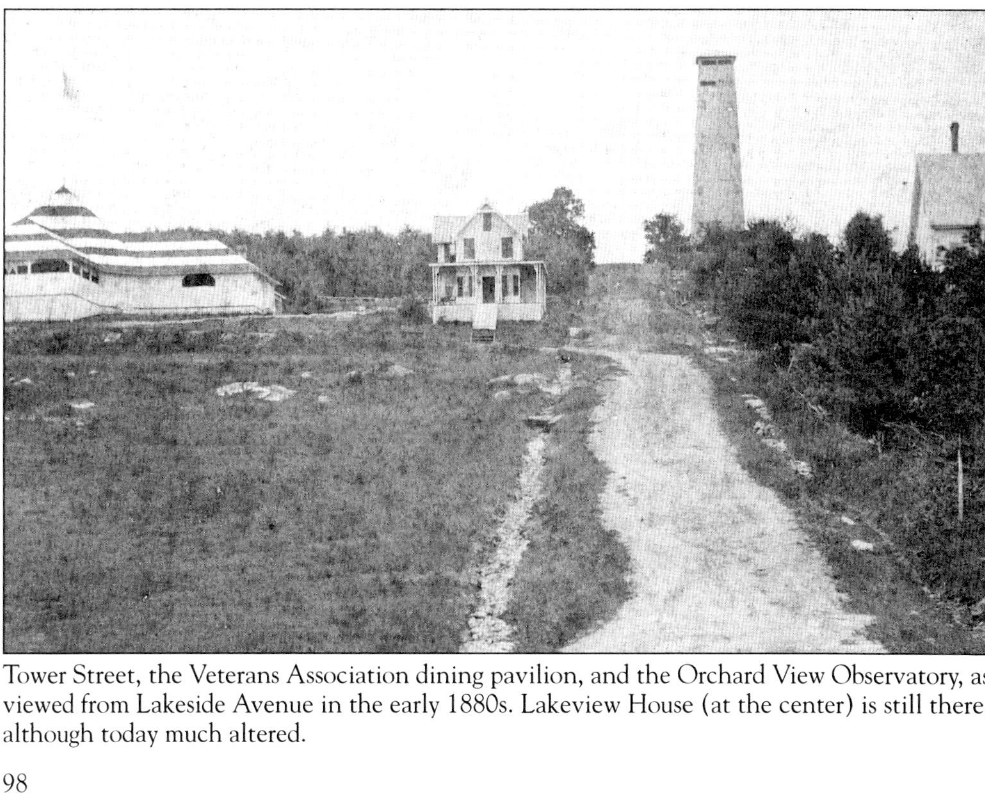

Tower Street, the Veterans Association dining pavilion, and the Orchard View Observatory, as viewed from Lakeside Avenue in the early 1880s. Lakeview House (at the center) is still there, although today much altered.

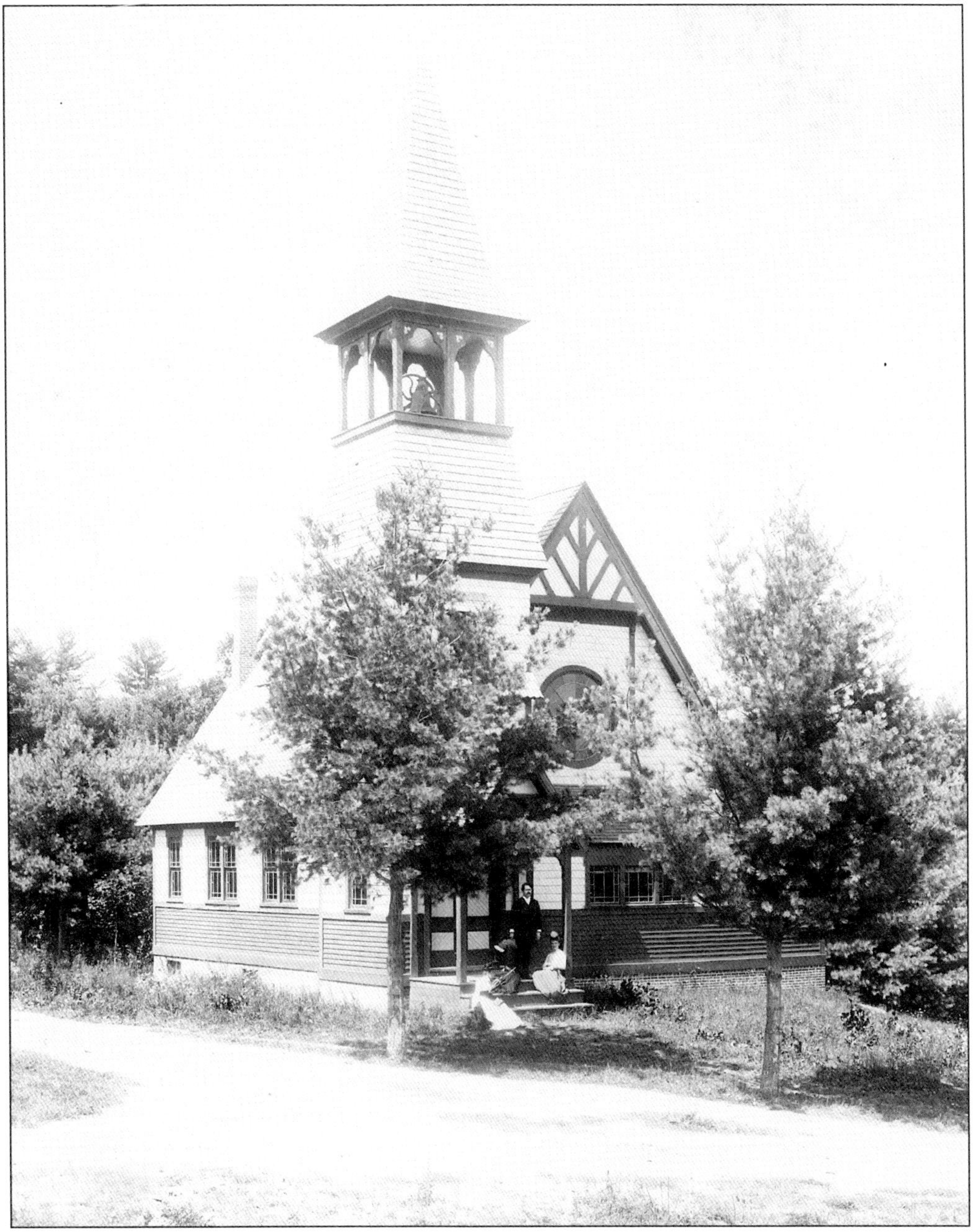

The original Trinity Methodist Episcopal Church, Tower Street. Inspired by memories of the stirring summer revival meetings that had begun in 1873 at the Methodist Campground, year-round residents met in April 1882 to establish a church. Initially conducting services in the Weirs Schoolhouse, by 1885 the group was ready to undertake a building campaign. Augustus Doe donated the lot, at the corner of Maple Street, in May of that year. The first service in the new edifice was held on October 17, 1886. The cost of the church was $2,290.21.

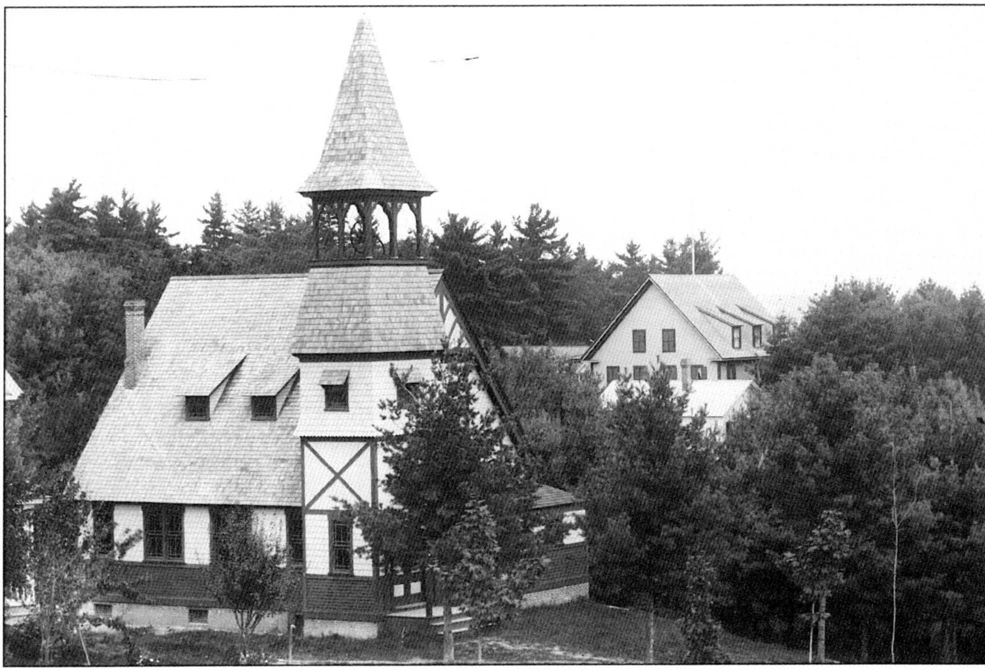

The original Trinity Methodist Episcopal Church, Tower Street, with Lakeside House in the background. The church burned to the ground in the fire of 1924, but was rebuilt on the site and rededicated in August 1926.

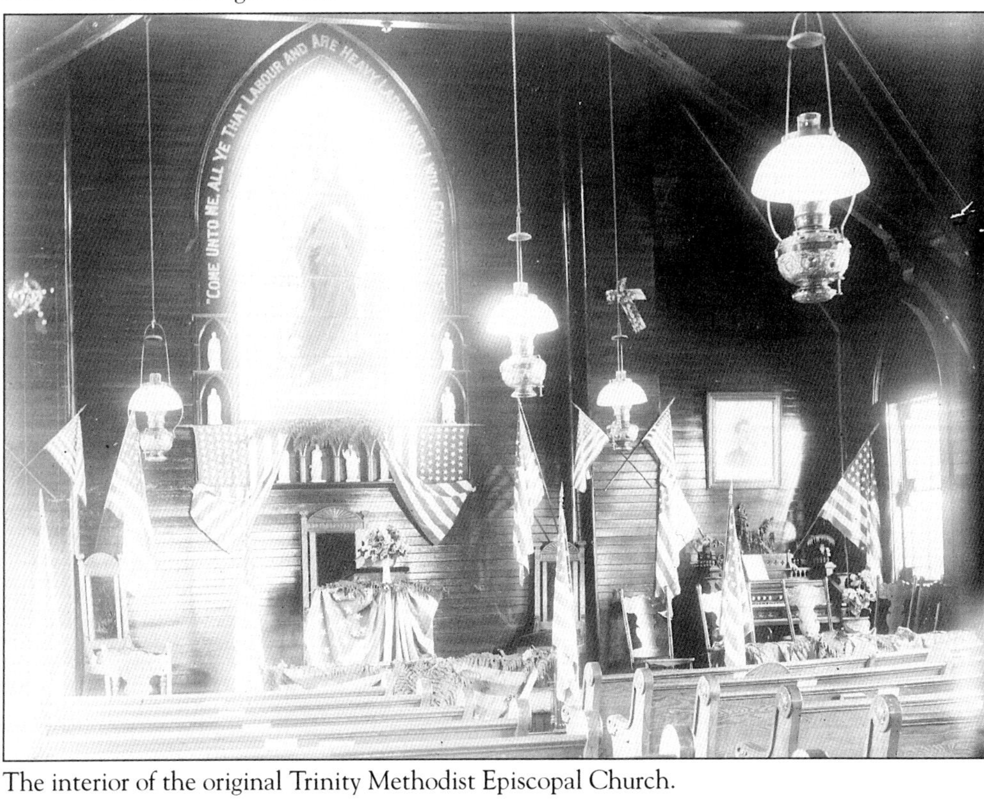

The interior of the original Trinity Methodist Episcopal Church.

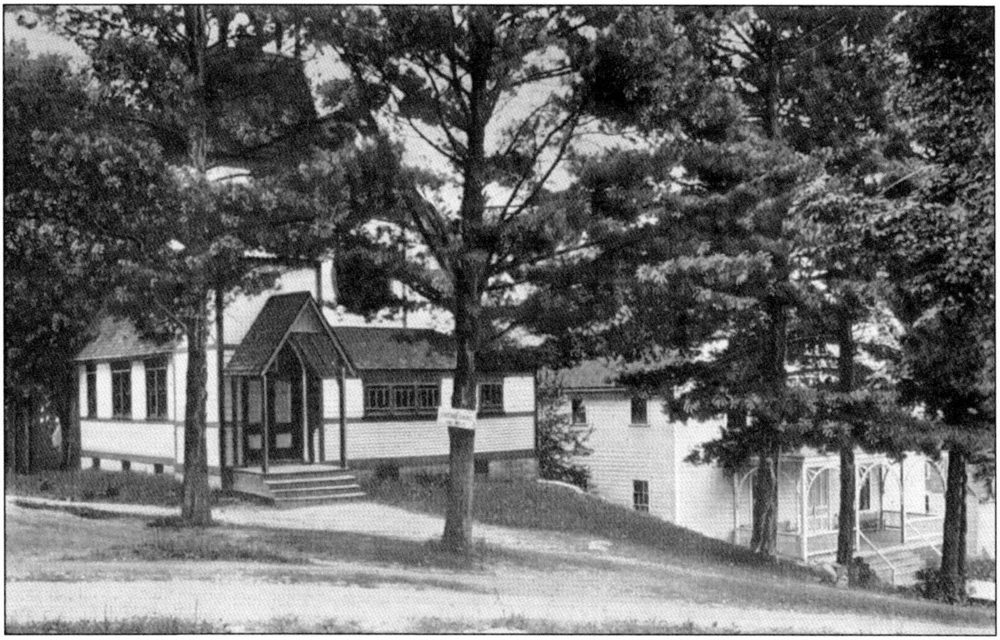

Trinity Methodist Episcopal Church and adjacent Music Hall on Tower Street.

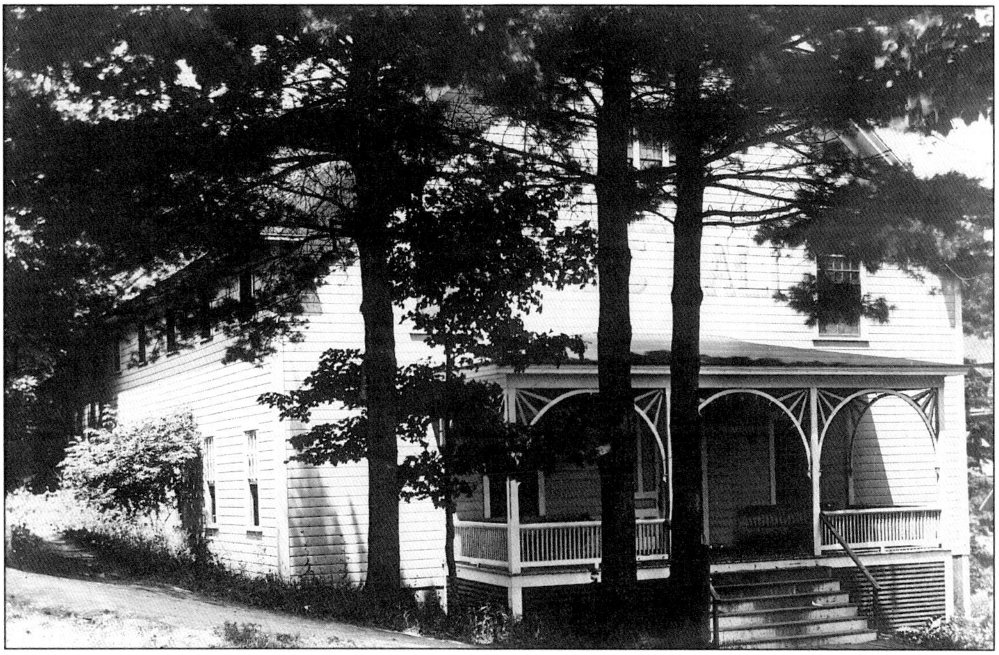

The Music Hall, on Tower Street, dedicated in 1903. This building replaced the structure which had collapsed during the previous winter in what is now Endicott Rock Park. In this 1903 building, burned in the fire of 1924, James Irwin Sr. first played at The Weirs with his dance band. After the fire, Irwin acquired the Winnipesaukee Pier (see p. 83) and built his Winnipesaukee Gardens (see p. 127) which opened in 1925.

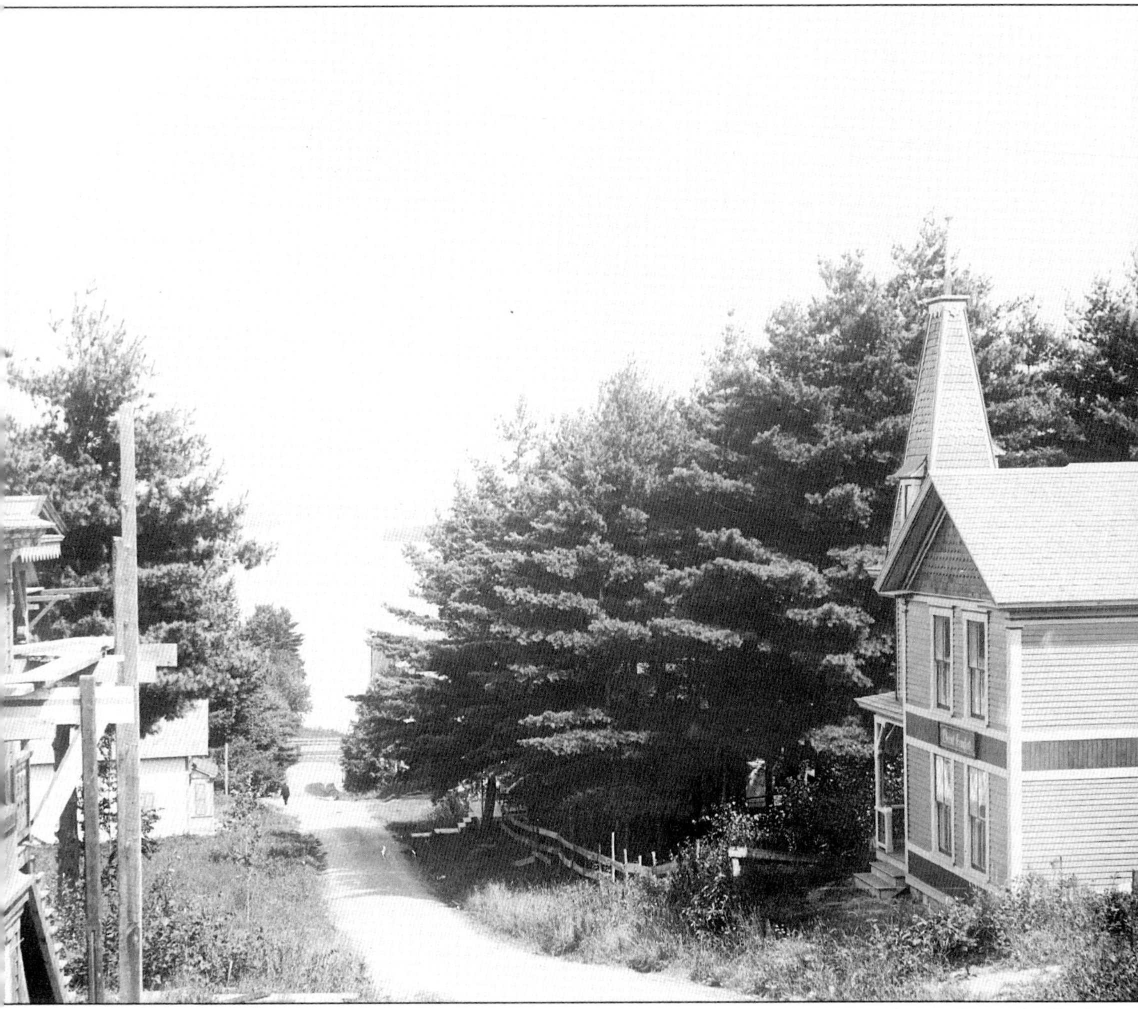

Dwelling, on the right, at 80 Tower Street, around the turn of the century. The building (called The Overlook), minus the tower, is still there. The Lakeview House is hidden just beyond the trees at right.

Six

Lakeside Avenue North

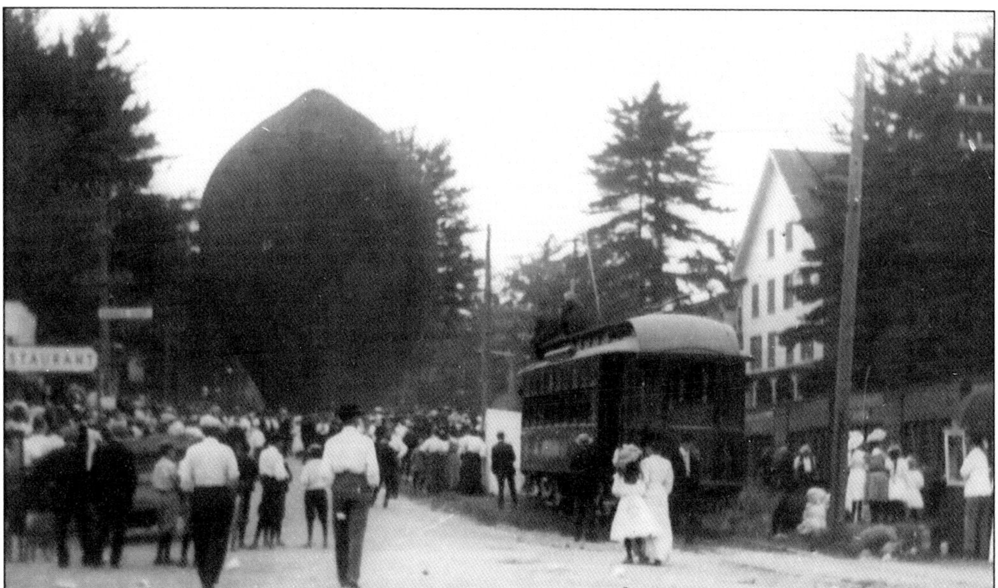

A balloon ascension attracts a crowd at the northern end of Lakeside Avenue, early in the twentieth century. Lakeside House is on the right. A trolley car of the Laconia Street Railway prepares to head toward Laconia.

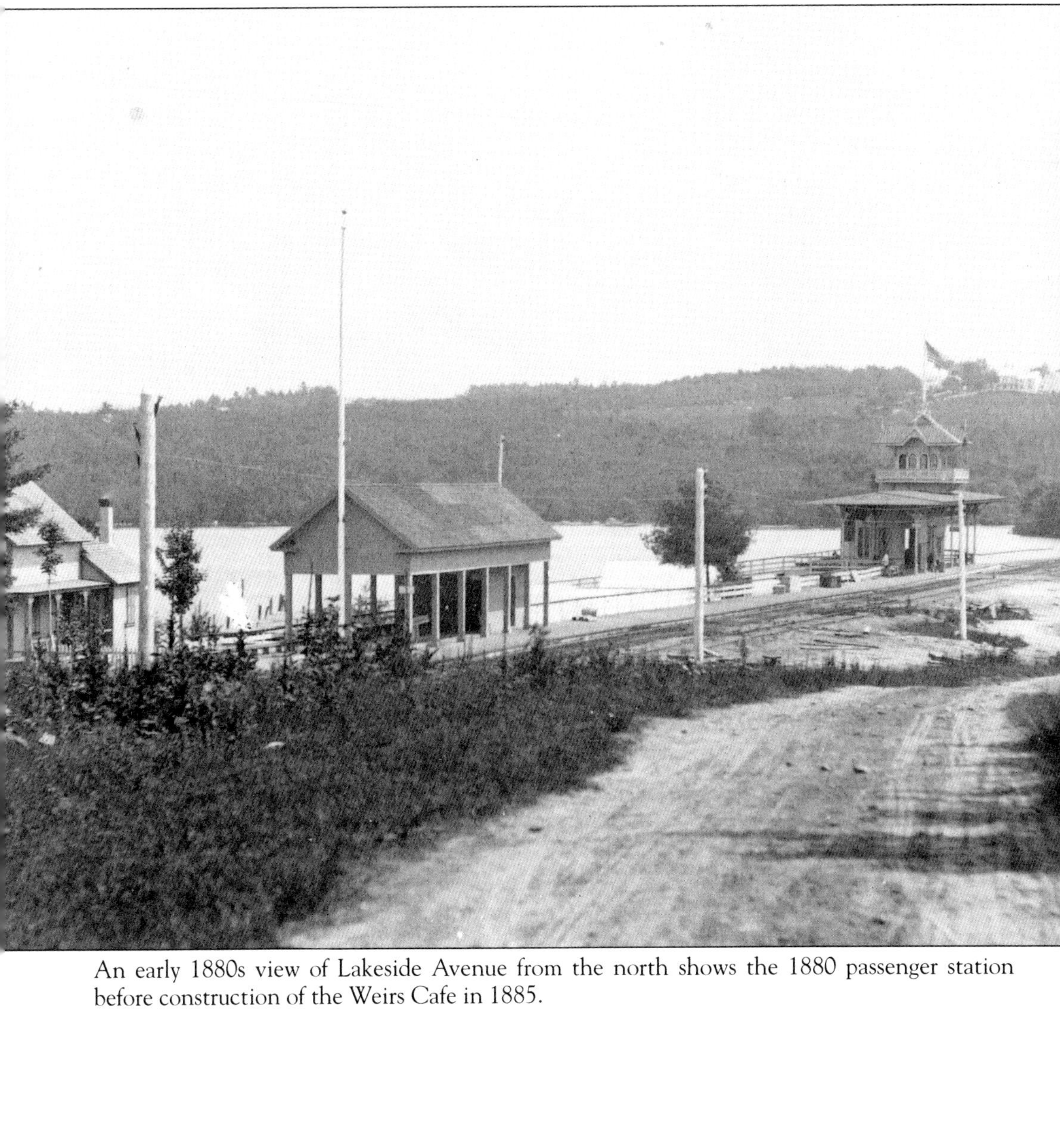

An early 1880s view of Lakeside Avenue from the north shows the 1880 passenger station before construction of the Weirs Cafe in 1885.

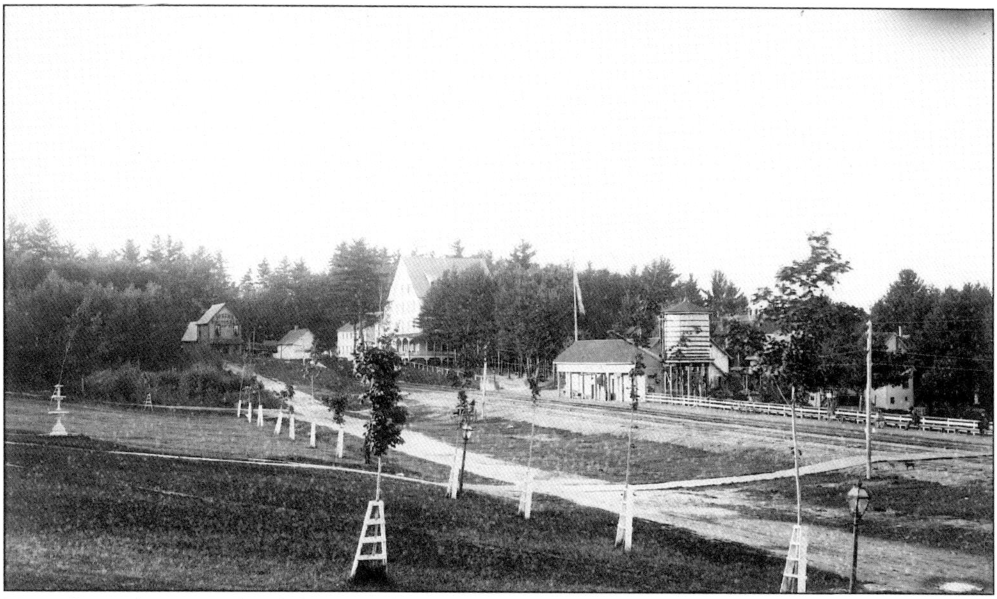

View from the grounds of the Hotel Weirs, looking northeast toward Lakeside House, with railroad waiting area and water tank alongside the railroad track. The ticket office is off the photograph to the right.

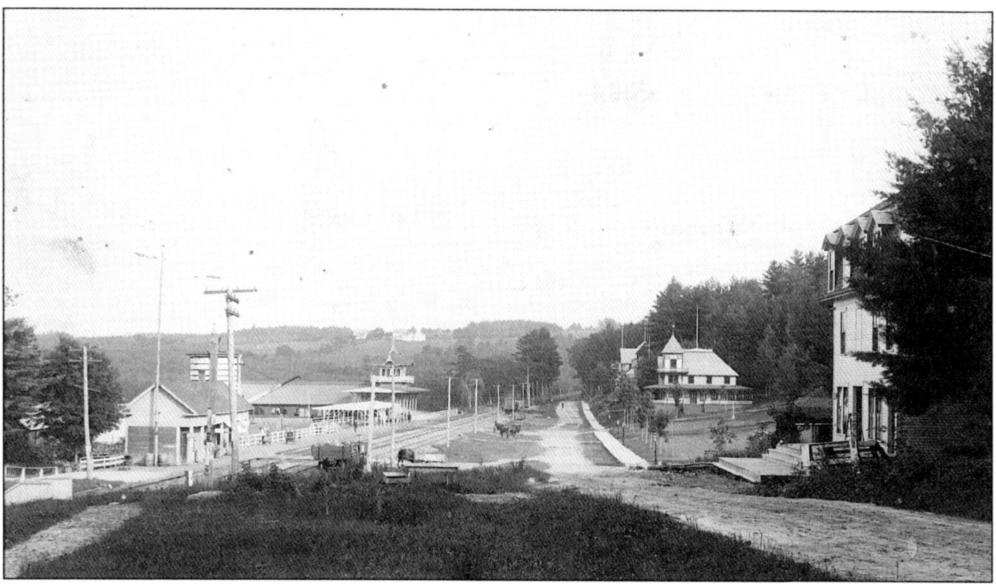

The same area from the north, with the grocery store (right) of George W. Weeks, later owned by George W. Tarlson, and the New Hampshire Veterans Association Headquarters Building in middle distance at right. George W. Tarlson opened a new store in 1911, across the street between Lakeside Avenue and the railroad tracks.

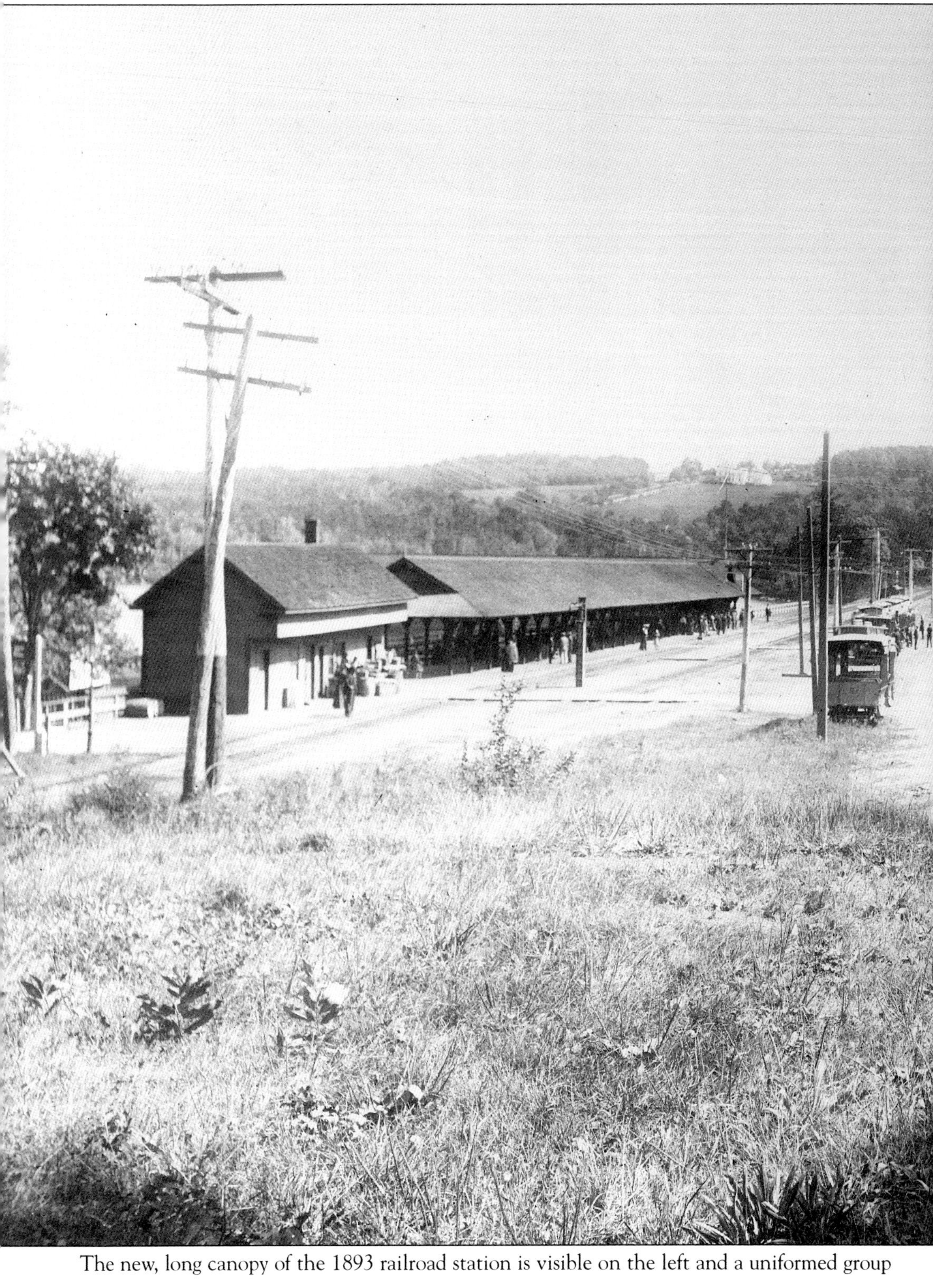

The new, long canopy of the 1893 railroad station is visible on the left and a uniformed group

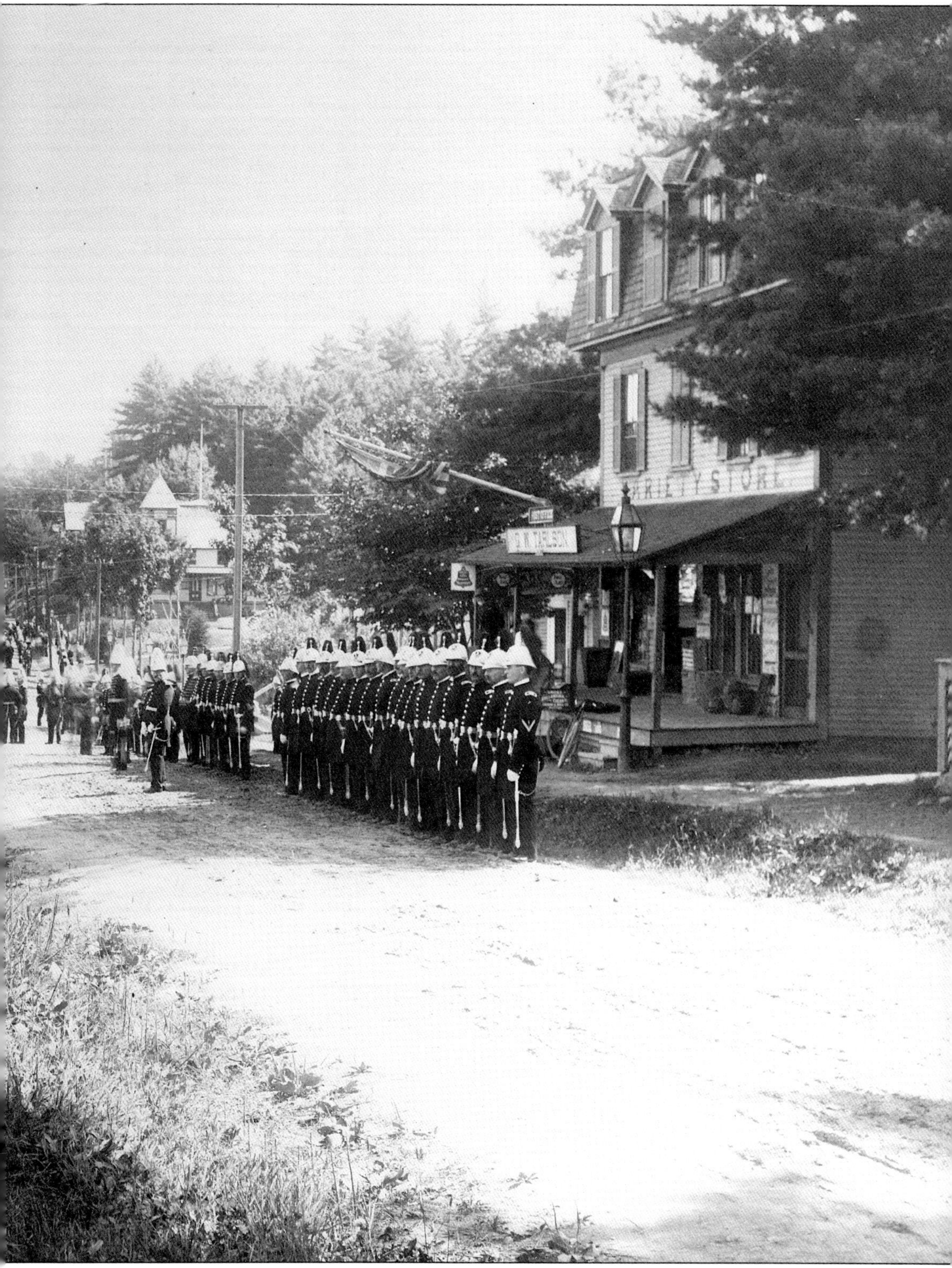

stands at attention in front of Tarlson's Store in this view of Lakeside Avenue from the north.

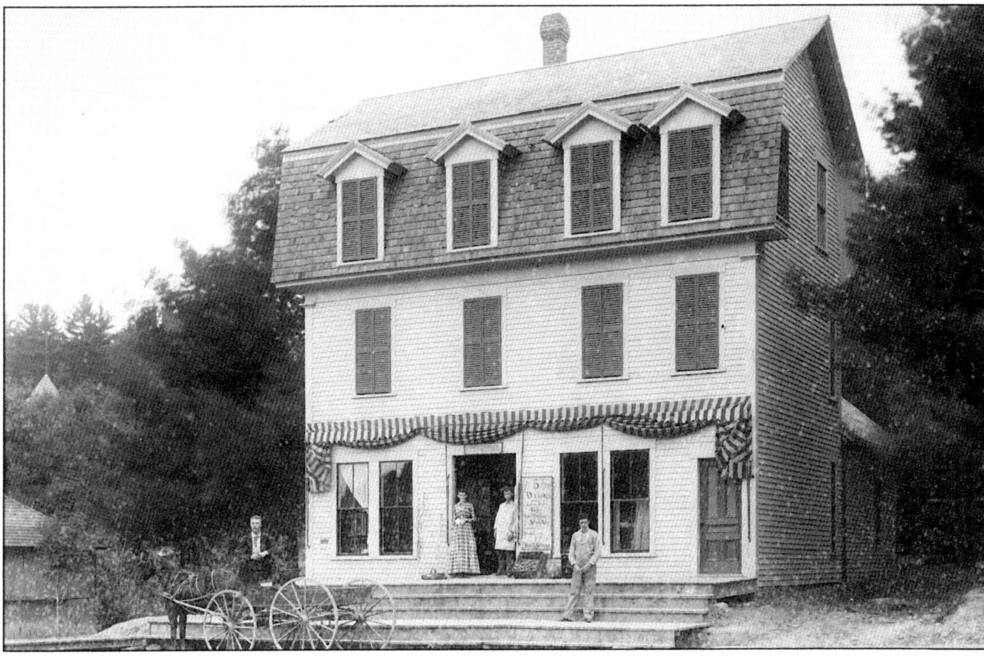

Grocery store of George W. Weeks, on the west side of Lakeside Avenue. Among later operators of the store were George W. Tarlson, followed by W.T. Cram and then Oscar Hall, under the ownership of Arthur C. Kinsman.

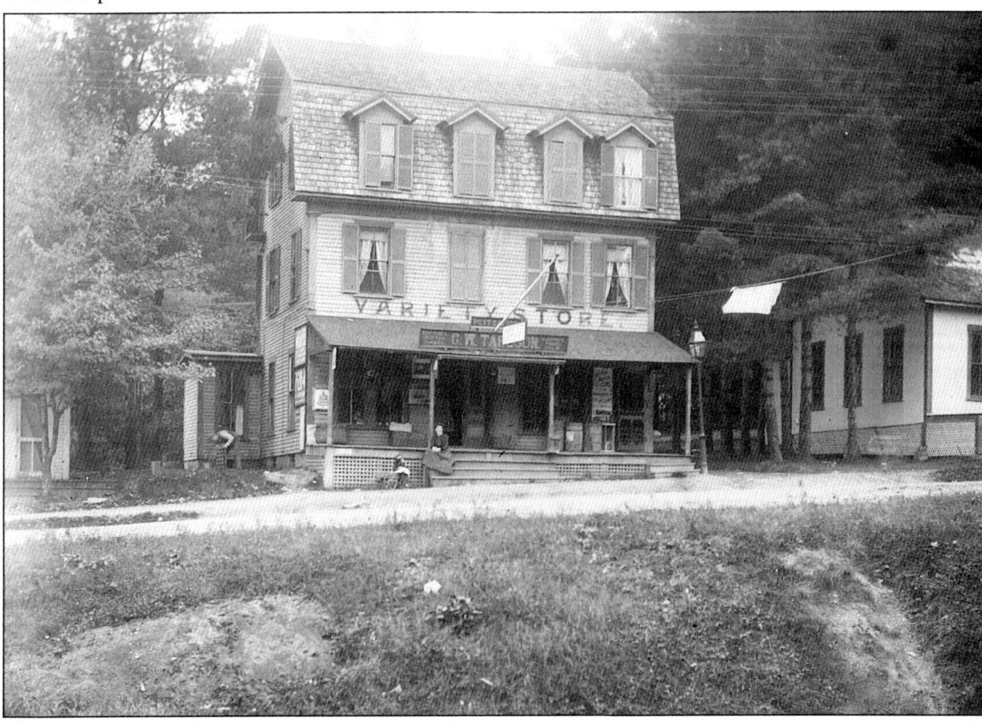

G.W. Tarlson store on the west side of Lakeside Avenue. An employee of George W. Weeks for five years, George W. Tarlson purchased the business in 1895, but relocated, early in the twentieth century, across the street.

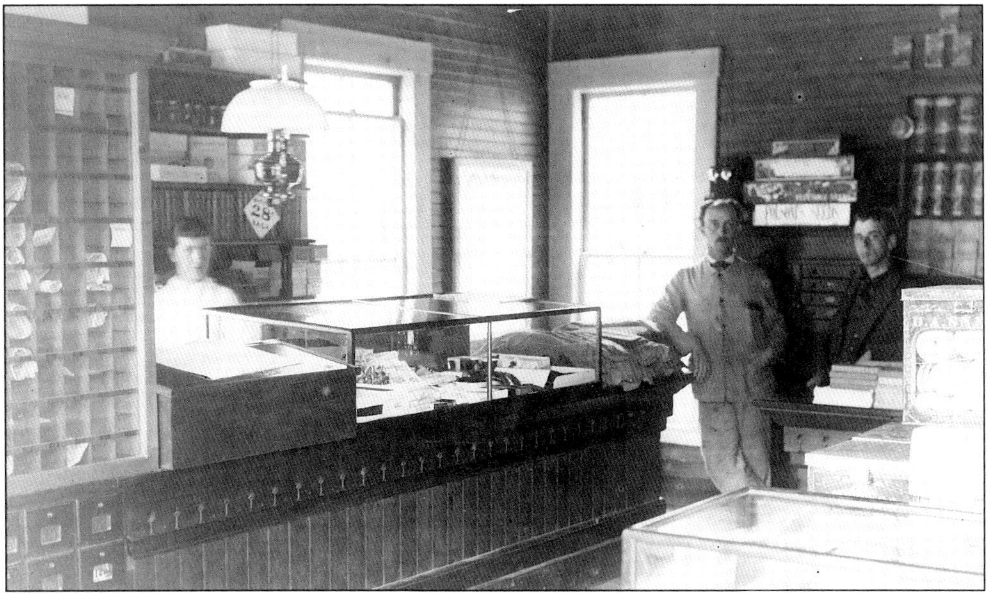

The interior of Tarlson's first store, which also housed the post office, in the late 1890s.

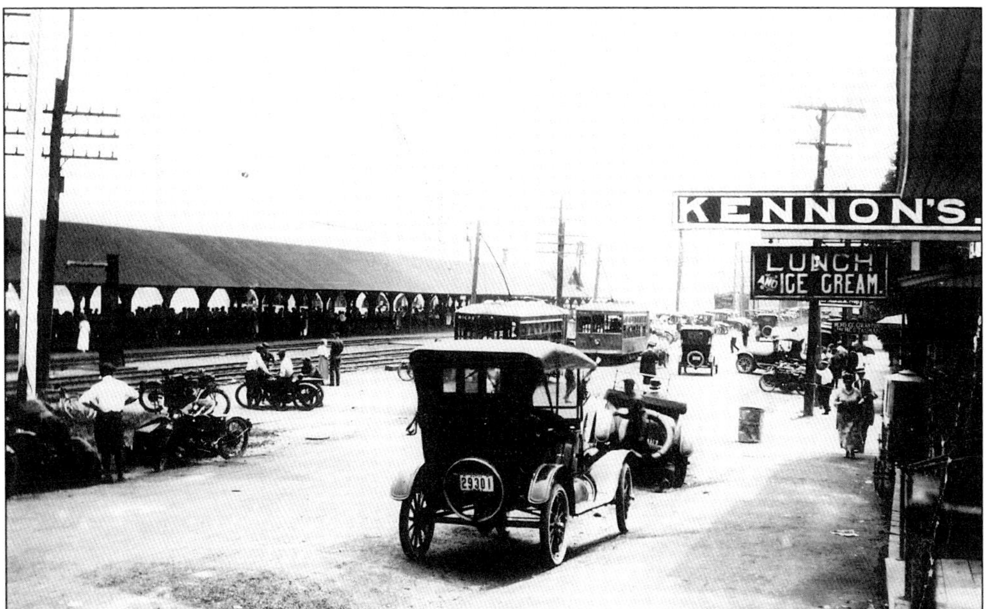

Looking south on Lakeside Avenue, summer 1924. Two cars of the Laconia Street Railway are at the center, with vintage motorcycles on the left.

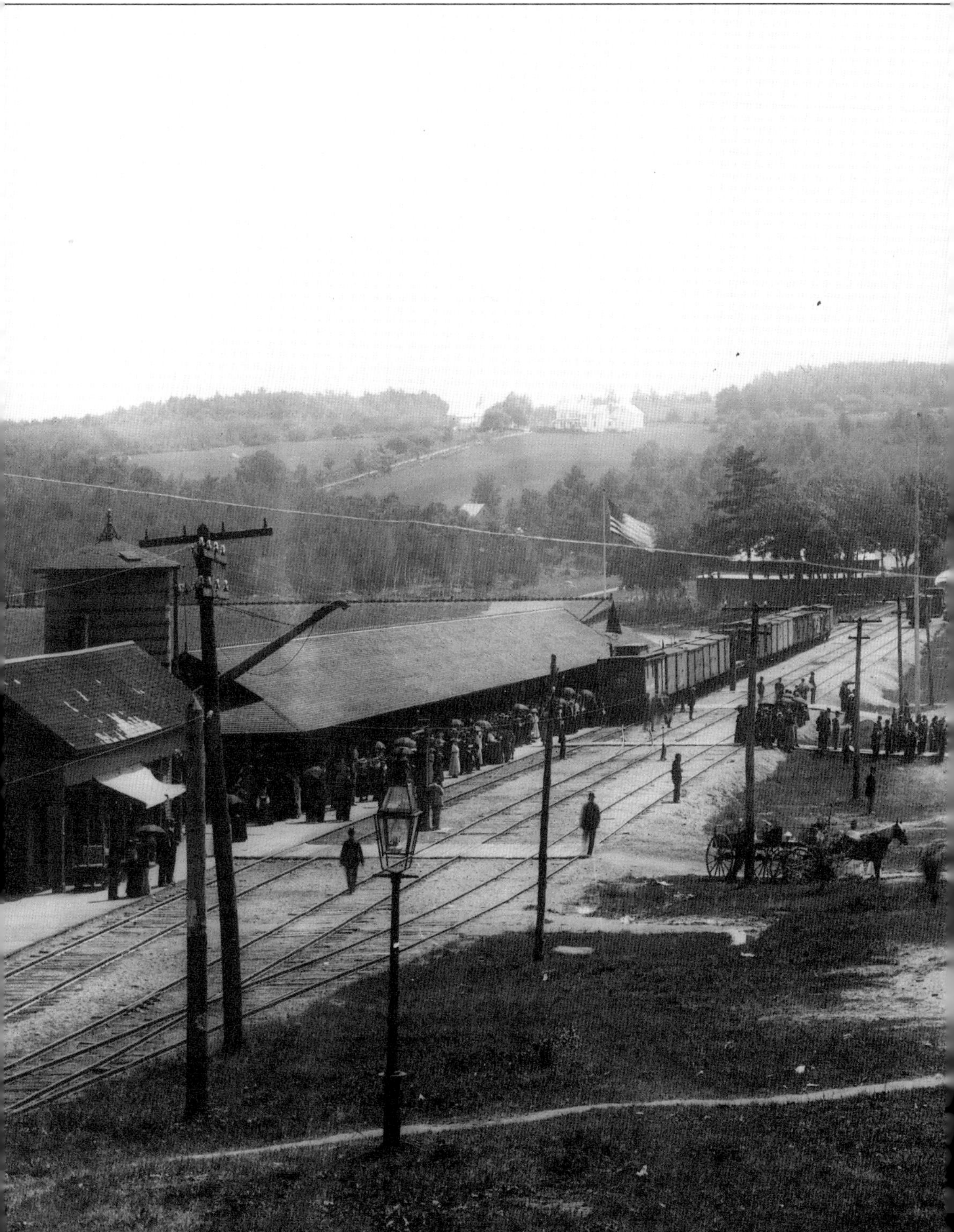

Lakeside Avenue looking south, with freight cars on the main line in front of the passenger station. Tarlson's first store is at right and the Headquarters Building of the New Hampshire

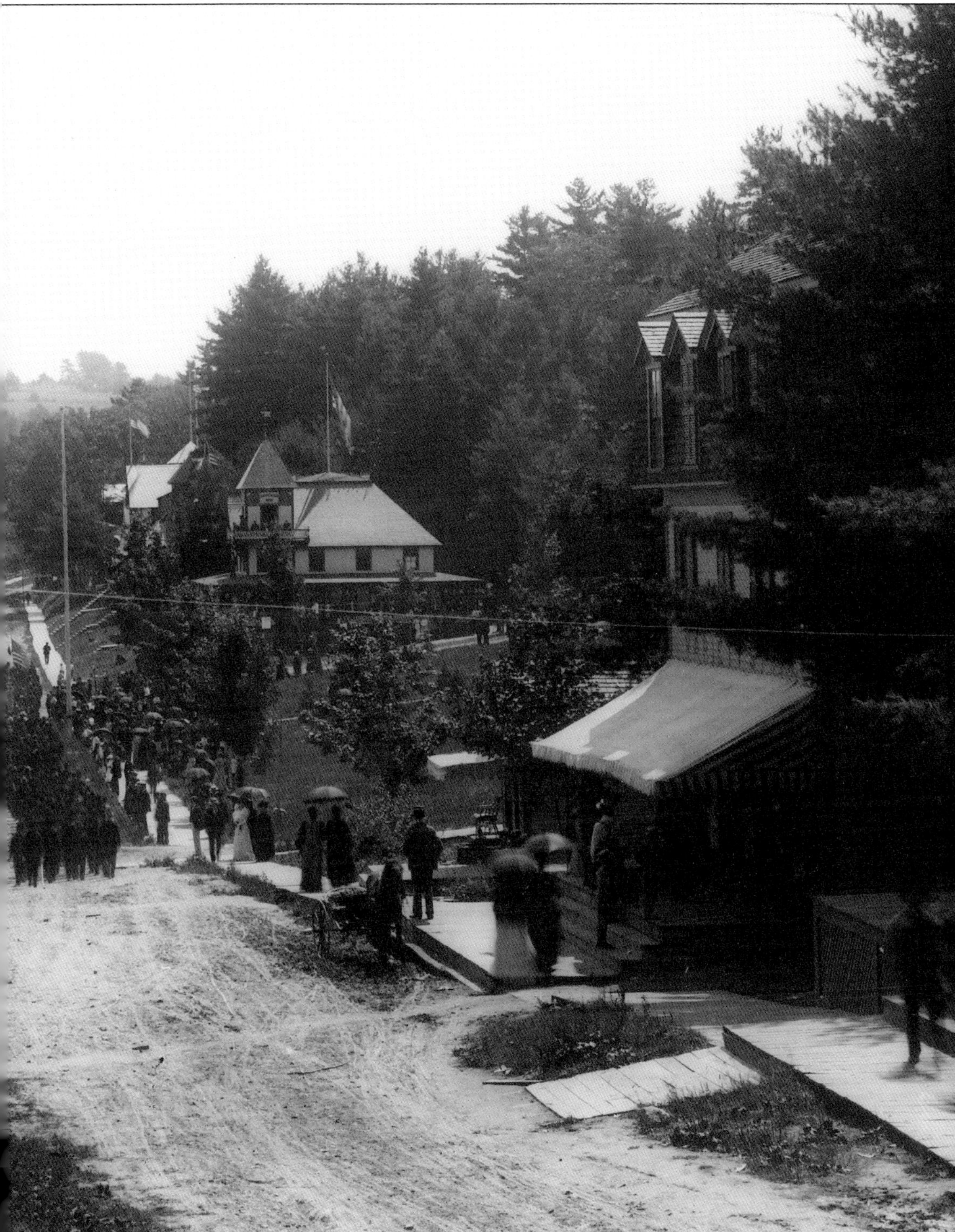

Veterans Association is in the middle distance on the right. The New Hotel Weirs is off the photograph to the right beyond Tarlson's first store and Tower Street.

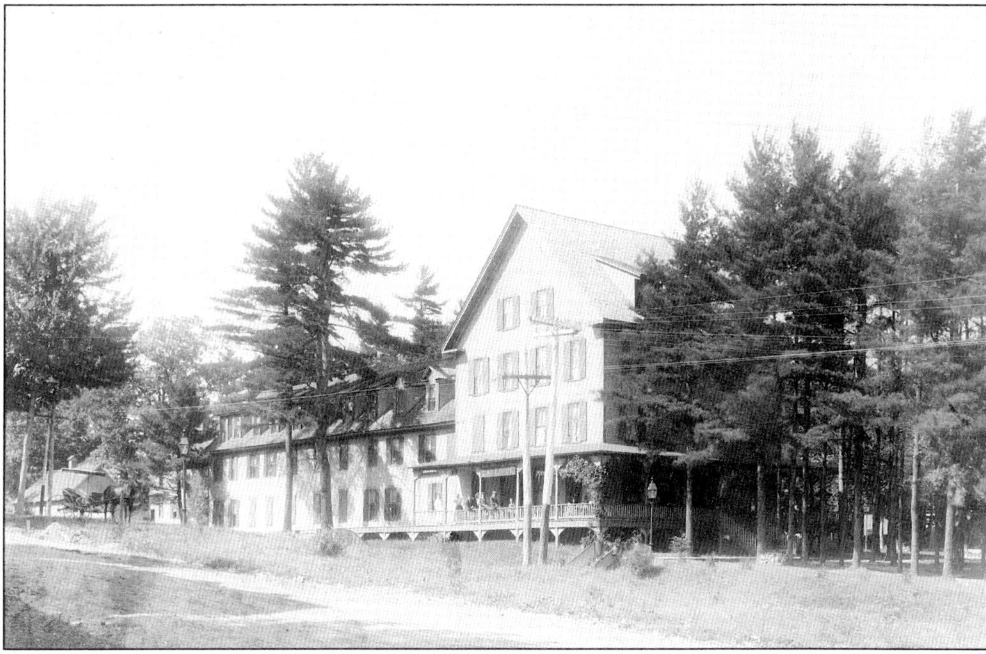

Lakeside House. Adjoining the Methodist Campground, the Lakeside House began with "eight sleeping apartments as an addition to a rough unfinished Methodist boarding house" in 1877. A new hotel was erected in 1880 and, with constant additions, by 1899 contained seventy-five sleeping rooms and "a spacious dining hall" as well as the adjoining Lakeside Cafe (see next page) to the east. Ultimately, the hotel included 118 rooms.

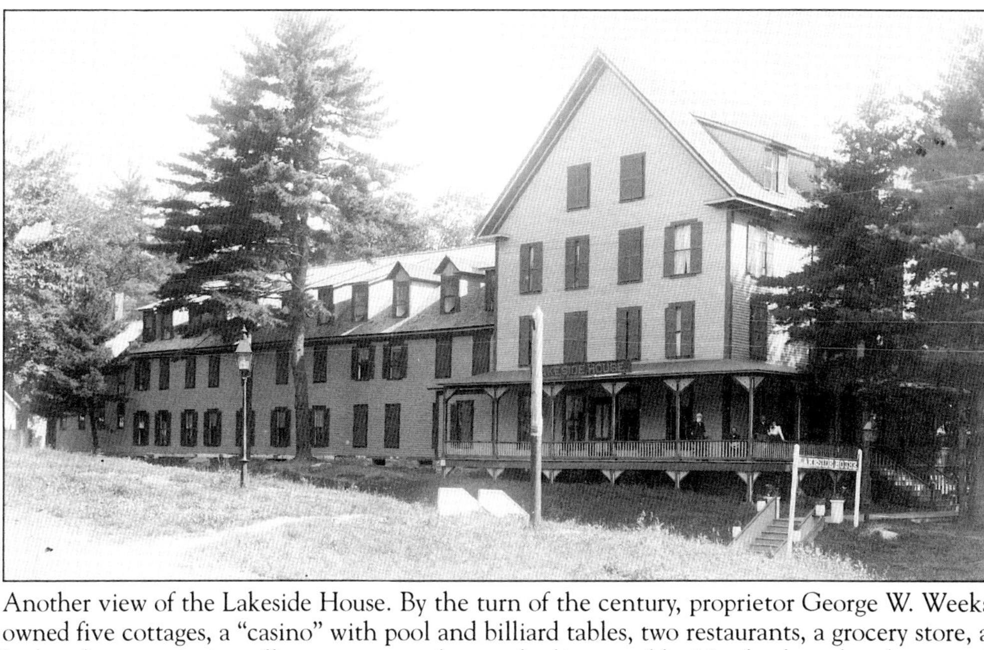

Another view of the Lakeside House. By the turn of the century, proprietor George W. Weeks owned five cottages, a "casino" with pool and billiard tables, two restaurants, a grocery store, a barber shop, a printing office, a meat market, and a livery stable. He also leased and operated the Hotel Winnicoette.

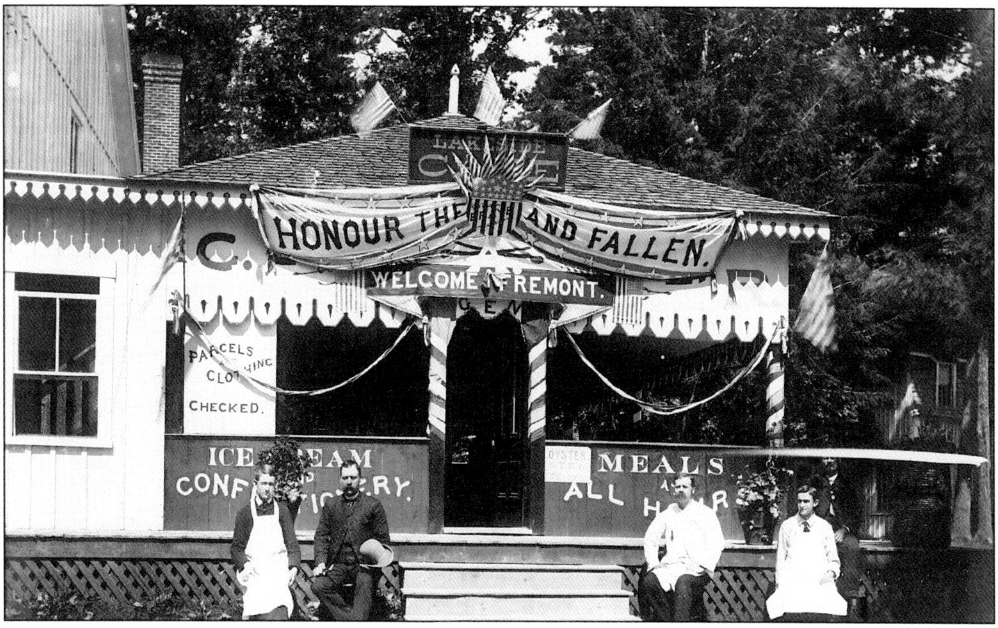

Lakeside Cafe, which adjoined the Lakeside House to the east. The sign over the door commemorates the visit of General John C. Fremont in August 1887. Fremont was one of six generals, seven colonels, three state governors, and assorted other notables in attendance, including Harriet P. Dame—known to the veterans as the "Florence Nightingale" of the war. The dignataries arrived "amidst great noise of cannon, music and vociferous acclamation of the crowd." From six to fifteen thousand people were present over the three days of that reunion.

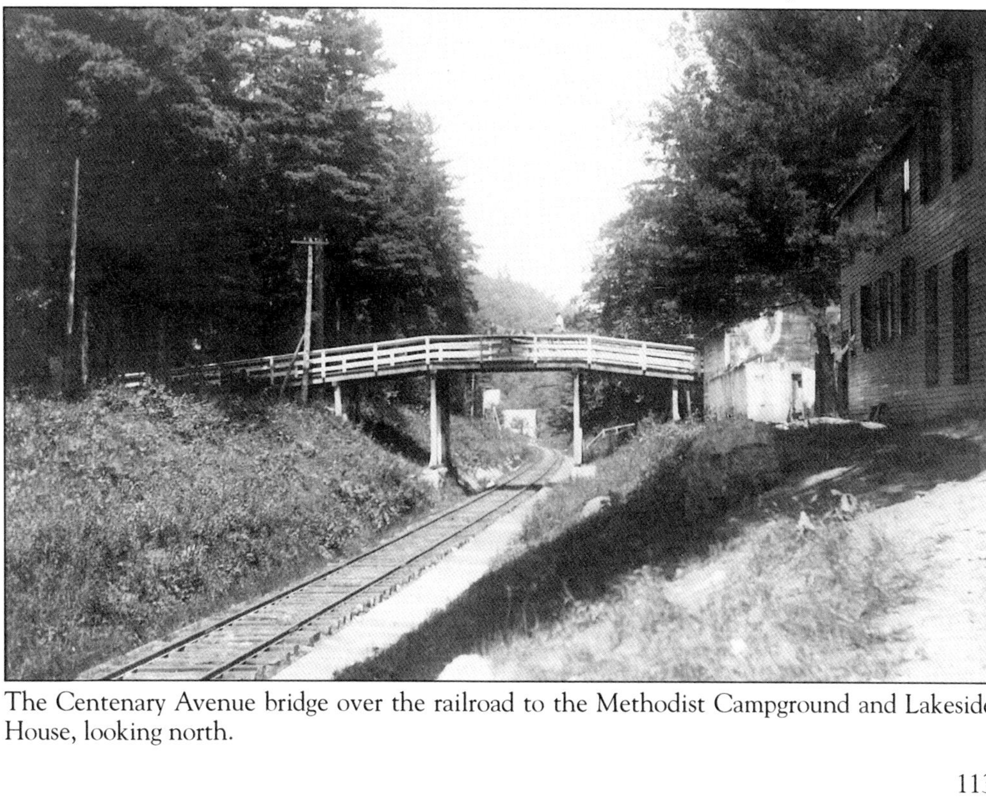

The Centenary Avenue bridge over the railroad to the Methodist Campground and Lakeside House, looking north.

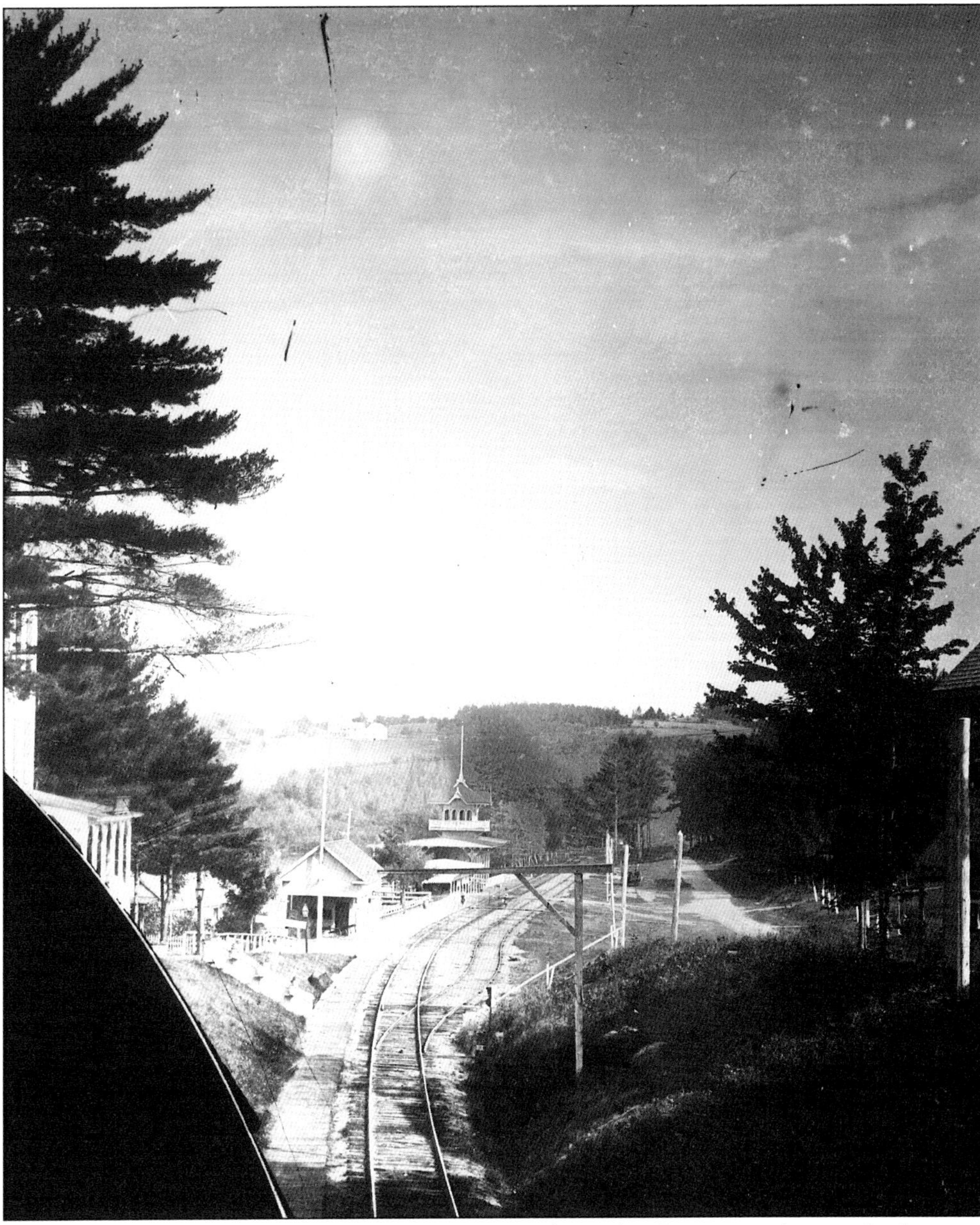

Looking south toward the 1880 passenger station from the Centenary Avenue bridge over the railroad tracks.

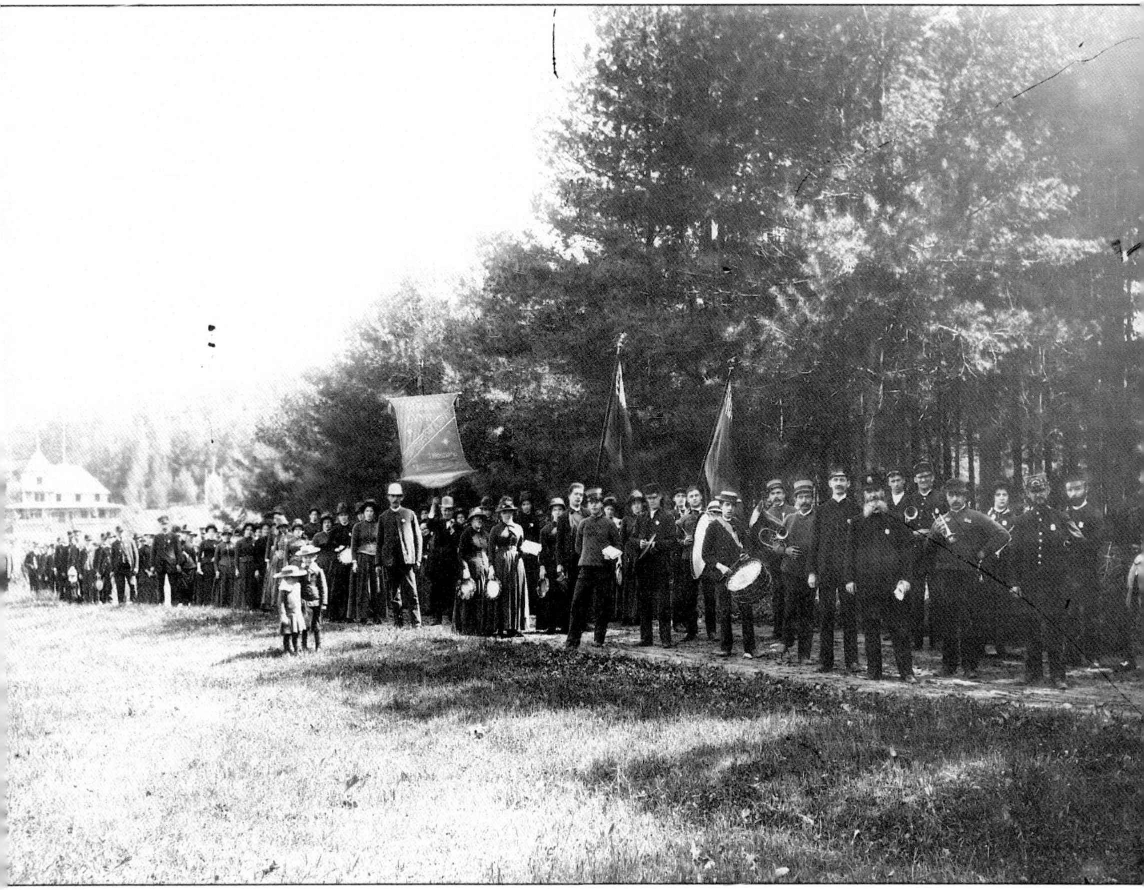

A Salvation Army delegation with band, early 1890s. Lakeside House is hidden behind the pine grove on the right and the Veterans Association Headquarters Building is visible on the left in the background. The banner reads "6th Mass., Lynn, Incorporated Oct. 1884." In this photograph, the Veterans Association arch is located halfway up the hill. By 1894, when the soldier's monument was dedicated, the arch had been moved down nearer Lakeside Avenue on a line with the front porch of the Veterans Association Headquarters Building. The policeman with the helmet strongly resembles Michael Whelan, a "hard boiled Laconia cop" of the period. The officer to the far left with cap and badge could be John M. Guay, who was city marshal in 1893.

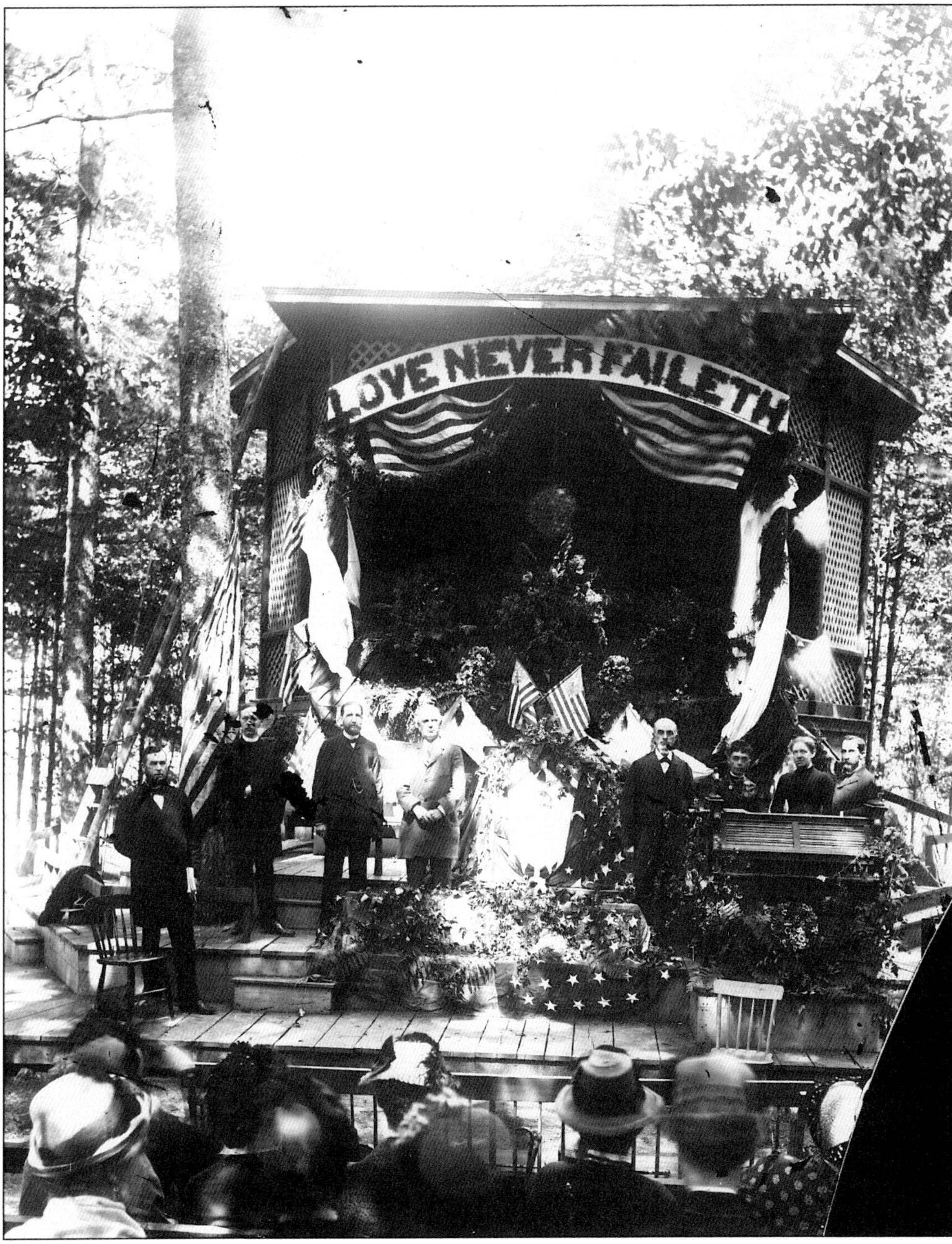

Funeral service at Methodist Grove, *c.* 1888. According to notes by local historian Andrew L. Childs, the coffin rests on the steps (center left) of the speakers' stand. Directly below the crossed flags (center) is a photograph of the deceased (which appears on the glass negative but didn't come out in this print). He was an old gentleman with a long beard. Above the crossed flags is a photograph that resembles General U.S. Grant. Hence; the conclusion is that the deceased was a Civil War veteran.

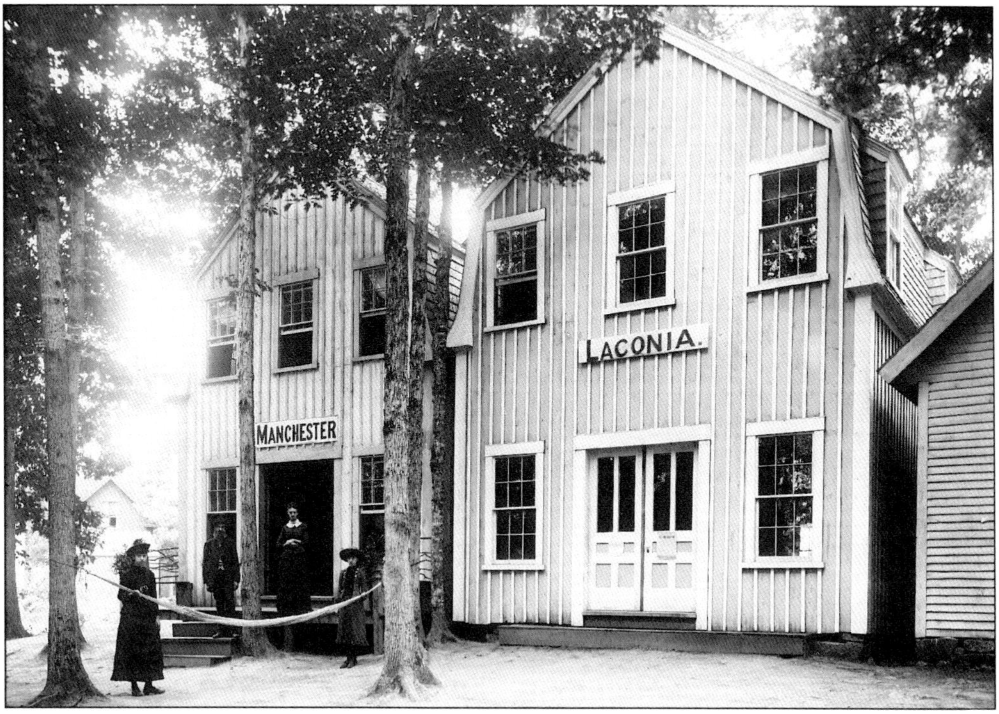

Two of the cottages of the Methodist Campground, *c.* 1885. In 1873, the Lisbon Campmeeting Association had relocated to The Weirs and had been renamed the Winnipisiogee Campmeeting Association. For decades, members of various Methodist churches held an annual one-week meeting here.

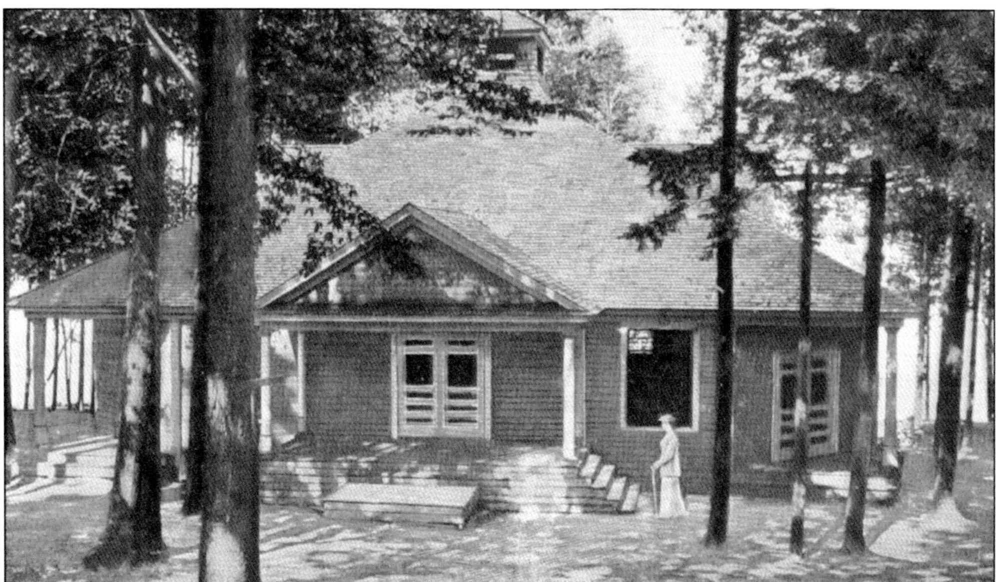

The auditorium of the Methodist Campground. This structure replaced the earlier out-of-doors tabernacles, one of which is depicted on p. 116. When the Methodists were not in session, other denominations, including Unitarians and Baptists, used the site for their own campmeetings.

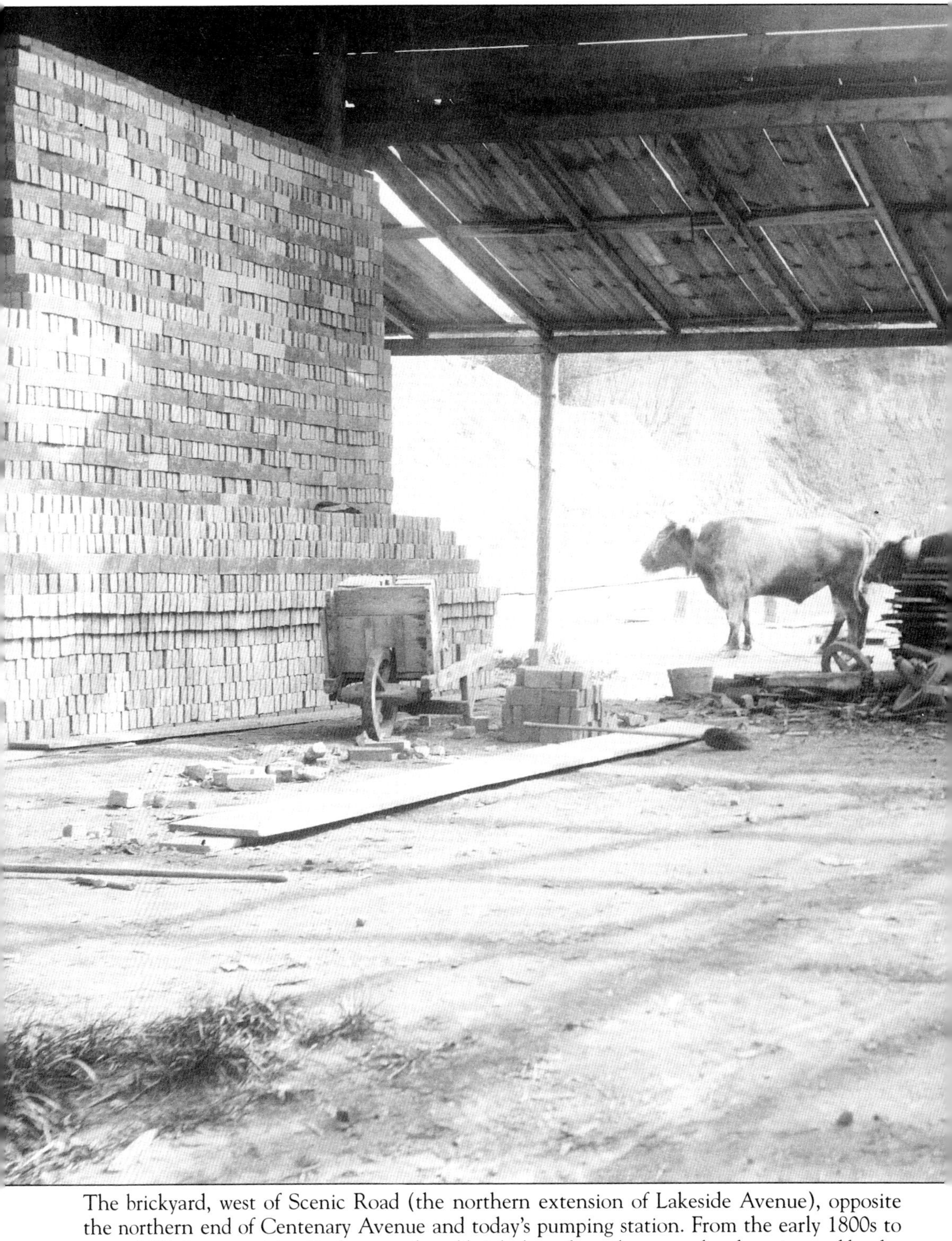

The brickyard, west of Scenic Road (the northern extension of Lakeside Avenue), opposite the northern end of Centenary Avenue and today's pumping station. From the early 1800s to around 1915, enterprising Yankees produced bricks here from the same clay deposits used by the American Indians of Aquedoctan village to make pottery, almost 10,000 years earlier. Many of

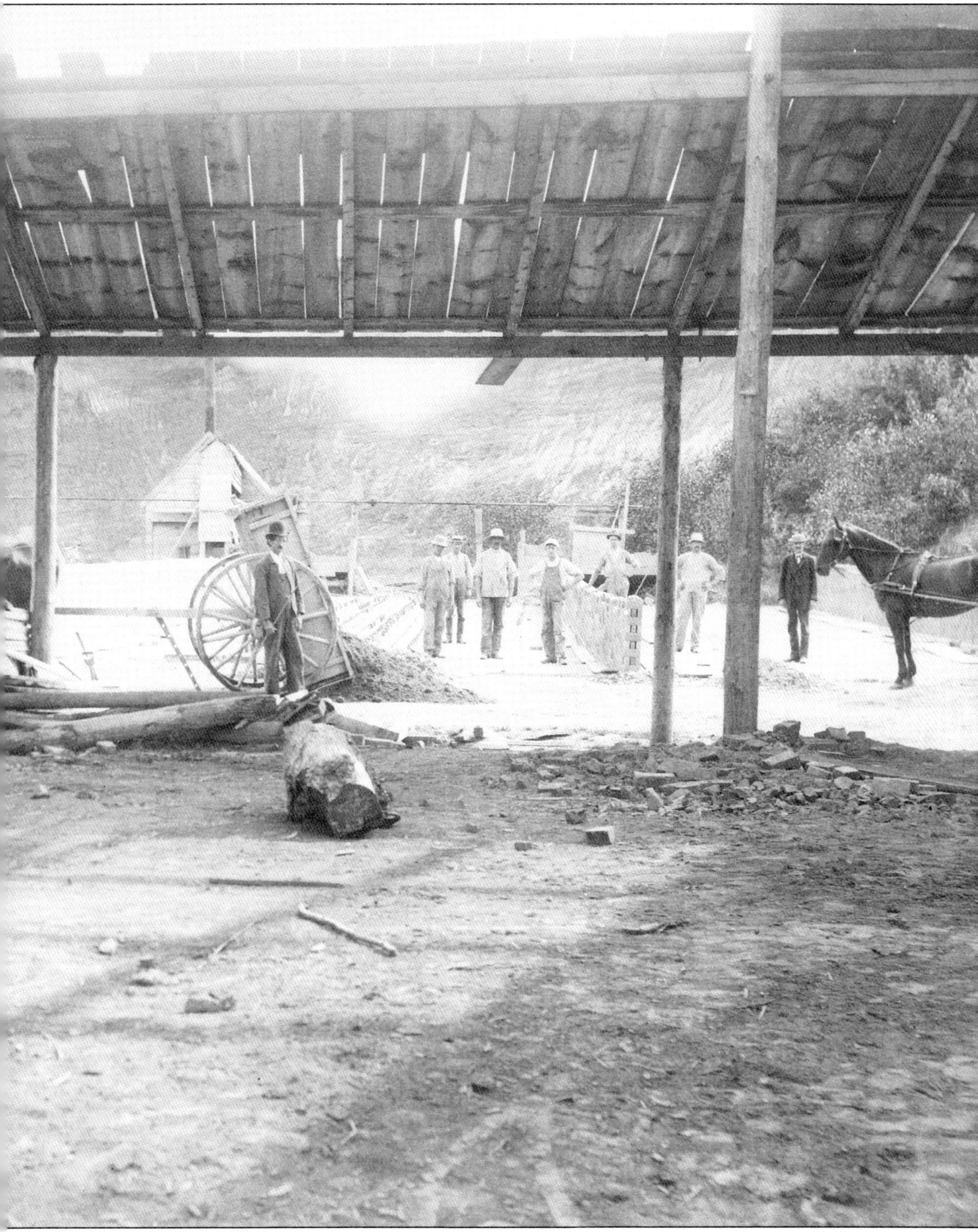

the old buildings in Downtown Laconia, including the 1886 Moulton Opera House, were made from Weirs brick. News reports in 1905 told of firing 400,000 bricks that season. Because of this industry, Doe Mountain became popularly known as Brickyard Mountain.

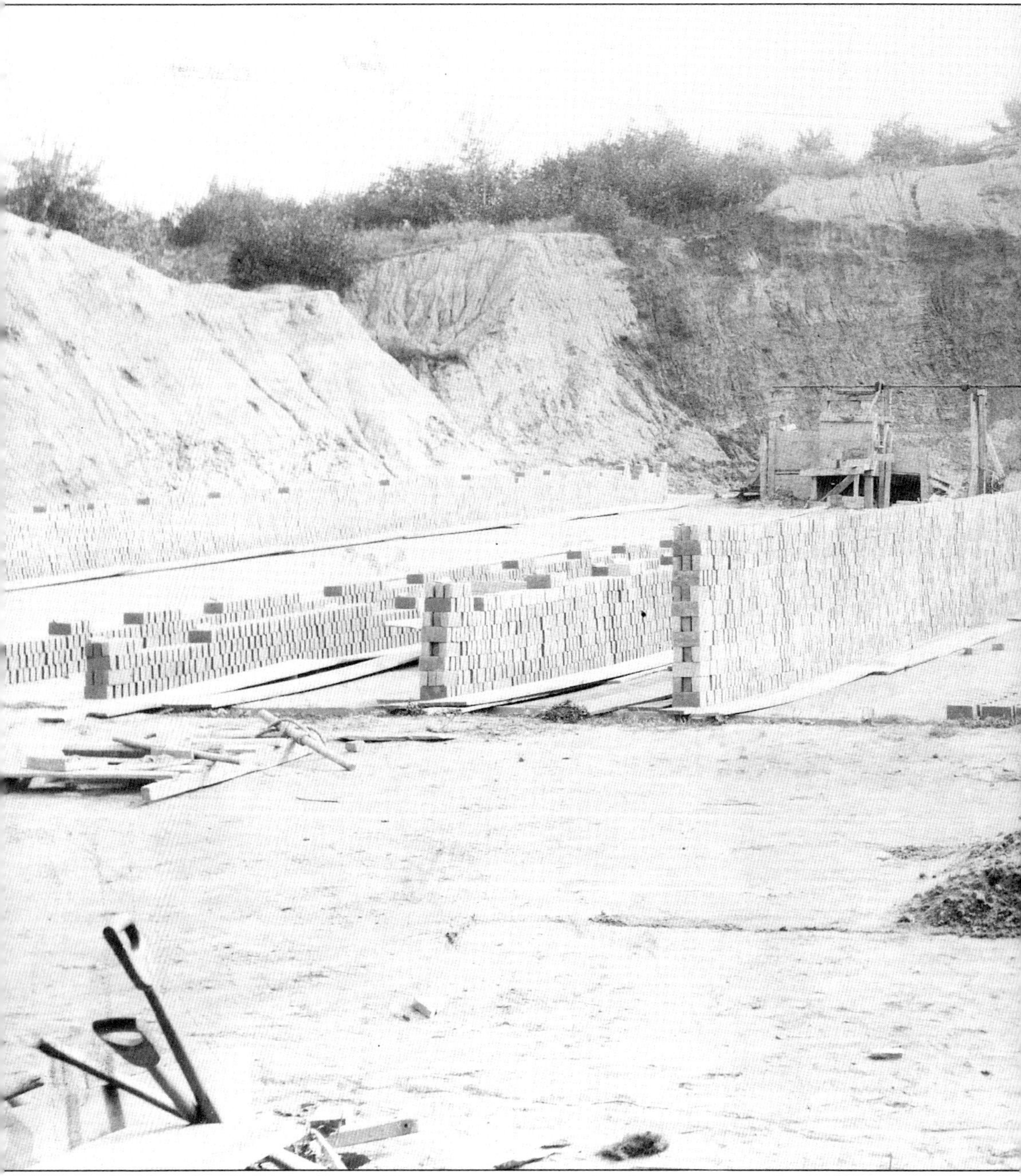

Another view of the brickyard. The kiln area was on the flat space near the road and was fired by wood. Eventually, the nearby supply of wood was depleted and wood was brought in from surrounding areas, as well as by barge from around the lake. Sand for the operation came from "Hatter" Bean's, later known as the Zebley Place (see p. 13). The sand was fine and had a lot of mica and silica, which, in combination, made very hard bricks. The clay was some of the best in the state for brickmaking—very hard and dark gray-green. The brickyard had its best years under the direction of Augustus Doe, farmer and large landowner, whose holdings at one time

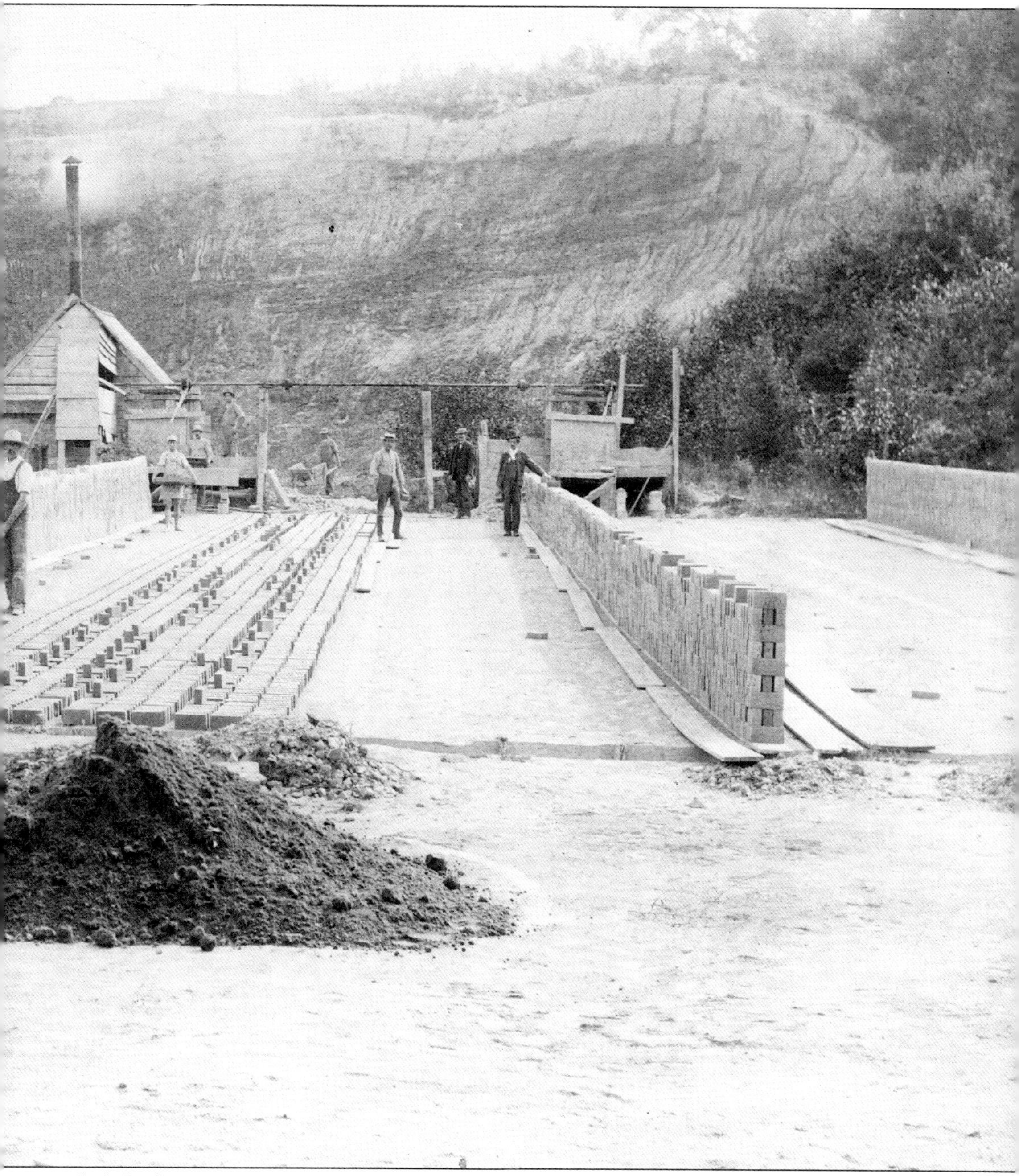

included a large portion of Tower Hill and the land upon which the Methodist Campground was later built. Doe's seventeen-room mansion, at the top of Doe Avenue on Tower Hill, was later known as Lawrence Manor. A brick house of the Doe family, across the street from the brickyard, was built to show off the brickyard's wares. After Doe's death in 1887, his son-in-law, William J. Morrison, carried on the business for a number of years. Morrison was a member of Laconia's first City Council.

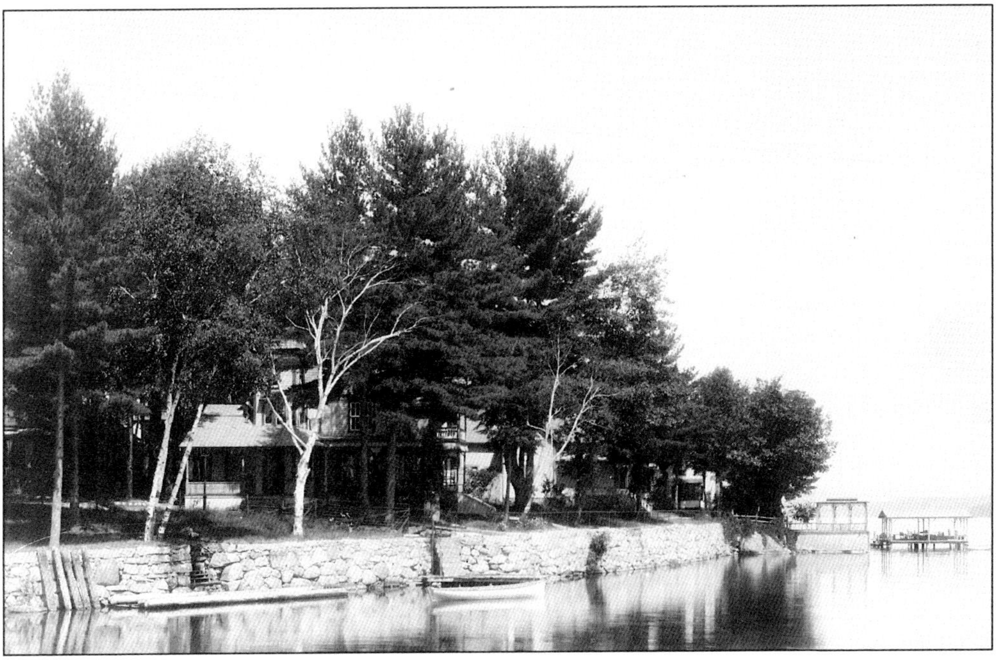

The shoreline north of The Weirs.

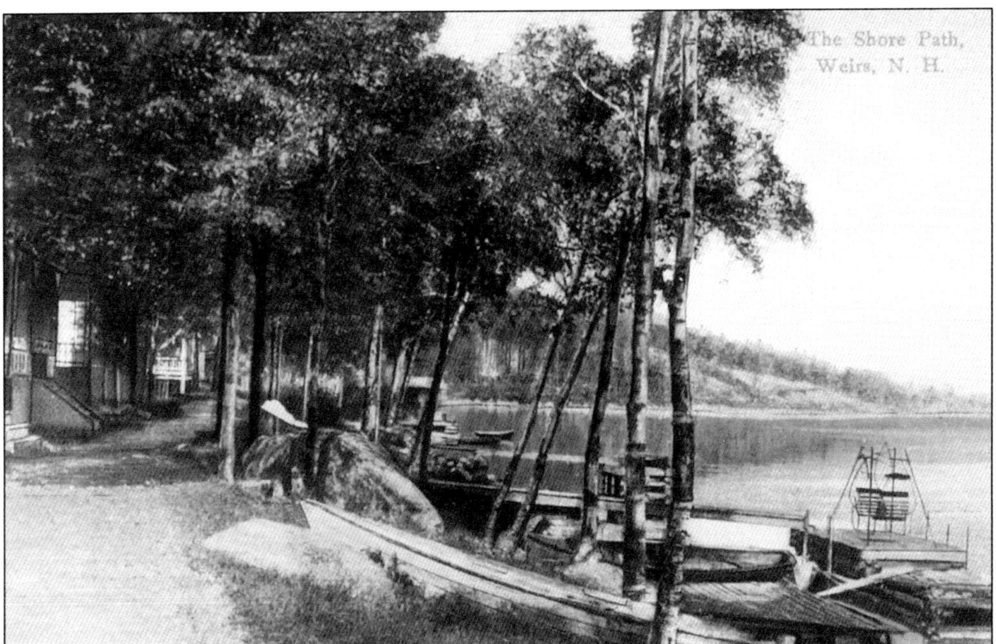

The shore path, around 1900.

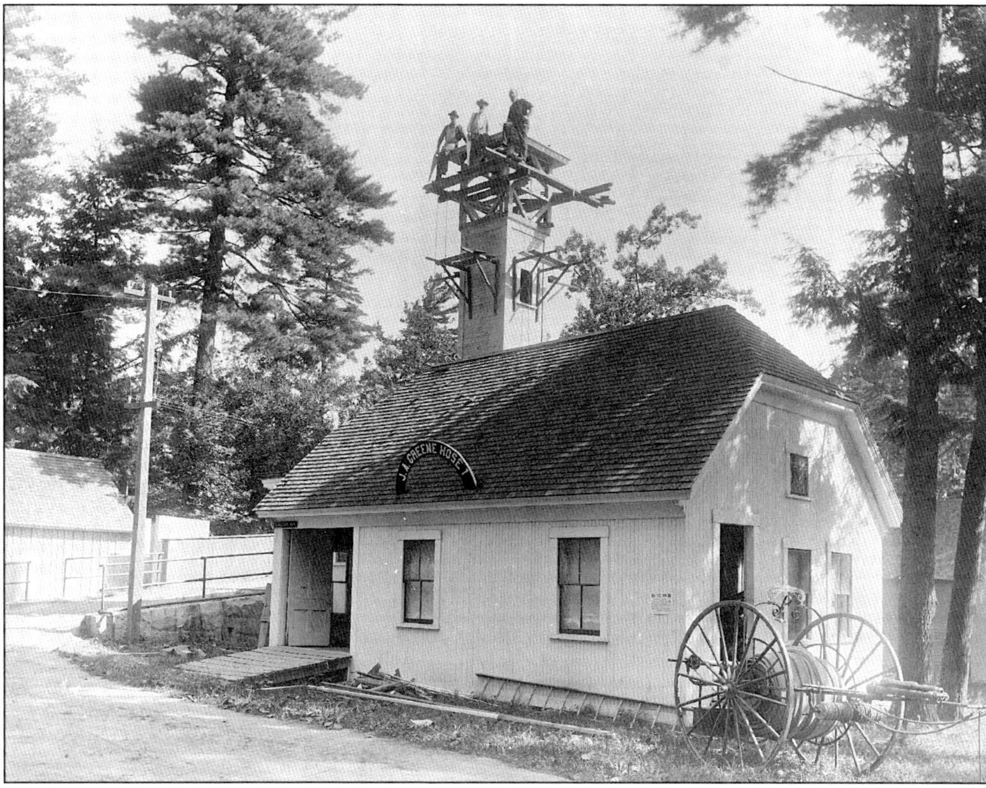

J.A. Greene Hose Co. No. 1, on Lakeside Avenue, with the Centenary Avenue bridge (left) to the Methodist Campground and Lakeside House. The new hose and ward room was built in 1893. This building still exists.

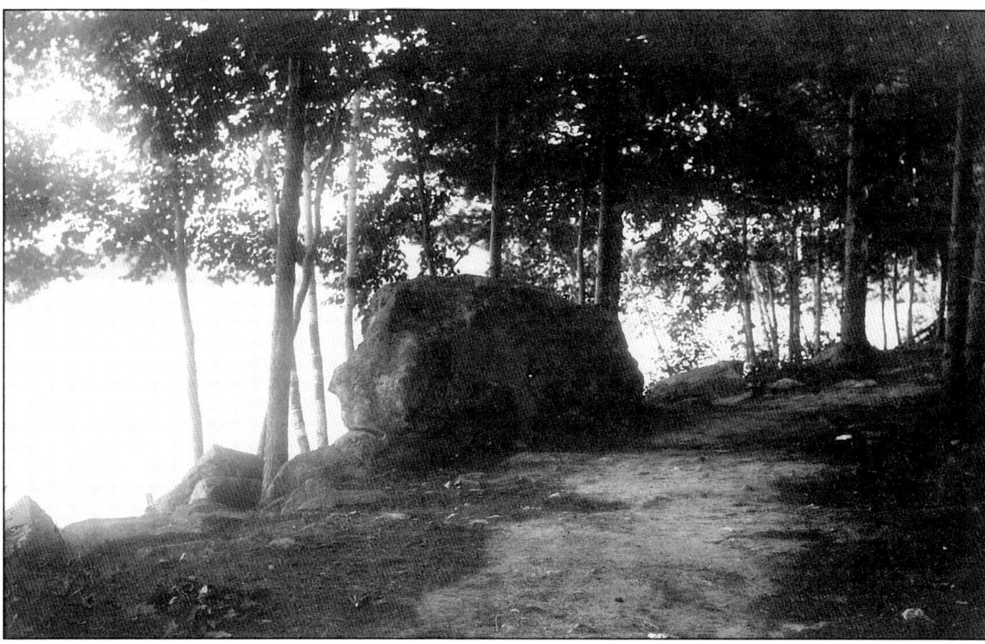

The boulder on the lake shore north of The Weirs, popularly known as "Profile Rock."

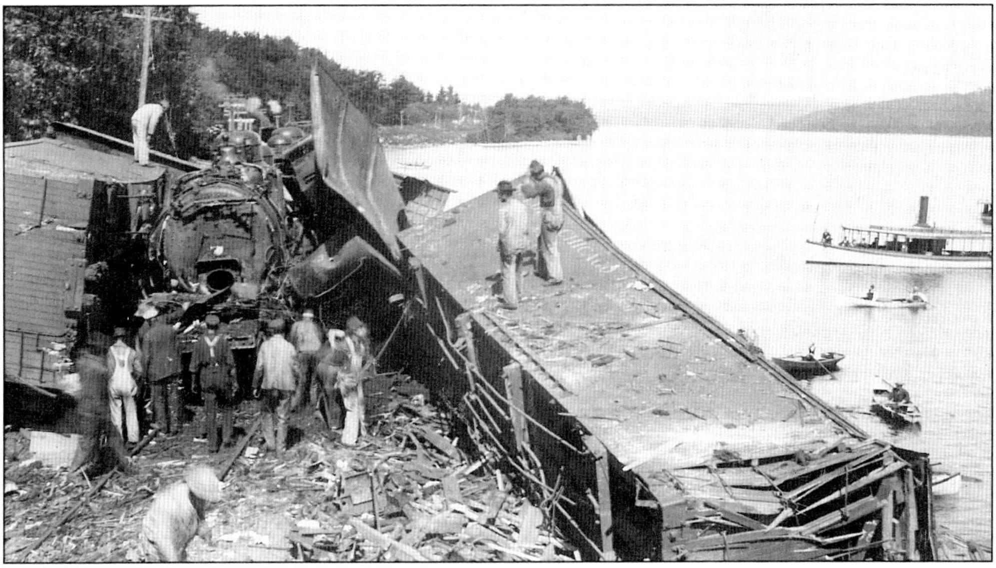

Train wreck on Saturday, September 15, 1900, just above The Weirs. This disaster was called the worst freight wreck that ever happened on the White Mountain Division of the Boston & Maine Railroad, at least to that date. Two men were killed almost instantly and four other trainmen were injured seriously in the middle-of-the-night collision. Two locomotives were demolished and twenty to thirty freight cars and their contents were "piled up into a confused heap on the track," according to *The Laconia Democrat*, Friday, September 21, 1900.

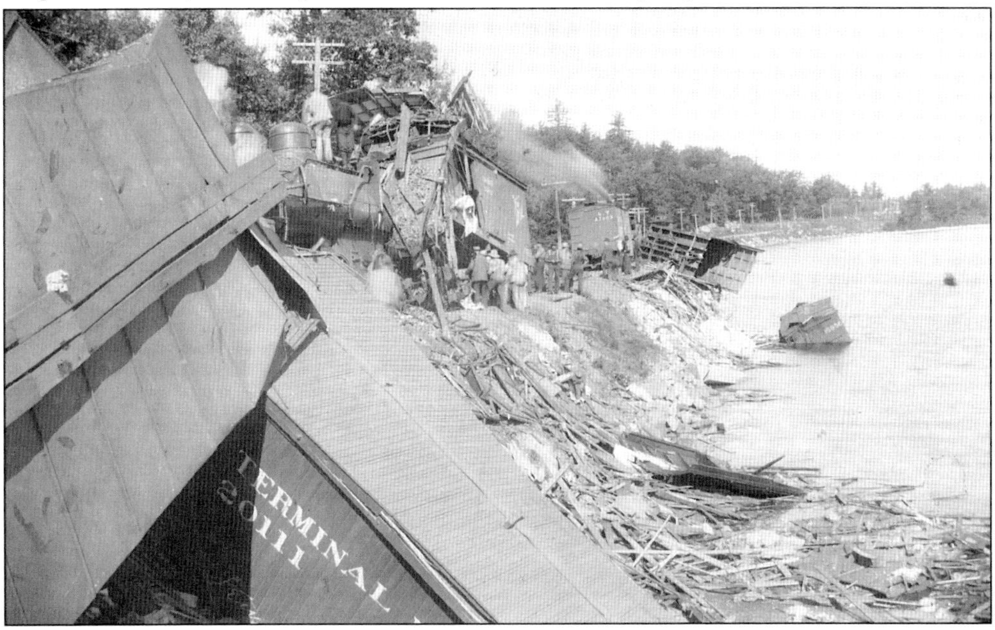

The regular northbound freight was made up of refrigerator cars loaded with perishables. An extra southbound freight was "loaded with what is known as dead freight." The trains came together with terrific force in a rock cut just above the pumping station at The Weirs, with a high bank of rocks on one side and another steep bank dropping down into the lake on the other. A confusion in the orders issued to the crew of the extra freight was believed to be the cause of the collision.

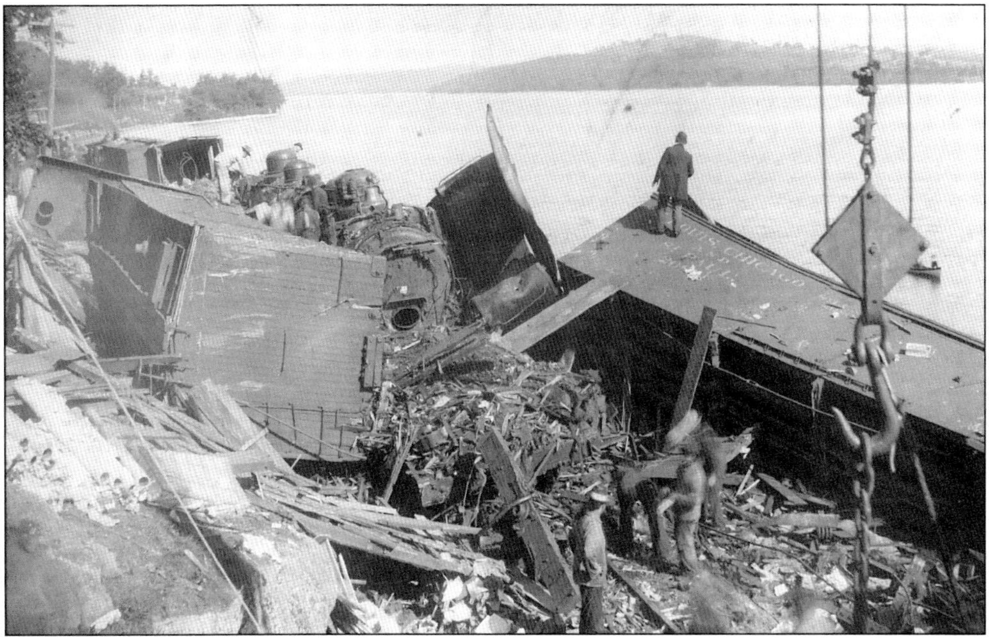

The engineer of the southbound freight said "that the first intimation of danger came to him in the glare from the headlight of the north-bound locomotive on the rails as he rounded the curve, and the next moment the engines were together." Wrecking teams were on the scene early in the morning, but the track was not cleared for traffic until late Saturday night, as the narrow cut around the curve where the accident took place made removing the wreckage a slow job.

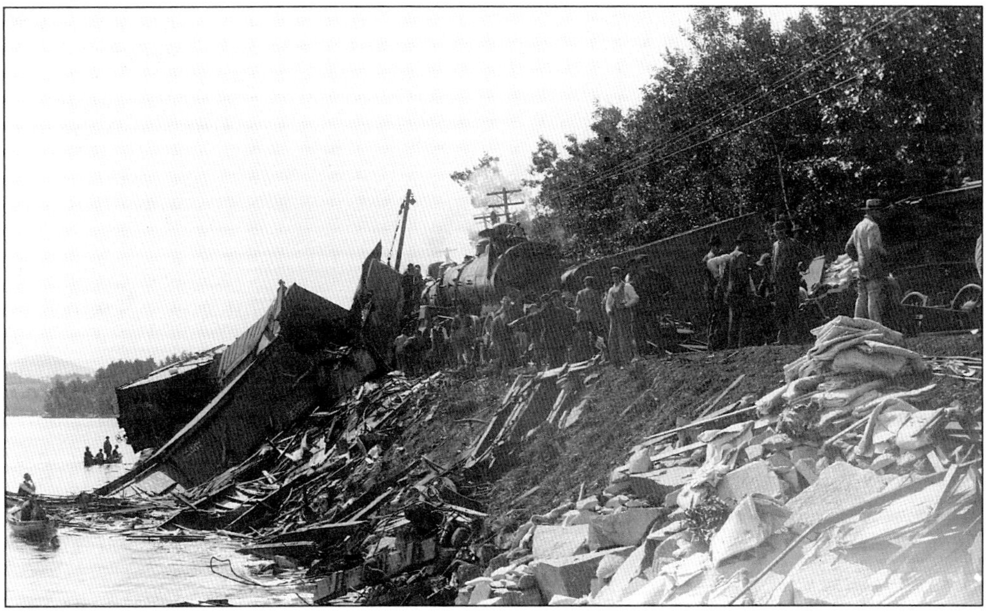

"So great was the force of the collision that the locomotives were simply welded together, and then the forward cars, impelled by the momentum, jumped onto and over them in a wild game of leap-frog, stripping them of all their top works and transforming them in a twinkling from powerful machines into heaps of junk."

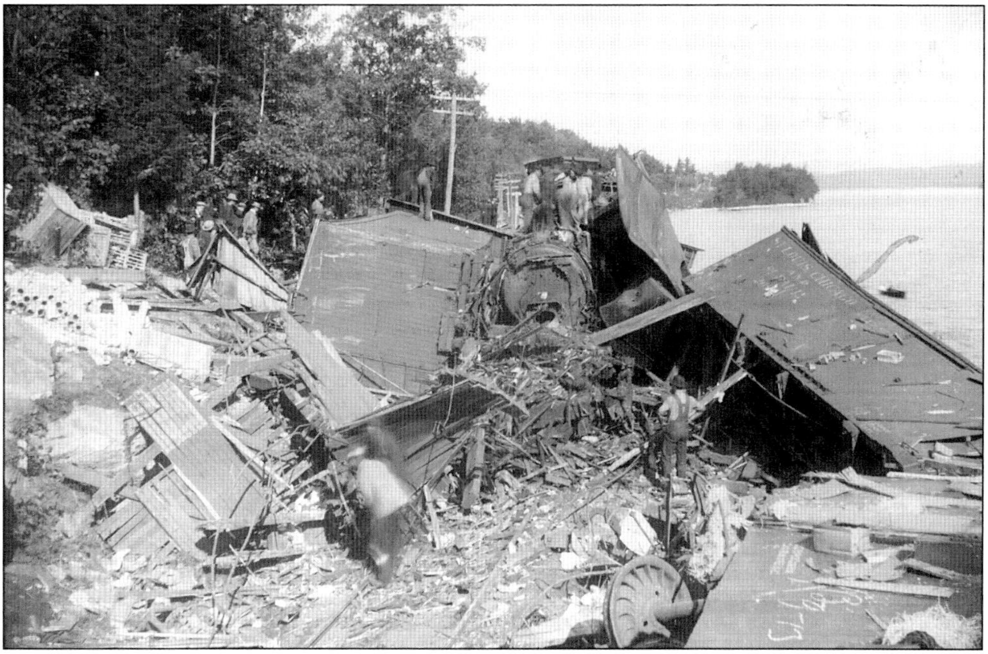

The two locomotives were telescoped together, while the freight cars and their contents were "piled around the spot in almost hopeless confusion." Some of the cars were reduced to kindling wood, and the ground was covered with their contents, including lumber, processed pulp, canned goods, barrels of beer, dressed beef, chickens, and vegetables.

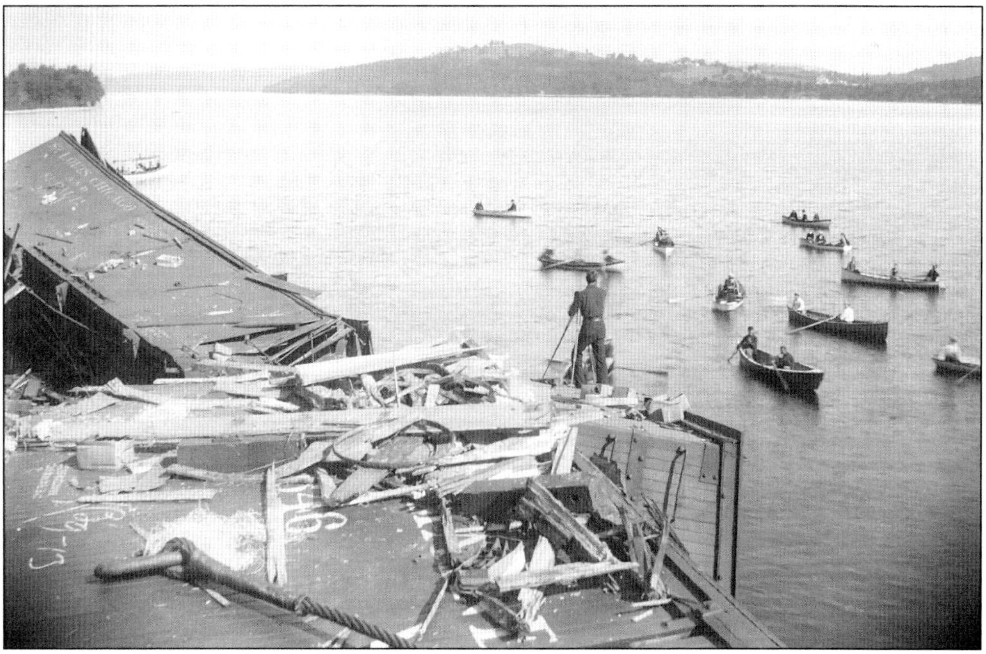

Thousands of people visited the scene on the day after the accident. The smashed freight cars and much of the merchandise were "piled into a heap Sunday afternoon and burned. Considerable of the perishable freight from the wreck was secured by residents near the scene of the accident and by parties who came in steamers, row and sail-boats."

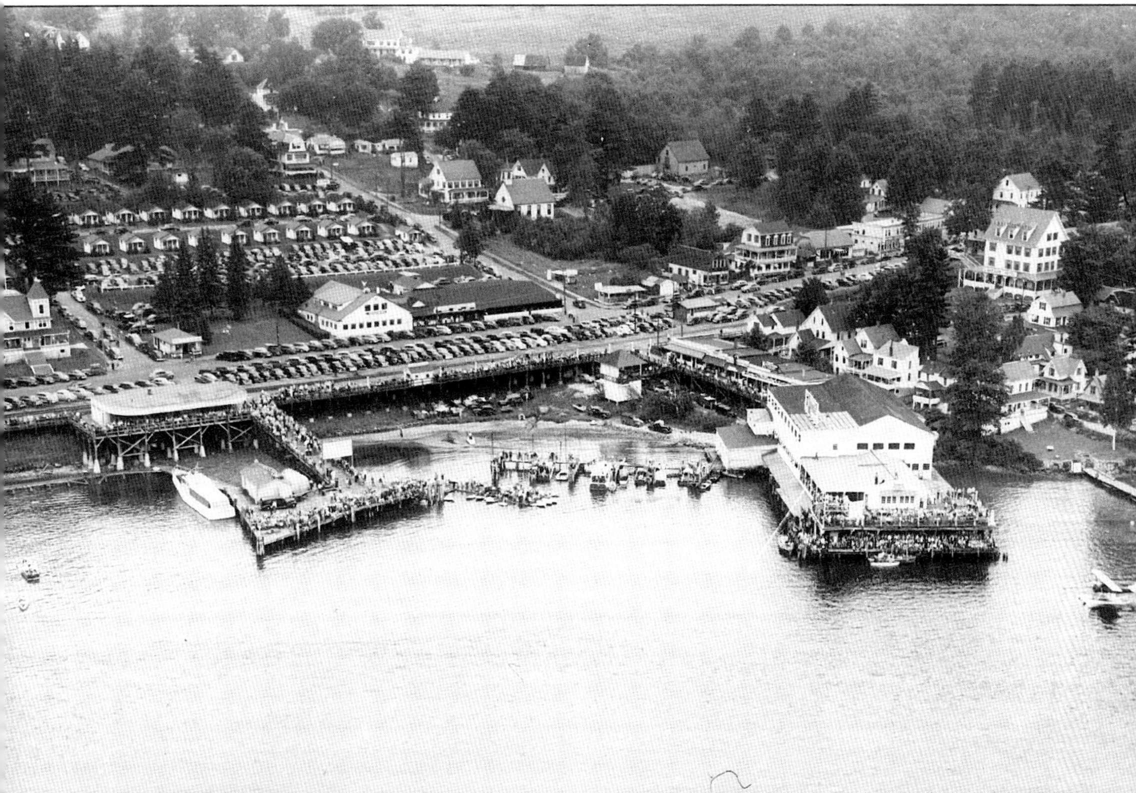

An aerial view of The Weirs, September 14, 1947, with the 1940s railroad station and wharf (left), Irwin's Winnipesaukee Gardens (right), and Lakeside House (top right). Half Moon Cabins and Lakeside Avenue arcades (upper left) had by then replaced the New Hotel Weirs. This photograph reflects changes as a result of the fires of 1924 (which had destroyed the New Hotel Weirs and other structures) and 1939 (which had turned the wharf, 1893 railroad station, and the steamer *Mount Washington* into ashes and rubble).

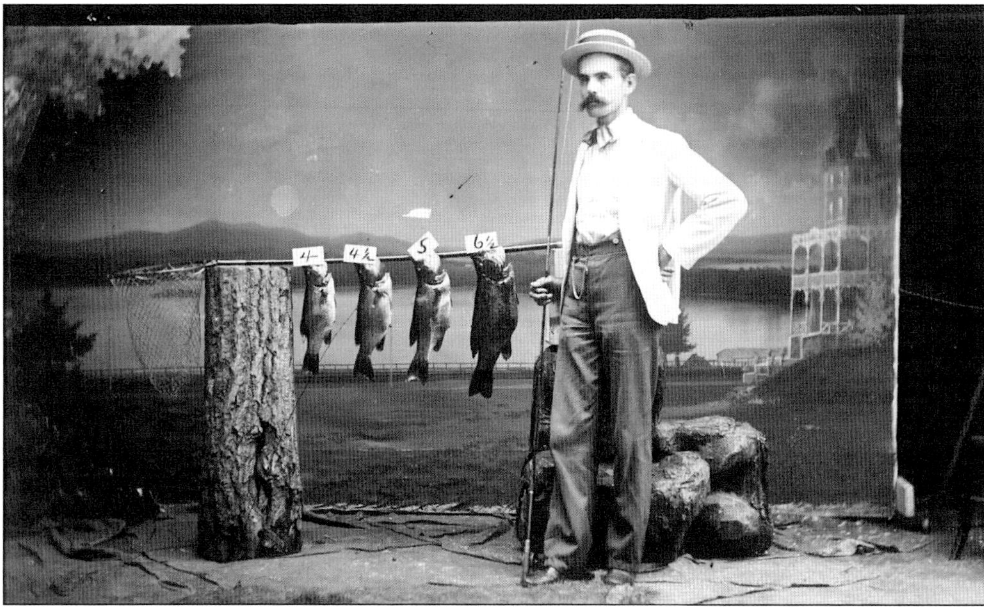

Fashionable fisherman poses proudly in photographer's studio, 1890s. Painted backdrop faithfully suggests the New Hotel Weirs on the right, with the railroad station, boardwalk, and lake in the distance.

Acknowledgments

While most of these photographs appear here for the first time in book form, seven of them were included in *Slates, Shingles and Shakes*, published by the City of Laconia in 1978. Douglas B. McGowan made available the photographs on pp. 39, 44, 66, 99, 108, and 112; at the top of pp. 24–25, 36, 38, 48, 57, 59, 70, 105, and 109; and at the bottom of pp. 19, 24, 40, 58, and 123. Robert F. Dearborn made available the cover photograph, as well as those on pp. 67, 79, and 99; at the top of pp. 22, 56, 69, 71, 83, and 98; and at the bottom of pp. 21, 47, 68, and 96. In addition, O.R. Cummings made available the photographs on p. 92 and the bottom of p. 90; Dr. David E. Livingston, DDS, those on pp. 72–73 and 97; Robert G. Holbrook, top of p. 74; and the Evangelical Baptist Church, Laconia, bottom of pp. 93 and 98.